Peace Power
for Adolescents

Peace Power
for Adolescents
Strategies for a Culture of Nonviolence

Mark A. Mattaini
with the *PEACE POWER* Working Group

NASW PRESS

National Association of Social Workers
Washington, DC

Terry Mizrahi, MSW, PhD, *President*
Elizabeth Clark, PhD, ACSW, *Executive Director*

Cheryl Y. Bradley, Director, Member Services and Publications
Paula L. Delo, Executive Editor
Susan Fisher, Editor
January Layman-Wood, Acquisitions Editor
Gail Martin, Editorial Associates, Copy Editor
Louise Goines, Proofreader
Leonard S. Rosenbaum, Indexer

Royalties for this book are dedicated to further development of *PEACE POWER* and related work.

Library of Congress Cataloging-in-Publication Data

Mattaini, Mark A.
    Peace power for adolescents : strategies for a culture of nonviolence / Mark A. Mattaini.
        p. cm.
    Includes bibliographical references and index.
    ISBN 0-87101-329-0 (alk. paper)
    1. Nonviolence. 2. Conflict management. 3. Teenagers. I. Title.

HM1281 .M38 2001
303.6'1—dc21

                                                    2001031724

The Power to enact a true Peace is the product of a unified people on the path of Righteousness and Reason.

Basic Call to Consciousness
(*Akwesasne Notes* of the Haudenosaunee, 1978)

If we can revere how things are, and can find a way to express gratitude for our existence, then we should be able to figure out, with a great deal of work and good will, how to share the Earth with one another and with other creatures, how to restore and preserve its elegance and grace, and how to commit ourselves to love and joy and laughter and hope.

The Sacred Depths of Nature (Goodenough, 1998)

Blessed are the peacemakers . . .

Matthew 5:9

Contents

Contents

About the Author

Mark A. Mattaini, DSW, ACSW, is associate professor and director of the doctoral program, Jane Addams College of Social Work, University of Illinois at Chicago, and editor of *Behavior and Social Issues*, a professional journal. His writing and research focus on prevention of and intervention with issues that carry significant social justice implications, often in collaboration with his partner Christine T. Lowery, PhD (Laguna/Hopi), associate professor, School of Social Welfare, University of Wisconsin at Milwaukee. With experience in child and family, mental health, developmental disabilities, juvenile corrections, and substance abuse settings, Dr. Mattaini continues to do part-time direct and community practice and is chair of Behaviorists for Social Responsibility.

Acknowledgments

Many individuals have contributed to this work, acting for extended or brief periods as members of the *PEACE POWER* Working Group. The most important has been Christine T. Lowery, PhD (Laguna/Hopi), my life partner, who initiated the discussions of shared power that found their way into the core *PEACE POWER* model, pointed us toward the many potential contributions of indigenous peoples to this work, and has often participated in *PEACE POWER* training. Also critical was Dr. Janet Twyman, who was extensively involved in the early work producing the underlying theoretical framework for the *PEACE POWER* strategy, and provided considerable conceptual assistance in developing the approach. Others who have been involved with our projects in significant ways, listed in alphabetical order, include Jay Blankenship (COA Youth and Family Centers, Milwaukee), Dominic Brancato (You Participate in Solutions, Staten Island), Wendy Chin (New York City), Jennifer DiNoia (New York City), Karen Herrera (You Participate in Solutions, New York City), John Humphrey (Metro High School, Cedar Rapids), George Kamps (Oneida Tribal Social Services, Wisconsin), Richard Malott (Western Michigan University), Kyung Nam Lee (Jewish Board of Family and Children's Services, New York City), Helen Perez (Jewish Board of Family and Children's Services, New York City), Dawn Rannie (You Participate in Solutions, Staten Island), and Frank Wood (New York State), as well as many program staff, all of the young people who have helped in the development and refinement of the strategy, their families, and my students at Columbia University, the University of Wisconsin at Milwaukee, and Jane Addams College of Social Work at the University of Illinois at Chicago. I also am deeply grateful for inspiration from B. F. Skinner, Dennis Embry, G. Roy Mayer, the Haudenosaunee and many other indigenous peoples, Rupert Ross, and so many others. All our relations.

Introduction

Our children are at enormous risk; therefore, so is our society. Youth violence captures a great deal of media and public attention, but the problem is even deeper than is at first apparent. The violence that comes to official attention is only a small portion of the violence that occurs, and the violence that occurs is only the extreme end of a continuum of threat and coercion within which children, and the rest of society, are deeply embedded (Sidman, 2001). According to Garbarino (1995), youth and their families today are living in an increasingly toxic social environment. The social and behavioral sciences already tell us a great deal about the causes of, and possible responses to, violence and coercion that naturally emerge from that environment. Given current knowledge, consistent efforts over a reasonable period of time could probably reduce violence and other coercive acts among youth by more than half (see the studies listed below under "Promising Programs"). Doing so, however, would require (1) commitments of resources—primarily time and the personal gifts each person carries—and (2) a willingness to recognize and address the many ways cultural networks in society support and encourage coercion and violence. Perspectives from other cultures can be particularly useful for recognizing those cultural processes, since it is difficult to see possible alternatives to existing practices from the inside.

Society in the United States is far more deeply rooted in coercive and adversarial power than may be immediately evident. When problems arise, whether the misbehavior of a child or Medicaid fraud, a perceived slight on the highway or the success of a disliked coworker, individuals in this society have been powerfully conditioned to turn to punishment and threat in order to elicit immediate change. Sidman (2001) documents the extensive reliance on coercion in families, friendships, schools, workplaces, law enforcement, government, churches—in fact, in every major system and institution in our society. Sidman then describes what behavioral science tells us is the natural outcome of repeated exposure to coercion, punishment, and threat: aggression and depression. Similarly, Garbarino (1999) describes the exposure that many youth, particularly young men, have in our society to aversive events and deprivation, and indicates that it is possible "to make sense of how their violent acts flow from their experiences in our society" (p. 20). Lane (1997) traces the historical roots of the high numbers of homicides in the United States for centuries and suggests a link between (1) the violence (actual and potential) that established and maintained slavery and perpetuated Native American genocide, and (2) current problems with violence.

The negative impact of these cultural factors is considered in detail later, but it is important to begin here. The only practical way to reduce violence is to encourage shifts toward different cultural practices. Perhaps surprisingly, the material in this book strongly suggests that such a shift is not as difficult as it may seem, at least within well-defined systems like schools, residential programs, or families. Cultural change, according to the data, is possible. The issue involves choosing between two kinds of power: coercive, competitive, adversarial power, which is ultimately limited and associated with many personal and social side-effects, and constructive power, which heals and strengthens personal and community networks. Science and experience converge here to provide concrete guidance for moving from the former to the latter; this book introduces tools to facilitate the process.

As discussed in chapter 1, a wide range of risk and protective factors and population indicators for violence have been discovered through hundreds of millions of dollars of research. This book is not meant to be another review of the epidemiology of youth violence. Although there is much more to be learned about that epidemiology, our most critical need now may be for an applied "science of action" (Elliott & Tolan, 1999, p.18). Elliott and Tolan, paraphrasing Moore (1994), note:

> In many respects, our limited success in influencing prevention and intervention programming and policy is the result of failures to translate theoretical propositions and basic research findings into operational programs and policies that have some realistic

chance of modifying the predisposing causes and conditions leading to violent behavior and that could be successfully implemented
by local communities and agencies with their existing resources.
(1999, p. 18)

The goal of this volume is to make a beginning toward such a trans-
lation, bringing both well-validated theory and empirical evidence to
the development of a coherent set of practical tools that can be used to
construct effective local programs.

A number of recent reviews provide initial guidance about the kinds
of programs likely to be effective and those almost certain to be ineffective (e.g., American Psychological Association [APA], 1993; Elliott &
Tolan, 1999; Embry & Flannery, 1999; Jenson & Howard, 1999c; Reiss
& Roth, 1993; Sandhu & Aspy, 2000). Effective prevention and intervention programs appear to share several common characteristics. Such
programs

- Are grounded in well-validated theory and knowledge of youth
  development,
- Target known risk and protective factors,
- Involve action at and among the multiple cultural networks within
  which youth live out their lives (including family, peer, school,
  and community),
- Focus on changing the entire ecological web of transactions among
  people within such networks, rather than on youth alone, and
- Are "constructional" (Goldiamond, 1974), emphasizing the construction of alternative practices, rather than being primarily punitive.

These basic principles apply to both preventive and interventive action.
In fact, prevention and intervention are best viewed not so much as
inextricably linked processes but rather as parts of the same process
(Embry & Flannery, 1999). The intervention programs likely to be most
powerful, as will be seen, involve higher intensity application of the
same basic strategies as those on which effective prevention relies.

Some increasingly common strategies are known to be ineffective.
"Control" strategies such as transfers of juveniles to adult courts, long
sentences, and shock incarceration programs like "boot camps" for
youth are demonstrably without value and are often damaging (Elliott
& Tolan, 1999). Ineffective programs for reducing school violence,
according to a review by Astor, Vargas, Pitner, and Meyer (1999), are
characterized by

- "A singular focus on the source of the problem" (p. 145), for example, focusing only on the child, or the family, or the school setting;
- "A psychological focus" (p. 145), focusing on characteristics and behaviors of individual youth, viewing youths as the "carriers" (p. 147) of violence;
- "Underuse of the school context" (p. 146), relying on add-on programs rather than changes in the basic social ecology within which children live out their lives; and
- An emphasis on the "deficits in children" (p. 147), therefore responding primarily by trying to repair children's pathologies or teach missing skills.

Similar emphases in programs other than those in schools produce similar poor results.

It is not surprising, given this information, that narrow skills-building approaches like anger management training or conflict resolution and peer mediation programs often produce disappointing results (DeJong, Spiro, Wilson-Brewer, Vince-Whitman, & Prothrow-Stith, n.d.; Elliott & Tolan, 1999; Samples & Aber, 1998). What is required is not primarily developing an additional curriculum or add-on program but rather constructing and maintaining a "new way of life" for everyone involved in the child's world. Doing so requires changes in interlocking practices within family, school, peer, and community cultures. For this reason, PEACE POWER is designed as a flexible strategy for cultural change that is deeply grounded in what is known about effective prevention and intervention, rather than as a narrow curriculum or a rigid program unlikely to be widely useful in a diverse social world.

The PEACE POWER Working Group has spent the past several years testing and refining a strategy based on the known causes of youth violence (chapter 2). Members of the working group, many of whom are listed in the acknowledgments, have included academic researchers as well as professionals in youth-serving agencies and schools, community members, and youth. The extensive available literature, as well as our own efforts, has made it clear to us that the most powerful solution for prevention and intervention is the co-construction of cultures in families, organizations, and communities—cultures that are characterized by high levels of four interlocking practices. The evidence for this assertion is found in subsequent chapters of the book. The four core PEACE POWER practices are shown in Figure 1.

4

Figure 1

The *PEACE POWER* Wheel. (The *PEACE POWER* Wheel is a registered service mark, used with permission of Mark A. Mattaini.)

The *PEACE POWER* Wheel, which draws on certain indigenous medicine wheel concepts (Lowery, 1998), suggests that the four core practices actually constitute an integrated whole. Much more detail regarding this framework will be presented in Section II of this book.

There are many empirically supported ways to increase levels of recognition and respect, as well as to help everyone in the culture find and use nonviolent power to build community. When conflict arises, there is more than one route to healing. Those involved need to design the specific approaches taken—one size clearly does not fit all, given variations in values, resources, cultures, and individuals in different settings.

The *PEACE POWER* Working Group has worked with regular and special education schools, after-school programs, camps, indigenous groups, shelters, and juvenile justice programs; naturally, each has required different emphases. For this reason, *PEACE POWER* is not a structured curriculum addressed only to youth who participate only for a limited time, nor a standardized program implemented in the same way everywhere. It involves, rather, a strategic change in cultural practices, a change shaped and supported in family, peer, organization, and community cultures in ways that are unique to the setting, but incorporate evidence-based tools and activities. Because it is possible to build such a strategy into everyday activities (e.g., in the classroom or the playground), it need not take time away from regular programming. The purpose of this volume is to present tools and activities that support such change, drawing on the experiences of members of the Working Group, as well as on a great deal of other research. The *PEACE POWER* strategy builds on a number of other evidence-based programs developed in recent years.

Promising Programs

A number of promising programs consistent with the science of behavior have emerged, in some cases demonstrating quite persuasive outcome data (for reviews, particularly of school-based approaches, see Astor et al., 1999; Lawler, 2000). The Center for the Study and Prevention of Violence at the University of Colorado selected 10 programs as Blueprint Programs, well-developed programs with persuasive evidence of efficacy (Muller & Mihalic, 1999). A number of other programs also appear to have reasonable to excellent empirical support. The *PEACE POWER* strategy draws and expands on a number of programs from both categories.

Bullying Prevention Programs

The vast majority of children in the United States report that they have been bullied at some point, with at least 15% bullied regularly—at school, on the street, even at church-sponsored activities. Similarly, most students participate in bullying at some point, with over 10% involved regularly (Walker, Colvin, & Ramsey, 1995). Despite the dangers associated with bullying, it is clearly deeply rooted in U.S. culture. The state of the art in bullying prevention is the model developed by Olweus (1993), an ecologically based approach that includes multiple actors and systems, and emphasizes that prevention of bullying is everyone's responsibility. This program is one of 10 identified by the Center for the Study and Prevention of Violence as a Blueprint Program (Muller & Mihalic, 1999). Effective bullying prevention and intervention programs are discussed in detail in chapter 4 of this volume.

PeaceBuilders

A school-anchored, but communitywide, approach to violence prevention, PeaceBuilders targets elementary school–aged children (Embry, Flannery, Vazsonyi, Powell, & Atha, 1996). The approach is heavily science based and, when well implemented, has reduced disciplinary actions and violence between 50% and 60%, with 77% of teachers indicating that the program made their jobs easier (see note 1). The *PEACE POWER* strategy has drawn extensively on the science underlying PeaceBuilders, adapting the general approach for youth at older developmental levels, with particular attention to flexible applications for varying community and cultural settings.

The Work of G. Roy Mayer and Colleagues

If PeaceBuilders can be viewed as a parent of *PEACE POWER,* the work of G. Roy Mayer and his colleagues must be seen as the grandparent, because the developers of PeaceBuilders drew heavily on that work. In the early 1980s, for example, Mayer and his colleagues (Mayer, Butterworth, Nafpaktitis, & Sulzer-Azaroff, 1983) implemented a program in Los Angeles County elementary and junior high schools in which high levels of social recognition produced dramatic reductions in vandalism costs (often an accessible marker variable for the range of antisocial behaviors) and improved discipline significantly. Mayer, Mitchell, Clementi, Clement-Robertson, Myatt, and Bullara (1993) implemented a dropout prevention program that relied substantially on changing the balance of positive versus punitive exchanges among high-risk ninth graders and staff working with them. Students involved in this program, formerly on task from 8% to 35% of the time, worked on task 70% to 100% of the time; suspensions dropped, and their dropout rate declined to less than the district average. These studies are examples of a program of research that spanned two decades, producing technologies with potentially wide applicability.

Aggression Replacement Training

Goldstein and his colleagues developed and refined an approach called aggression replacement training (ART) over many years. The full ART package includes three components: social skills training, anger management, and moral education. Among youth released from a correctional setting, 15% of those trained in ART were rearrested, compared to 43% of those who did not receive the training (Goldstein & Glick, 1994a). In a similar project with New York City street gangs, 52% of those not receiving the training were arrested during an eight-month period, compared to 13% of those who did receive it (Goldstein & Glick, 1994b). When offered to all residents in a runaway shelter, ART significantly reduced the rate of antisocial behavior (Nugent, Bruley, & Allen, 1998). Other studies of the procedure produced similar effects; ART must, therefore, be regarded as among the best practices in the field for work with high-risk populations. ART is discussed further in chapter 9.

Other Programs for High-Risk Youth

A number of other approaches have been demonstrated to be effective for youth at the high-risk end of the continuum. Among these are functional family therapy (Barton & Alexander, 1991) for those in the early stages of antisocial behavior, multisystemic treatment (Henggeler, Schoenwald, Borduin, Rowland, & Cunningham, 1998) for those displaying more serious problems, and the teaching family model for residential care, used extensively at Boys Town. A number of these approaches have contributed to the intensive PEACE POWER approach discussed in chapter 9.

Other Empirically Supported Programs

In addition to programs for high-risk youth, a few programs have been demonstrated to be effective in preventing youth violence. Among these are the I Can Problem Solve (ICPS) program developed by Shure (1992, 1999); prenatal and infancy nurse home visitation, a Blueprint Program; Big Brothers/Big Sisters of America, also a Blueprint Program; some service learning programs for at-risk youth (Waterman, 1997); and Quantum Opportunities, an educational incentives program for disadvantaged teens (a Blueprint Program; see note 2). The strategy presented in this book draws on, and expands on, many of the tools and activities in the useful programs mentioned. It provides, however, a single, integrated approach that is empirically grounded, but highly flexible; that is adaptable to local conditions and values; and that can be sustained with modest, locally available resources. The material is organized into three major sections. The first clarifies the extent of the problem of youth violence and offers a data-based perspective for understanding this often apparently mystifying issue. The second section presents the core *PEACE POWER* strategy, including a conceptual framework for action and an extensive menu of tools and activities for implementation. The final section discusses supporting practices that can help strengthen and sustain the core strategy, including organization level approaches and tools for working intensively with youth who are already involved in, or at high risk for, violence. Throughout, the emphasis is on constructing cultures of nonviolent empowerment among youth and the adults with whom they live out their lives.

Violence and Cultures of Coercion

The National Research Council defined violent acts as "behaviors by individuals that intentionally threaten, attempt, or inflict physical harm on others" (Reiss & Roth, 1993, p. 2). This definition is a useful starting point, but has several limitations. Another useful, but still somewhat narrow, definition is offered by Elliott and Tolan (1999):

> Violence is the use or credible threat of use of physical force intended to physically harm other persons or property. Our focus here is on interpersonal [as opposed to collective] violence, the use of physical force on another person with the intent to cause injury. This definition also includes the use of physical force to intentionally damage or destroy another's property. (p. 21)

One issue in these definitions is the use of the word "intentionally" or "intended." A scientific understanding of human behavior suggests that people often act without being fully aware of why they are doing so (Mattaini, Twyman, Chin, & Lee, 1996). In addition, many incidents that are of concern here are to some extent "accidental"—as when a bystander is hit by gunfire. An even more important consideration, however, is that there are many forms of coercion, oppression, exploitation, and threat that produce terrible harm, even though they may not involve primarily physical action. Physical violence and threats of the same are simply examples of coercive behavior that are particularly easy to observe. The *PEACE POWER* Working Group has addressed action to prevent the full spectrum of violence and coercion, and the strategy and tools developed by the Group attempt to construct cultural practices that will decrease these in a context of nonviolent empowerment.

The two chapters in this first section introduce the issues and set the stage for the *PEACE POWER* strategy. Chapter 1 sketches the epidemiology of violent behavior among youth. Chapter 2 outlines a number of explanatory perspectives for understanding the problem and elaborates a three-level (biobehavioral, experiential, and cultural) framework that integrates what is known in ways that lead directly to preventive and interventive strategies.

1

The Problem of Youth Violence

To understand the reasons for violent behavior among youth, it is necessary to examine a number of important epidemiological questions. How much violence occurs? Who is involved? What factors increase or decrease the risk of involvement? How stable is violent behavior over time? What is the impact of exposure to high levels of violence?

Several excellent summaries of the incidence and prevalence of violence, youth violence in particular, have been published (e.g., Jenson & Howard, 1999b; Reiss & Roth, 1993). A few key statistics may help to establish the breadth of the issues. About 3,000 persons under the age of 18 are murdered each year (only about 1% at school, despite attention to a few high-visibility cases; Kaufman et al., 1998). Not included in this figure are the roughly 5,000 children who die as the result of violence turned back upon themselves every year. (As it turns out, the basic strategies for preventing violence toward others are consistent with those required for preventing suicide.)

Rates of arrest for violent crimes among youth increased dramatically from 1987 through 1994 (especially, but not exclusively, in large urban areas); since that time, they have generally declined, although quite unevenly. For example, the juvenile homicide rate dropped by two-thirds between 1993 and 1999, while the rate of aggravated assault declined less dramatically and the rate of simple assault declined very little (Figure 2; Snyder, 2000).

Despite recent declines, the numbers for the United States are still much higher than those for other developed countries. Young people between the ages of 12 and 24 are the victims of violent crimes at least 2 million times a year, with peak risks between the ages of 16 and 19; the peak age

Figure 2

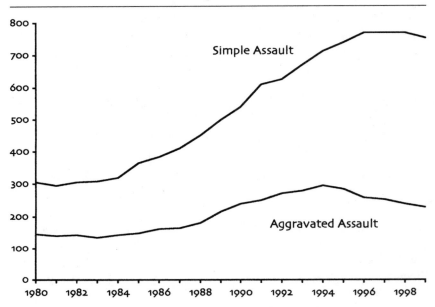

Juvenile arrest rates per 100,000 for simple and aggravated assault, 1980–1999, ages 10–17. Source: Data derived from Snyder, 2000.

for violent offenders is only a bit higher (Perkins, 1997). In 1999, rates of victimization continued to be two to three times higher for youth than for adults (Bureau of Justice Statistics, 2000). Risks for gay and lesbian youth are exceptionally high. Battering in dating relationships and sexual assault are even more common for teenaged girls than for adult women (Chesney-Lind & Brown, 1999). More than one in three high school students does not feel safe at school, and 14% of high school students (in some studies, many more) report having carried weapons to school, usually out of fear (Josephson Institute of Ethics, 2001); and 80% to 90% of youth report being bullied at some point, with 15% reporting serious and persistent bullying (Walker, Colvin, & Ramsey, 1995). Overall, the problem of violent victimization among youth is clearly serious.

Population Indicators

Howard and Jenson (1999) cite Earls' (1994) recommendation that certain indicators such as race, ethnicity, and gender not be presented as "risk factors," since they are not "causes" of violent behavior but are merely predictive indicators of what groups may be particularly vulnerable. Race and gender, for example, do not cause violence, but they are markers of vulnerability. Garbarino (1999) persuasively suggests that economic and social mechanisms (e.g., poverty and discrimination) are likely to be responsible for increased vulnerability among some groups.

Gender

Violence among youth is perpetrated primarily by males, who are arrested about nine times as often as females for violent crimes. In addition, males report much higher rates of violent behavior in surveys. These rates are changing, as rates of violence-associated arrests for young women have been increasing throughout the early 1990s, while rates for males remained relatively stable (Potter, 1999). The extent of change can be overstated, however; although young women now account for about one-quarter of juvenile arrests, only a tiny proportion (about 2%) of those arrests are for serious violent crimes (Chesney-Lind & Brown, 1999).

Some studies indicate that the level of gang involvement for girls may be increasing, but the data are inconsistent and do not always indicate that the role of the "gang" for those who are members is primarily criminal or violent. The gang often provides significant social support, sometimes substituting for missing family support (Chesney-Lind & Brown, 1999). It is clear, however, that young women involved in gangs are at high risk for sexual abuse and assault. Girls involved in juvenile offenses have more extensive histories of physical and sexual abuse than do boys of the same age, and they experience more serious mental health problems (Chesney-Lind & Brown; Potter, 1999). Factors that contribute to girls' involvement in violence may be different from those that affect young men, and somewhat different preventive and interventive strategies may therefore be required.

Race

Rates of victimization by violent crimes are much lower for whites than for most youth of color (Perkins, 1997). Rates of arrest for violent crimes are also higher for African American and Latino youth than for whites, although the differences are not as great in self-report surveys of involvement in violent crime (Howard & Jenson, 1999). This is not surprising, given the deep and longstanding biases built into the justice system in the United States. Still, minority youth are more likely to report being involved in violent behavior, including the use of weapons, than are white youth. Socioeconomic factors, as well as family education and stability, moderate these differences (Franke, 2000). Socioeconomic and family factors do not account for all of the variance among races, which is to be expected given the complexity of differences in the experience of youth of different racial and ethnic groups. Differences that go beyond simply financial and educational factors include, for example, variations in community stability and opportunity structures, and the deeper effects of oppression that have impact at the personal and collective levels. Differences among groups, therefore, should perhaps be viewed primarily as indicators of the level of social justice in society.

Risk and Protective Factors

Table 1 lists both population indicators and risk factors that are associated with increased risk for youth violence, drawn from a number of reviews of the related research.

The table is organized according to individual, situational, and macrocontextual factors. One serious limitation of this kind of listing is that it makes no provision for transactional effects; for example, high rates of truancy and low bonding to school are likely to be related to conditions in schools, rather than being exclusively "individual." (See discussion of such transactional questions in chapter 2.) Nevertheless, the listing in Table 1 is helpful in several ways. It makes clear that simplistic explanations for violence, and correspondingly simplistic solutions (as often arise in political discussions), are likely to be of only marginal benefit. Recognition of multiple transactional contributors points to the importance of approaches that target multiple systems (peer, family, school, and macroculture). In addition, factors contributing to violent behavior are likely to vary substantially among both communities and individuals affected, so flexibility and individualization in program development are essential.

Most studies of risk factors are correlational, meaning that the direction of causation is unknown; there is evidence, for example, that aggressive youth seek out antisocial peers early in their developmental trajectories (Patterson, Reid, & Dishion, 1992). Association with delinquent peers, then, can only loosely be seen as a risk factor, even though

Table 1. Risk Factors for Youth Violence

Individual Factors

Population Indicators
Male gender
Age 15–25
African American or Hispanic
American race or ethnicity
Low SES

Biological Factors
High testosterone levels
High levels of lead
Low resting heart rate
Low CNS serotonin levels

Psychological Characteristics
Impulsivity/hyperactivity/restlessness
Concentration problems
Risk-taking/sensation-seeking
orientation
Early involvement in problem
behaviors (e.g., sexual intercourse)
Early aggressiveness
Neuropsychological dysfunction
Low verbal skills

Family Factors
Parental criminality and proviolence
attitudes
Child neglect/abuse
Marital and family conflict
Low levels of parent–child interaction
and family bonding
Excessively punitive or permissive
family management practices
Frequent changes of residence
Leaving home before age 16

School Factors
High rates of truancy
Suspension
Dropping out
Low academic expectations
Low bonding to school
Poor school performance
Enrollment in a school attended by a
large number of delinquents

Peer Factors
Delinquent/violent peers
Delinquent/violent siblings
Gang membership

Situational Factors
Victim–victimizer relationship
Role of bystanders or witnesses
Behavior of victim
Substance abuse
Presence/availability of a weapon

Macrocontextual Factors
Neighborhood poverty and popula-
tion density
High residential mobility among
neighborhood residents
Community disorganization
Media influences

Source: Jenson & Howard, 1999.
SES, socioeconomic status; CNS, central nervous system.

delinquent peer cultures are likely to support continued antisocial behavior among the group members. As discussed in chapter 2, the multiple cultures (family, peer, organization, community, and sociocultural) within which youth are embedded are probably the most powerful and manipulable factors that violence prevention programs have to work with. It is also important in examining lists of risk factors like that in Table 1 to look carefully at the underlying information. For example, high levels of testosterone are "associated" with high levels of aggression, but some data indicate that increased levels of the hormone may be a result, rather than a cause, of aggression. Also notable are some factors not listed, such as genetic factors, which have generally not shown the associations with violence that some expect.

One factor on Table 1 that is clearly central to reducing the damage associated with violent behavior is the ready availability of weapons. Canada (1995), in his instructively titled book, *Fist Stick Knife Gun,* indicates that a critical factor in the increasing rates of serious injury and death by violence during the last half of the twentieth century was the availability of more lethal weaponry. Those attacked are much more likely to suffer a severe injury if the attacker is using a high-powered handgun or assault weapon than a fist. Further, the immediate risk of injury to an attacker is higher *without* a firearm, as the attacker may also be injured in close combat. Firearms—if used quickly and first—maintain a "safe distance." Of course, this advantage does not hold in the long run, if the person with the firearm is dealing with many other similarly armed individuals. For youth who have limited rule-governed behavior repertoires and who tend to respond impulsively, however, the thought of long-term consequences may not be a powerful influence. The research on risks associated with availability of weapons for individual adults yields mixed results (Reiss & Roth, 1993), but the best current thinking in the field views firearms as "criminogenic" (Moore, Prothrow-Stith, Guyer, & Spivak, 1994) and certainly dangerous among youth. On a populationwide basis, firearms are much more likely to be directed against oneself, one's family, or friends than toward unknown criminals.

Small local programs can sometimes meaningfully, but often only modestly, affect factors like weapons availability. The same is true in regard to a number of other macrocultural and community factors. Communities with high levels of disorganization and transience, poor schools that shatter hope and self-recognition, poverty, widespread drug availability, few opportunities except those that are illegal, and frequent exposure to older persons who are deeply involved in criminal behavior rather than legitimate pursuits, not surprisingly, produce many social problems, including violence (Williams & Van Dorn, 1999). These are not, of course, simply personal problems, but rather major social issues with profound social justice implications. Local programs can in many cases have some effect even on such factors, but the importance of policy advocacy directed toward recognizing and addressing larger issues of oppression must also be emphasized.

The flip side of risks is the identification of protective factors, including those associated with resilience even in the face of risk factors. Most youth exposed to multiple risk factors do not become violent (Jonson-Reid, 1999). Understanding resilience requires a framework for understanding both violence and its alternatives, the subject of chapter 2. For the present, however, it is useful to note that meaningful, positive relationships with adults (e.g., parents, mentors); positive involvement in community activities, churches, and schools; and individual strengths of some kinds are associated with decreased risk for violence (see Biglan & Taylor, 2000, for an excellent recent review). A straightforward public health approach (e.g., Moore et al., 1994) aims to decrease exposure to risk factors and to increase exposure to protective factors. Such an approach is eminently sensible; just how to carry it out is complex, however, and often requires a deeper analytic understanding of the mechanisms involved.

Stability of Violent Behavior over Time?

Many researchers in the field have asserted that patterns of aggression are quite stable over the life course. As Elliott and Tolan (1999) note, "From this perspective, violence is established in early childhood, and subsequent life course events in adolescence and adulthood have little or no impact on this behavior" (p. 33). The authors continue, however, by noting that researchers have recently identified serious weaknesses in this hypothesis. For example, "although antisocial behavior in childhood is a good predictor of antisocial behavior (and violence) in adolescence and adulthood, most antisocial children do not grow up to be antisocial or violent adults" (p. 33). Embry and Flannery (1999) further refine our understanding of this issue, as follows: If predictions of who will and who will not be violent at a later age, based on aggression and violence at an earlier age, are 80% accurate, the number of false positives will outnumber the number of true positives, because only about 2% of a cohort of youth are likely to become violent criminals. With a 20% error rate, 1,968 young people who would not become antisocial adults will be misidentified as potential criminals from a group of 10,000, while only 160 true positives will be correctly identified. As a result, many youth who would not have become seriously antisocial adults may be labeled as troubled, which in itself may cause additional problems.

A critical consideration is whether any existing stability should be attributed to individual level variables like "personality traits" or underlying biological factors, or whether contextual stability is the real issue. Changes, both personal and contextual, at later developmental points can very significantly change trajectories for better or for worse. Extensive data indicate that changing experiences change both biology and behavior (see chapter 2). It seems particularly likely, based on current knowledge of human behavior, that stability in aggressive and violent behavior is rooted largely in ecological stability (Elliott & Tolan, 1999). The work of Patterson and his colleagues (Patterson et al., 1992, as well as earlier studies) is important here. Walker and colleagues (1995) summarize the findings of Patterson's program of research:

A host of family stressors . . . pressure family members severely. Under the influence of these stressors, normal parenting practices are disrupted and family routines become chaotic and unpredictable. Disrupted parenting practices, in turn, lead to social interactions among family members that are reflected in negative-aggressive escalations, the use of coercive techniques to force the submission of others, and the aversive control of behavior by others. . . . Children from these homes come to school with negative attitudes about schooling, a limited repertoire of cooperative behavior, and a predilection to use coercive tactics to control and manipulate others. If a young child brings an antisocial behavior pattern to school . . . he or she has a severely elevated risk status for rejection by both peers and teachers. Peer and teacher rejection, in turn, is associated with academic failure, and the child is increasingly isolated. Because of this rejection and social isolation, the antisocial child seeks out others who share the same status, attitudes, and behavioral characteristics. (p. 19)

In addition, the educational system often relies heavily on coercive control, which tends to spark further coercive countercontrol from the youth involved. The stage is now set; 70% of these youth will have a felony arrest within two years. It is not just the child's behavior that is "stable" by this point; few changes are likely at home, at school, or with peers once the patterns Patterson described are established. Given stability in those conditions that shape and maintain the child's repertoires, it is not surprising that the young person's behavior appears "stable." There is very persuasive evidence that changing a child's world will change his or her behavior, however. Stability, therefore, should be viewed as descriptively often true, but by no means inevitable.

One final point. The most antisocial youth are typically exposed to extremely high levels of coercion, but in U.S. society, compared with that of all other developed countries, the *average* exposure to both violence and coercion is extraordinarily high. One particularly evident dimension of this exposure involves experience with and observation of physical violence. The problem of coercive cultures and contexts extends much deeper than this, however. In fact, a strong case can be made that everyday forms of coercion nurture, encourage, and structure the factors that produce violence.

Exposure to Violence

The rates and effects of children's and youths' exposure to violence are further considerations with serious social justice implications. The data reported in a review by Chapin and Singer (1999) are staggering. Among fifth- and sixth-grade students in a low-income Washington, DC, neighborhood, 43% had witnessed a mugging; 31%, a shooting (Richters & Martinez, 1993). In a survey of large inner-city high schools, one-quarter of the boys indicated that they had been shot at, and 45% had witnessed someone being shot at (Singer, Miller, & Slovak, 1997). One-quarter of youth on the south side of Chicago had witnessed a homicide by age 17 (Bell & Jenkins, 1993). A child growing up in Chicago is 15 times more likely to be the victim of homicide than is a child in Northern Ireland (Chapin & Singer). In another study of youth in high-risk communities in New York and Washington, DC,

> [v]ery high percentages of adolescents reported having been exposed to such events as "seen another selling drugs," "seen another

being arrested," or "seen another with a weapon" (81%, 89%, and 82%, respectively). . . . More strikingly, more than half (59%) reported having "seen another being severely beaten" and almost a third have "seen another attacked with a knife" (32%) or "seen another shot with a gun" (32%). Finally, 24% reported having "seen another killed." Overall, subjects witnessed an average of 7 of the 13 events [asked about in the study]." (Allen, Jones, Seidman, & Aber, 1999, p. 126)

Chapin and Singer (1999) make a powerful argument that, given these extremely high levels of exposure, it may be necessary to turn to the information available about combat stress and battle fatigue to work with youth living their lives under such conditions. Even exposure to relatively mild violent events can have seriously negative effects on young people, but this exposure is something more. Rather than treating such children as patients suffering from mental disorders, Chapin and Singer suggest viewing them as victims struggling with the effects of trauma, responding in normal ways to abnormal conditions. This approach would call for such strategies as debriefing victims, helping them give meaning to what they have seen in political and social justice terms, and providing emotional reassurance that the rest of the world is not like what they have experienced. For many of these youth, of course, the question is whether the world really is as they have experienced it—do they live in a world of coercion and oppression in which fear, anger, and countercontrol are the most adaptive responses?

Many of our children, at times probably even most, live in environments of fear and threat, in some cases very severe and life-threatening threat. As Jenson and Howard (1999b) indicate, "Youth violence has deep roots in American society" (p. 3). The heart of the problem lies in the deep and, in many sectors, almost exclusive reliance of U.S. society on coercive and adversarial processes.

Understanding
Youth Violence

They fear the world. They destroy what they fear. They fear themselves.

(Silko, 1977, p. 142)

In her novel, *Ceremony*, from which this quote comes, Laguna Pueblo author Leslie Marmon Silko narrates the story of a gathering of witches, metaphorically describing how the basic trust in the universe characteristic of most indigenous peoples the world over shifted to the fear, threat, and anxiety so common in modern society. Gerald Vizenor, an Anishinaabe "crossblood" (in his own terms), describes modern U.S. culture as a "culture of death" (1991, p. 9). These assertions go beyond fiction. Historian Calvin Luther Martin (1999), who uses Silko's work as one of numerous examples of the contrasts between Native American cultures and European cultures, indicates, "This, I think, has been our most devastating and enduring impact on this continent and its indigenes: Europeans furnished it all in fear" (p. 168). This is not to say that fear, and evil, have not been present in all cultures; rather, rapid cultural changes in North America in recent centuries, including colonialism and slavery, have perhaps taken our society beyond a critical tipping point.

The problem goes beyond the oppression of indigenous peoples and other minorities, critical though this is. A report from the National Research Council (Shonkoff & Phillips, 2000) indicates that modern life exposes children and families to dramatically increased stresses and that these can have profoundly negative effects. More specifically, renowned behavioral scientist Murray Sidman (2001) decries "the almost exclusive use of coercion in all spheres of human interaction" (p. 1) in contemporary society, despite scientific evidence that in the long run such reliance is self-defeating. As Sidman further notes, "Yes, we can get people to do what we want by punishing or threatening to punish them for doing anything else, but when we do, we sow the seeds of personal disengagement, isolation from society, neurosis, intellectual rigidity, hostility, and rebellion" (p. 2). Later, describing research into this almost universal social dynamic, Sidman indicates, "punishment and deprivation . . . spawn aggression. But coercion induces more than just the aggressive act itself. After being punished, a subject will do anything it can just to gain access to another subject it can attack" (p. 201). There is, in other words, something seriously wrong in a culture that relies so heavily on coercive strategies; further, that wrongness contributes in important ways to the levels of violence present.

Perspectives on Violence

After decades of study and research, multiple perspectives on violence have emerged, and many have something to contribute to our understanding of youth violence. Particularly important in choosing a primary viewpoint are two questions: Is the approach consistent with the available data, and does it clarify accessible points for intervention?

Biobehavioral and Biogenetic Perspectives

Although individual genetic differences no doubt result in varying predispositions for many forms of behavior, even sociobiologists agree that genetics cannot account for differences observed in rates of violent behavior among population groups and rapid changes observed in the incidence of violence; the patterns are not consistent with genetic mechanisms, and genes do not change as quickly and erratically as the incidence of violence does in population groups (Wilson & Herrnstein, 1985). Some persons are more prone to violence than others, but such variation appears to be a universal phenomenon that some cultures apparently handle better than do others. Other physiological factors, including exposure to environmental toxins (e.g., lead), exposure to alcohol or certain other drugs *in utero*, and poor nutrition early in life apparently do affect propensities for violence, however (Mirsky & Siegel, 1994).

A major issue is whether the primary determinant of violent behavior is usually biological. For example, Mirsky and Siegel (1994) view

24

violence as "maladaptive" and indicate that violent behavior is performed by "abnormal (presumably) human subjects" (p. 9). Further, they state that "it seems reasonable to hypothesize that humans who are engaging in maladaptive, violent behavior have some brain abnormality" (p. 79). According to other biobehaviorists and behavioral scientists, there are serious problems with this analysis. Existing data consistently suggest that biology alone can at best account for only a small and highly inconsistent amount of the variance in violent behavior (Miczek, Mirsky, Carey, DeBold, & Raine, 1994). Rather, the evidence available suggests that biological influences act in concert with environmental events as part of complex causal mechanisms (Jonson-Reid, 1999).

Social Learning Approaches

Social learning theory (e.g., Bandura, 1986) suggests that imitation and modeling are primary determinants of human behavior and, therefore, are likely to be involved both in the development of aggressive and violent behaviors, and in the construction of effective responses. For example, although the relationship between viewing violence and perpetrating it is not simple and linear, major studies now make clear that viewing violence, especially violence that "works," in the media or in real life is likely to be associated with higher levels of violent behavior (American Psychological Association [APA], 1993; Reiss & Roth, 1993). In a related vein, the "catharsis" theory (i.e., that watching violence reduces violence) is clearly incorrect (Goldstein, Glick, & Gibbs, 1998); watching aggression and violence is associated with increases in aggression and violence. In addition, the evidence shows that reliance on physical punishment in raising children increases the rate of antisocial behavior in which those children engage (Gunnoe & Mariner, 1997; Straus, Sugarman, & Giles-Sims, 1997). Although qualifications and cautions are necessary in each of these research areas, the basic conclusion is clear: Those who live with violence are more likely to become violent. The mechanisms probably go beyond social learning, but social learning clearly plays a role.

Developmental Pathways

Longitudinal studies of child development among antisocial boys help to clarify how social learning takes place (and can also in some cases suggest links to biobehavioral factors). Important studies conducted by

Patterson and his colleagues (Patterson, DeBaryshe, & Ramsey, 1989; Patterson, Reid, & Dishion, 1992) suggest that the most common developmental pathway for seriously antisocial youth is as follows:

1. Early in life, parenting is chaotic and coercive; an accumulation of severe environmental and intrafamilial aversives (e.g., poverty, drug abuse, family violence) is often present. Temperaments of both parent and child, which may include biological dimensions, may contribute to these problems. Antisocial models are common in the home, as is extensive reliance on physical punishment and other forms of harsh, inconsistent discipline (Biglan, 1995). By early childhood, antisocial children have learned that aggressive and other antisocial repertoires help them to escape aversives and obtain reinforcers in the family; often, they have learned few other repertoires for doing so. This learning may begin with observation, but personal experience reinforces it.
2. When the child begins school, he (most, but not all, are male) brings those social repertoires with him. As a result, both prosocial peers and teachers often rapidly reject the child.
3. Academic failure follows quickly, and bullying may develop as one way to obtain some level of social contact and control.
4. The child often finds that other antisocial children, whose behavioral repertoires are familiar, make up the only peer group available to him. By about grade 4 or 5, many antisocial children become members of such deviant peer groups, which then encourage further antisocial behavior (Walker, Colvin, & Ramsey, 1995). Some, however, remain socially isolated and may engage primarily in covert antisocial behaviors.

Consistent with these findings and others that indicate the effects of multiple community level factors through processes of social learning and social control, the social developmental model (Catalano & Hawkins, 1996) emphasizes the need to focus on constructing healthy bonds between youth and the multiple systems that shape their lives.

Feminist Thought

The perspectives on violence discussed thus far, while not inconsistent with recognition of systematic oppression, do not explicitly address it to the extent that feminist thought does. There are at least two areas in which feminist perspectives provide important insights. One has to do with the differential pathways to antisocial behavior that are characteristic of girls as contrasted with those that are characteristic of boys. Developmentally, feminist research indicates that for many girls, adolescence is "a painful process of losing both voice and relationship" (Potter, 1999, p. 126). Girls may be more involved in, and damaged by, *relational aggression*, "which is characterized by the threat of withdrawal of relationship to control the behavior of others" (Potter, p. 127), than in and by physical aggression.

Feminist thinking also emphasizes the need to look explicitly at gender and power dynamics. With regard to girls, it is clearly essential to address societal acceptance of systematic oppression in both subtle and overt ways (including sexual coercion; Biglan, 1996) as part of any comprehensive strategy to reduce violence. But, as noted by Chesney-Lind and Brown (1999), the dynamics of power as played out in gender relations also support violence by boys and men. Not only are aggression and violence by males more socially acceptable, but also many social groups actually encourage the use of coercive control strategies in ways that are likely to generalize beyond gender relations. Programs need to take the specific victimization experiences of women seriously, including male violence and coercion toward women, in order to build respect across genders and address specific issues of power and voice.

Indigenous Thought

If, as indicated at the beginning of this chapter, indigenous people see fear and punishment as the wrong approach, one likely to exacerbate an already problematic situation, what are the alternatives? And does indigenous thought in this area have anything to contribute to those who are immersed in mainstream Western cultures? Rupert Ross, a Canadian attorney who has studied indigenous justice systems around the world, but especially among Canadian First Nations peoples (1992, 1996), believes that the answer to the second question is yes, and other data support the assertion. Ross begins his 1996 book by quoting from a First Nations justice proposal:

> Probably one of the most serious gaps in the system is the different perception of wrongdoing and how best to treat it. In the non-Indian community, committing a crime seems to mean that the

individual is a *bad person* and therefore must be punished. . . . The Indian communities view a wrongdoing as *a misbehaviour which requires teaching or an illness which requires healing*" [emphasis added by Ross]. (p. 5)

The statement hints at the developmental processes required for prevention of violence, as well as potentially effective approaches for intervention. What do children need to learn to become effective adults? Among other things, Ross's informants indicate that they need to learn that they are "born into a network of relationships and responsibilities" (1996, p. 129):

> They had to learn to see themselves not as separate, individual beings but as active participants in webs of complex interdependencies with the animals, the plants, the earth and the waters. Their first obligation, then, was to look for all the connections and relationships that surrounded them, to understand "things" in that dynamic way. The second was to learn, as best they could, over a lifetime of study, how they all worked together. Third, they had to forever look for ways to accommodate themselves to those dynamics, rather than trying to dominate them. At its most basic, life was taught to be a process of *connecting* yourself, in accommodating ways, to everything and everyone around you. (1996, p. 66)

Teaching about connectedness and healing breaches in connectedness then become the keys to prevention and intervention in human problems, including violence. Social isolation and exclusion (present in several recent high-visibility violent crimes committed by youth) naturally lead to imbalance and "misbehavior." There is little room for ego or hierarchy in this view of life. Martin (1999), echoing Napoleon (1991), labels living in recognition of connectedness as "the way of the human being," the way of knowing who one is in context. Contemporary sociocultural structures often fail entirely to help young people reach this essential developmental cusp and, in fact, often work against such complete development.

Links among Multiple Perspectives on Violence

Each of these perspectives has something to contribute to effective prevention of violence and intervention when it does occur, and there are obvious links among them. Biology is involved in all behavior and is profoundly affected by environmental events. The life course in context shapes personal and collective outcomes, in part through social learning. Realities of context include, for many youth, experiences of oppression, coercion, and threat. Developmental pathways toward antisocial behavior and pathways toward deeply prosocial behavior appear to be profoundly different.

Contemporary behavioral science is consistent with these multiple transactional perspectives to a significant degree. That science, in turn, suggests the key dimensions of an integrated strategy. It is important to note, however, that although different viewpoints can contribute to each other and some integration is possible, they remain different. That diversity, as is true for other forms of diversity, should be valued and respected. For that reason, the integrated strategy should not be understood as an eclectic amalgam of biobehavioral, social learning, developmental, feminist, indigenous, ecobehavioral, and other approaches, but rather as a strategy drawn from behavioral science that has its own coherence, which has been substantially enriched by these other views, especially by indigenous perspectives.

Ecobehavioral Science and Violence

"Violence is learned behavior" (Flannery & Huff, 1999, p. 294). This simple statement provides more information than may be immediately evident, since in fact a great deal is known about behavior and how it is learned. Violent and coercive behaviors are not a single class of behaviors, of course. The topography of coercion (i.e., what one observes when it occurs) varies tremendously (e.g., verbal threats, subtle threatening looks, physical attacks, the use of weapons, state-sponsored terrorism). The functions of violent behavior, which involve its effects on the environment, are complex and multiple. The "causes" of violent actions are even more so. Violence and other coercive behaviors are parts of ongoing, transactional webs of events that always occur in the context of many other events and conditions, which reciprocally affect each other.

In the work of the *PEACE POWER* Working Group, we have relied on an integrated framework that incorporates these considerations, but which is still simple enough to deal with conceptually. This framework, emerging from the science of behavior (in which researchers attempt to understand behavior in terms of natural science), has proven very robust, has led to many predictions that have proven to be true, and has been widely applied to important human issues (see, e.g., Malott, Whaley, & Malott, 1997; Mattaini & Thyer, 1996).

The approach that we rely on for integration is selectionist, indicating that behavior is selected by consequences at three levels: the biological/genetic, the experiential, and the cultural (Skinner, 1981; see also Rottschaefer, 2000, for a similar division from a slightly different viewpoint):

1. At the biological level, the process of natural selection, in which effective variations are selected by a particular environment, is well established. Other biological factors interact with genetically determined physiology in many ways, some of which directly affect potential for violence.

2. Extensive data confirm that, all else being equal, people tend to repeat behavior that produces positive outcomes and not to repeat behavior that produces pain. This is the experiential level, in which behavior is selected by its consequences for the person over the life course. (The "all else" phrase emphasizes the importance of the biological and cultural levels, as well as the many concurrent factors present in a person's experience.)

3. The cultural level is actually a special case of the experiential level; groups shape and maintain certain practices among members of the group (a reasonably accurate description of a "culture"), often in part because of the outcomes for the group as a whole (Glenn, 1991).

Considerable data are now available about how coercion and violence are selected at each of these levels. Crucially, there is now a good deal of information about the connections among levels. When aggregated and integrated, this information provides substantial guidance for the development of an effective strategy for violence prevention and intervention. Community-based prevention programs can target particular manipulable variables.

Biological Factors

As mentioned earlier, increases and decreases in rates of violence in communities and within particular social groups are not primarily genetic and also do not appear to result from other sudden biological shifts. Like driving a car or conducting a symphony, violent behavior requires a physical body, and also like those other actions, violence is not organized at the physiological level. Violence is not a simple response to biological factors, but such factors can affect an individual's sensitivity to environmental transactions and conditions. These biological effects operate in significant part at the level of hormones and neurotransmitters (Carlson, 1998).

Although the actions and interactions of neurochemicals are extremely complex and are at best only partially understood, certain basic operations now appear to have clear connections with violent behavior. In particular, levels of serotonin, dopamine, norepinephrine, and certain steroids appear to play an important role in violence and response to preventive strategies (Embry & Flannery, 1999). High levels of serotonin in critical regions of the brain, for example, are associated with intrinsic motivation, learning, and experiences of satisfaction, while too little serotonin is associated with aggression and self-injury. Achieving adequately high levels of serotonin, therefore, is protective with regard to both violence against others and violence against oneself (i.e., suicide). High levels of dopamine in particular brain areas are associated with control of motor behavior and ability to socialize cooperatively; low levels are associated with hyperactivity and fighting. High levels of norepinephrine are associated with suspiciousness, as well as constant scanning for, and hypersensitivity to, environmental threat. Increased levels of certain steroids (e.g., cortisol, testosterone, and related hormones) are also associated with higher levels of aggression and may interfere with the biological structures needed to process serotonin, although the association is not direct, and is moderated by other experiential factors (Biegon, 1990). There are reasonable explanations for the evolution of these biobehavioral processes, since they would be protective under expectable conditions in prehistoric times (Embry & Flannery, 1999)— but our world has changed much more quickly than our biology can.

One crucial fact for violence prevention strategies is that levels of such neurotransmitters and steroids in children and youth are highly sensitive to environmental events; therefore, parents, teachers, and other environmental actors can directly affect the immediate physiological state of youth (which over the long term also affects neurological structure). Levels of dopamine in the primary reward centers of the brain, for example, are intimately related to experiences of reinforcement (Carlson, 1998). Hyperactive children, in particular, may require high levels of reinforcement. There are many kinds of reinforcers, however. Thus, fighting increases the level of dopamine, as does precision praise for positive effort (Embry & Flannery, 1999). Frequent, targeted rewards increase levels of dopamine, some of which is converted to serotonin. Social and affectionate exchanges, including kind words, praise, and physical touch, can also increase levels of serotonin. In contrast, threats increase levels of norepinephrine and cortisol, while rejections decrease levels of serotonin. Over time, exposure to high levels of traumatic experience, for example, observations of violence, affect youth at the level of brain structure. Their brains may become "tuned"—highly sensitized—to scan for possible threat. Many experience the classic symptoms of posttraumatic stress disorder, including a numbing effect that involves the release of beta-endorphins, the body's natural painkillers (see Embry & Flannery, 1999, for more detail).

Luckily, changes in environment can reliably and substantially change these biobehavioral factors (Shonkoff & Phillips, 2000). Environments that provide a great deal of recognition and affection in association with few coercive conditions (e.g., threat, punishment) will shift immediate neurochemical events and eventually modify structure as well. These changes may occur more quickly for younger youth, while those with longer histories of trauma may require prophylactic environments for extended period. (Not surprisingly, then, Wolf, Braukmann, and Ramp [1987] suggest that those with long histories of antisocial behavior perhaps should be viewed as having a disabling condition requiring extended support.) Well-designed programs that address these needs reliably produce dramatic changes in behavior, even for those with substantial antisocial history who may have already moved into the adult correctional system (Cohen & Filipczak, 1971). As noted earlier, however, there is more happening in violent and coercive behaviors than physiology; personal experience predictably changes both behavior and the underlying biology.

Experiential (Ecobehavioral) Selection

As violence is learned behavior, an individual's history of learning over the life course is critical to understanding what he or she does and why. Decades of extremely robust research have shown that "intentional" or instrumental behavior is selected over time because it works (Malott et al., 1997). Actions that "pay off," that produce positive outcomes, tend to be repeated, while those that do not eventually tend to fade. While there are many complexities and learning histories are difficult to capture in simple ways, behavior in general occurs because it is in some way functional, and violence is no exception (Mattaini, Twyman, Chin, & Lee, 1996). Youth who rely on coercive threats and violence have learned over time that by doing so they can sometimes escape or avoid negative events, obtain some level of positive payoffs, or both. Many such youth have not learned alternative ways to achieve those ends. Particularly challenging for many are behaviors that produce only cumulative, distant, and uncertain outcomes, with few immediate positive consequences. For example, for young people with a history of school failure and few skills, studying is likely to be productive, if at all, only over a long period of time. In the short run, there is often no obvious payoff, either practically or socially.

Not all of the functions of violent behavior need be in the person's awareness. For example, one subclass of violent action appears to relieve the biological–affective condition labeled "rage." Although such behavior is biologically different from that often labeled "instrumental," it is, nonetheless, functional—it produces an improved condition (Mattaini et al., 1996).

Violence, being functional, offers some influence over one's world, some "power," even if this power is limited and of poor quality. For persons with few alternatives, some power is better than none. Asking youth, therefore, to "Just Say No" to violence is a call to give up what may be the only power that they have so far discovered. Behavioral theory and research consistently indicate how unlikely the success of a strategy that provides no alternative path to reward is (Mattaini et al., 1996). What is required in such situations are new repertoires, alternative ways to exert influence, to "do power" in one's life.

The *PEACE POWER* Working Group conducted focus groups with students and school personnel in two co-located alternative schools. In the focus groups, we explored the apparent functions of violent and coercive behavior by young people, and identified several distinct clusters of violent and coercive actions (Mattaini & Lowery, 1999). Four of the major clusters involve rewards of one kind or another. One very common cluster involves gaining or maintaining status or "face"; this pattern emerges in many different situations and in a variety of ways, from bragging and tough posturing to "snapping"—verbal competitions involving rapid, creative put-downs. A second cluster of incidents begins with attempts to elicit sexual attention (often quite awkwardly). A third, sometimes quite serious in terms of the severity of threat involved, cluster appears to be motivated by the desire to get others to do what one wishes—to assert coercive power and control. Some of the examples given involve threats and violence within dating relationships, but the general pattern clearly operates in other situations as well. The fourth cluster, consistent with the biological research discussed earlier, consists of aggressive acts carried out for "fun" (i.e., to produce a "dopamine spike"). Students and teachers in the schools where this study was conducted were clear that there is a separate, fifth cluster of actions that produces escape or relief from aversive conditions. These acts of aggression distract observers and oneself when one's academic deficiency becomes obvious, for example, or when others are making comments about one's lack of expensive clothing or jewelry. Involvement in aggressive transactions also, in some cases, may distract youth from the pain associated with problems at home or in other life spheres.

Finally, there is a sixth cluster, which overlaps functionally with others discussed, but needs to be acknowledged separately. Behaviors in this cluster involve patterns that are functional in other settings, for example, rapid escalation of aggressive action when an individual feels threatened or disrespected (Anderson's [1999] "code of the street"). When these repertoires generalize to the school setting, however, they lead not to survival and problem solving, but to confrontations with school staff and peers. Maintaining a "tough" stance on the street is sometimes a survival skill, but the same behaviors at school can lead to failure (a case of situational overgeneralization). What young people in these enormously difficult situations need to learn is what Anderson calls "code-switching"—acting according to a different code, a different set of rules, in different settings.

The major issue in most of these behavioral clusters is not primarily anger that gets out of control, although many may escalate to that point. Effective prevention therefore requires much more than anger management skills, although these can be a useful focus as one component of an overall strategy (see chapter 8).

Other research supports the basic principle that there are multiple types of violent behavior, but that all are functional in some way. (If behavior is functional, incidentally, it is not "abnormal" as it has been described by those with a biological orientation.) Elliott and Tolan (1999), for example, describe four types of youth violence. The first they label *situational violence*. In these cases, contextual factors such as extreme heat or neighborhood disorder appear to catalyze violent behavior, substantially increasing its incidence among those who are susceptible for other reasons. The second, *relationship violence*, is a very large cluster of violent behaviors that arise from interpersonal disputes in ongoing relationships, including friendships, dating relationships, and family relationships. The third type of violence described by Elliott and Tolan is what they call *predatory violence*, a relatively small, but often very violent, category in which violence is used to obtain some gain, as in robbery or protection of a gang's territory or status. (This type overlaps with the more severe examples of the first, third, fifth, and perhaps sixth clusters that emerged in the *PEACE POWER* research.) The fourth, very rare, type of violence described by Elliott and Tolan is *psychopathological violence*, which results from serious personality disturbance; those authors suggest that this type may be rooted in physiology, severe trauma, or both.

Our work and that of Elliot and Tolan (1999) are somewhat different in perspective. The focus group categories are functional in nature, while Elliott and Tolan's four-way classification involves a mix of description and causation. In both typologies (and in others in the literature), however, violent behavior clearly is selected by its outcomes; it happens for reasons and is not simply random. This finding is consistent with well-established behavioral theory (Mattaini et al., 1996). *An effective prevention or intervention strategy must help youth learn alternative repertoires that are functionally similar to the problem behaviors, producing valued outcomes like respect and safety in other ways.* These may include, for example, finding new ways to gain recognition and respect, new ways to relate to boyfriends and girlfriends that produce security in relationships, and new ways to avoid or obtain relief from aversive conditions.

Violent and coercive behavior can be learned in multiple important spheres of life. As demonstrated by the work of Patterson and his colleagues (1989, 1992) discussed earlier in this chapter, both family and peers commonly contribute to shaping coercive and violent behaviors. There is often a false dichotomy drawn between the two, particularly in the popular literature. In fact, both the microculture of the family and cultures of antisocial peers help to establish antisocial patterns, in different ways and sometimes during different critical developmental periods. Larger sociocultural factors, the third level of behavioral selection, often substantially shape those microcultures in turn. It is not surprising that a society that glorifies violence in the media and relies heavily on coercive and adversarial processes in many realms, including economics, the justice system, education, and informal social relations, would support and maintain coercive repertoires in its children (Lowery & Mattaini, 2001; Sidman, 2001).

Cultural Selection

Not only family and friends but also larger cultural forces—including the culture of the street, the media, and even, paradoxically, the justice system—often shape and support violent acts. In his book, *Fist Stick Knife Gun*, Canada (1995) describes the changes that he has seen over four decades in the life experience of children in Harlem, where he grew up and now works with youth. In addition to discussing the increased lethality resulting from the easy availability of weapons, Canada notes how the culture of the street shapes and demands coercive and violent action, and how families may reluctantly come to believe that they must encourage their children to participate in that culture for their own protection and for that of the family. Anderson (1999) describes "the code of the street," in which respect may be valued more highly than life itself; in that world, it is essential to answer behavior viewed as disrespectful, regardless of risk. Historian Roger Lane (1997) has suggested that this readiness to scan for threat and to escalate aggressive behavior rapidly may be a residual pattern of Southern slave owners' practices to maintain tight control (which may now affect white and black alike)— perhaps yet another example of the spread of a culture of fear and death structured and maintained by coercion and oppression, and its terrible results for all concerned.

The easy availability of weapons, even very lethal weapons, is another important cultural phenomenon. Many youth (10% to 20%) indicate that they regularly carry weapons; 47% of high school students report that they have access to firearms (Josephon Institute of Ethics, 2001). Firearms are present in 35% of homes with children, and, in many of those homes, the weapons are accessible to the children (Schuster, Franke, Bastian, Sor, & Halfon, 2000). Over 10% of eleventh graders in Seattle report owning firearms, and most incarcerated youth report doing so (Rushforth & Flannery, 1999). Youth who carry weapons generally report that they do so for protection. But as Garbarino (1999) indicates, "It requires a highly controlled and healthy society to live with guns in its midst and not end up with people using those guns against other members of that society. The pervasive social toxicity of American life, coupled with our strong individualist impulse, makes us a bad risk when it comes to widespread availability of guns" (p. 201).

In recent years, people in the United States, especially youth, have also seen and heard increasingly realistic models of violence in movies, television, music, and video games. A recent study by the Federal Trade Commission (2000) indicates that many of these violent media have often been specifically marketed to youth. Although these media may not significantly affect behavior among those with strong rule-governed repertoires, scientific reviews clearly indicate that such exposure can powerfully affect many youth (APA, 1993). Given the number of models in the media; the support, even demands, for coercive and violent action from peers and family; and the ready availability of firearms, it is not surprising that the incidence and lethality of violent events are as high as they are.

The "social toxicity" described by Garbarino (1999) extends to many areas of modern life. The justice system in the United States incarcerates a far higher proportion of the population than any other developed country (Reiss & Roth, 1993) and increasingly turns to capital punishment, even though the Universal Declaration of Human Rights (United Nations, 1948) recognizes such punishment as a violation of basic human rights. The U.S. justice system relies on threats and punishment, and it is often difficult to even imagine alternatives—although effective alternatives do, in fact, exist (Cohen & Filipczak, 1971; Ross, 1996).

Societal reliance on coercion as a primary means of establishing and maintaining social institutions is a basic, critical issue that extends far beyond the "justice system," as Sidman extensively documents in his book, *Coercion and Its Fallout* (2001). Families rely on coercion in parenting; many organizations use threats to elicit desired performance from workers; reprimands and punishments occur at least twice as often as do recognition events in schools; even nation-states rely extensively on threats to maintain apparent security. All of this occurs despite strong scientific evidence that the exercise of coercive power is ultimately weak and produces a wide variety of undesirable side effects, ranging from counteraggression to depression (Sidman). Coercive arrangements are ever at risk of collapse and, therefore, require constant surveillance. They also damage the web of community relationships on which all of society depends, by increasing aggregate experiences and observations of interpersonal coercion, threat, and suspicion present in society. As discussed earlier, however, asking anyone, be it individual young people or the justice system, to simply give up what power they have (even if it is of minimum quality and of maximum cost) is unrealistic unless there is available to them another means of exercising some influence over their world. Alternatives in some cases already exist (Sidman) and, in other cases, can be constructed. The *PEACE POWER* strategy, described in the next section, is one effort to shape and maintain family, organizational, peer, and community cultures that provide higher quality, lower cost forms of personal empowerment.

The *PEACE POWER* Strategy

An understanding of the biological, experiential, and cultural roots of violent and coercive behavior, as discussed in chapter 2, provides powerful guidance for designing preventive and interventive strategies. Because cultural systems and cultural practices are the matrix within which individual lives are shaped, the central goal of the *PEACE POWER* strategy is to construct cultures of nonviolent empowerment among networks of all sizes, from the microculture of the family, to organizational cultures, to larger community networks. Extensive scientific data and practical experience suggest that four core cultural practices, if firmly embedded in a cultural system, not only will dramatically reduce the level of violence and coercion but also will dramatically increase personal and collective empowerment: (1) recognize contributions and successes, (2) act with respect, (3) share power to build community, and (4) make peace.

Structure of *PEACE POWER* Projects

The *PEACE POWER* Working Group determined from the literature and our own experiences that we needed to pursue a highly flexible and adaptable strategy rather than a tightly structured program or curriculum. We did not wish to design an add-on program requiring already busy youth workers and educators to do more; instead, our goal was to identify different ways to do what was already being done and ways to support those new practices within cultural networks.

Community psychologists and social workers have looked carefully at the kinds of projects that tend to thrive in family and community settings. Complex programs that involve substantial financial and other costs, or require adherence to a rigid structure, typically remain dependent on significant, ongoing investments of external resources. Our goal, however, was to provide an approach that could be established and maintained with modest, locally available resources. Fawcett and his colleagues, after extensive experience, have identified several critical characteristics of workable interventions for community settings (Fawcett, 1991; Fawcett, Mathews, & Fletcher, 1980). They characterize contextually appropriate prevention and intervention technologies as (1) quickly effective, (2) inexpensive, (3) decentralized, (4) flexible, (5) sustainable, (6) simple, and (7) compatible with the values, experiences, and needs of users. Our goal in developing the *PEACE POWER* strategy has been, to the extent possible, to remain consistent with those guidelines.

The strongest programs, of course, are those with support from multiple segments of the community. The Work Group on Health Promotion and Community Development at the University of Kansas has developed an extensive online resource, called the Community Tool Box, as well as a series of published manuals that describe a wide range of tools and activities to engage the community in prevention and change efforts (see note 3). Figure 3 is a diagram, from the University of Kansas Work Group *Action Planning Guide* for preventing youth violence, that identifies the multiple sectors that might be engaged in planning a communitywide prevention strategy.

The key, as indicated, is to engage multiple sectors of the community in prevention and change initiatives. This is one step toward shared power.

Constructing cultures of nonviolent empowerment is challenging. One objective of the Working Group was to identify a minimum set of cultural practices that should be emphasized in any *PEACE POWER* project, practices that have strong empirical support and that in combination can produce powerful effects. After several years of experimentation, we arrived at the core set of four practices noted earlier, all of which appear to be essential. We also recognized that simply encouraging people to take action in a general way was unlikely to be adequate, given the complexity of cultural change and the persistence of existing interlocking cultural practices. Therefore, we decided to develop a set of specific, practical tools from which organizational and community groups can choose, adapting the tools that fit their particular projects.

40

Figure 3

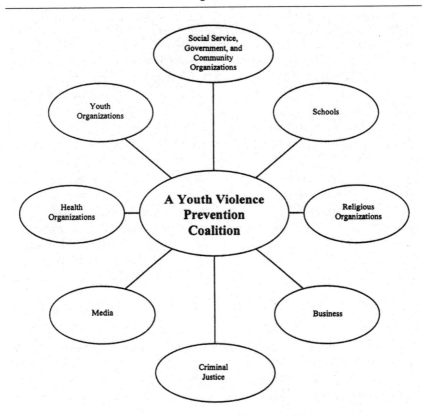

Sectors that can be involved in a community youth violence prevention coalition. Source: Reprinted with permission from Fawcett et al., 1994.

There are many different ways to design and implement a *PEACE POWER* project, although every program should incorporate each of the four core practices in meaningful ways. Language is important; common terms should be used throughout the groups and organizations involved to build common cultural language understood by all. Local programs can modify the *PEACE POWER* terminology according to local usage and values, so long as the use of the terms selected is consistent. On the other hand, we have found that the language used in this volume can speak to many people, youth and adults, so programs may want to consider using it.

The four core practices are portrayed on the *PEACE POWER* Wheel, shown in Figure 1 on page 5. There is substantial power, including scientific, spiritual, and collective power, in this simple figure and the cultural webs that it can help to construct—much more power than may be immediately evident. Each of the core practices included on the Wheel is discussed in detail in one of the following chapters. The first core practice, "Recognize Contributions and Successes," structures dramatic increases in the level of positive feedback provided both for contributions to collective well-being and for personal successes. A culture of recognition affects levels of neurotransmitters in key areas of the brain, as discussed in chapter 2, and also affects collective transactions and experiences in predictable and essential ways. The second core practice, "Act with Respect," structures reductions in the level of threat and coercion experienced in a cultural environment (again producing predictable biobehavioral effects), while teaching key repertoires for empowered action. "Sharing Power to Build Community" is a core practice that moves toward collective empowerment, inclusion, and social welfare. Finally, "Make Peace" is essential to resolve the inevitable conflicts that arise and to support collective healing.

These core practices are not slogans; each has specific behavioral referents, as well as specific tools and activities that can be used to operationalize the core practice in a practical way in community settings. Although each is presented as distinct, in fact, there are many interlocks among them. Experience shows that none of these practices can safely be ignored; all four appear to be necessary, and the four together sufficient, to achieve meaningful levels of change.

The *PEACE POWER* Wheel and strategy as presented in this volume are aimed primarily at preteen, teen, and adult groups. The same basic practices, of course, are also effective and crucial in work with younger children, although the language requires some adjustment. The *PEACE POWER* for Kids Wheel, shown in Figure 4, can be used for such programs.

This model still uses the word "Recognize," although not the words "Contributions and Successes"; an alternative, used by the PeaceBuilders program (Embry, Flannery, Vazsonyi, Powell, & Atha, 1996) is "praise people." Even young children can work with the single word "recognize," and its use maintains consistency with the *PEACE POWER* projects into which children will "graduate." The second practice, acting with respect, has been simplified to "Stop Putdowns," because reducing the often damaging teasing and criticism so common among young chil-

Figure 4

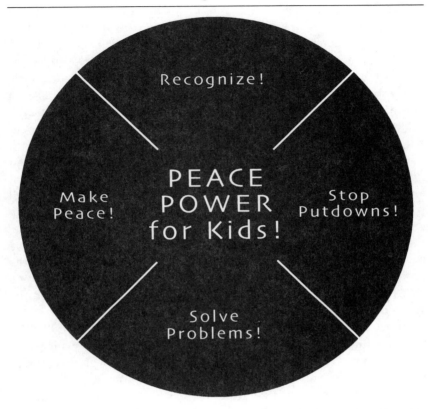

The *PEACE POWER* for Kids! Wheel. Source: Reprinted with permission from *PEACE POWER* Working Group, 1999.

dren appears to be the key change required to maintain an atmosphere of respect, thus decreasing social threat. Although sharing power is a complex construct, the process can begin with individual and group problem-solving skills, and there is considerable evidence that young children who learn problem solving exhibit less aggressive, violent, and antisocial behavior later. The fourth core practice, "Make Peace" by resolving conflict using simple tools like the Making Peace Tool presented subsequently, is as essential for younger children as for teens and adults. Many of the tools discussed in the chapters in this section can be used or easily adapted for children's programs as well.

PEACE POWER projects can be developed in many different organizations and systems. The *PEACE POWER* Working Group has partnered with alternative and special education schools, regular high schools, a nonviolent leadership camp for inner-city youth that blended the *PEACE POWER* strategy with the principles of nonviolence developed by the Martin Luther King, Jr., Center, Native American tribal organizations, recreation and after-school programs, and programs for court-referred youth. Community centers and church groups have also sponsored projects. At least one shelter has applied the strategy, and many residential settings would be ideal settings. In general, any system in which youth and adults have ongoing, regular contact over time can adopt *PEACE POWER*. Even a single classroom can develop its own project, although the effects are likely to be more powerful if an entire school participates. It is essential, however, that the primary leader of the group or organization be unambiguously involved. In one school, for example, the administrative assistant principal took the lead, with the principal being generally supportive, but uninvolved. The staff perceived the project as belonging largely to the assistant principal, with whom some staff had ongoing conflicts; as a result, the project never achieved the status of an organizational priority.

Impetus for developing a local program based on the *PEACE POWER* strategy can come from anyone: an executive director or principal, a parent group, a group of interested staff members, even a group of youth themselves. A social worker, school counselor, psychologist, or other professional often plays a key role in catalyzing and maintaining the program; such a leader is probably essential, but no one person can carry out a program alone. The programs that seem to produce the best results typically involve leadership from a committee or planning group representing the larger system or organization, with one or two key players keeping the project in focus over time. This core group is probably the single most crucial factor in structuring a *PEACE POWER* project.

Some *PEACE POWER* activities clearly require professional expertise (e.g., leading life and leadership skills training groups). Any group can implement the core strategy, however, because the core practices are straightforward and tools for operationalizing them have already been developed. Naturally, the more systems that are involved, the broader the potential influence of a *PEACE POWER* project. Parent and family involvement, in particular, can synergistically combine with the efforts of a youth program or school, although it may take time to build such involvement. Media involvement can rapidly disseminate information about and spark interest in the program. In each of the next four chapters, specific strategies for reaching out to families and the larger community are described.

Time and other resources are ordinarily not major issues when there is a commitment to the *PEACE POWER* strategy. For example, many schools and recreation programs already have art, theater, and video production projects in place. Implementation of the *PEACE POWER* strategy then becomes simply a matter of incorporating the core practices into those projects. Similarly, there are many ways to integrate *PEACE POWER* into regular classroom or recreation activities. The primary time commitment involves the planning group (task force, committee, or whatever term fits the setting best), who should meet on a regular and continuing basis—at least once or twice a month for the life of the project, which should extend over at least one to two years. Larger community-building activities may require some financial or material resources, but working with community groups and businesses to obtain such resources is often part of the project itself and can be excellent experience for staff and youth alike, extending connections more integrally into the community.

New and improved tools and activities will no doubt be developed over time, but the foundation presented in this book will allow well-trained professionals to create and refine their own programs, often with no outside consultation. There should be some form of initial training, whether by internal staff specialists or outside trainers, that offers an opportunity for participant buy-in, because developing a common culture requires everyone to know about and have opportunities to help shape the project. The particular tools and activities presented here are useful on their own, but the real power comes from the co-construction of an integrated culture. Each *PEACE POWER* project will, and should, look somewhat different, but each should in some way include each of the core practices and should change over time based on evaluation data and program experiences. For example, a local program based in a school may use the following during the first program year:

- Recognition Notes, Home Recognition Notes and parent workshops, and *PEACE POWER* circles (see chapter 3);
- A pledge campaign and intergroup tolerance work to build respect (see chapter 4);

- Group work for discovering personal power and environmental service for increasing shared power in collective action (see chapter 5); and
- The Making Peace Tool at school and home (see chapter 6).

The next year, some of those activities would probably be continued, others would be modified, and still others would be discontinued and replaced by new ones. Like any other culture, *PEACE POWER* cultures, if they are to survive, must be continually evolving, adapting to changing conditions.

Beginning a *PEACE POWER* Project

One way to begin a local *PEACE POWER* project is to invite one or more trainers from existing *PEACE POWER* projects to conduct a half-day workshop that offers training in the model and an opportunity for participants to think together about its possible application in their own setting. The trainers may then return periodically to consult with the planning group and other interested participants. As the strategy has evolved, an initial workshop, followed by consultations about every two months, seems to be a useful structure. The developers of the strategy have offered many *pro bono* consultations of this kind, but the *PEACE POWER* strategy is no one's "property" and, over time, staff members in programs that are working well can themselves offer consultation to others. In other cases, those involved in the planning group may feel prepared to conduct such a workshop themselves, relying on the material in this volume.

Once an organization or community is ready to implement a *PEACE POWER* program, in most cases some form of public commitment and announcement is appropriate to demonstrate the interest and involvement of key actors. The vehicle for this announcement may be an assembly, a newsletter to homes or to members, or some other approach that reaches a large proportion of the community. It is very helpful at this point to distribute small items (e.g., pocket cards, "respect" lapel buttons) and to organize one or more follow-up events like a poster contest in which the youth themselves develop posters related to the program, a mural painting project, or a project newsletter. The idea here is to make a statement that

- We are doing something really different;
- We are doing it as a collective, including youth, staff, administration, and community; and
- This could mean a new way of life for us.

Ideally, if the commitment is made as a public event, it should include entertainment, perhaps some improvisational theater related to the key practices, a recitation of the *PEACE POWER* Pledge, and other "change of pace" activities. There is plenty of room for creativity, and with collaborative planning, this event can be a highlight of the program year. It should be the beginning of a collaborative process that will be implemented continually. Representatives of all important stakeholder groups (e.g., staff, parents, youth) should be involved in both initial and ongoing planning.

Local programs, guided by the next four chapters, can assemble and adapt program components and tools to support the core *PEACE POWER* practices in ways consistent with local preference, need, and values. Chapter 7 then addresses simple, practical ways to monitor and evaluate a *PEACE POWER* project, which is usually essential to program survival and effectiveness.

If there is a "secret" to achieving lasting cultural change, the science of behavior tells us it is this: Genuine change is the result of substantial changes in the aggregate incidence of particular practices, rather than of single dramatic acts. Cultural change is the result of, and, in fact, consists of, the cumulative effects of thousands of acts of recognition, acts of respect, acts of shared power, and acts of peace making. The real heroes, then, are those who make plans to perform the core practices regularly, who find a way to structure such efforts into daily life, and who share their efforts with others (primarily as a check on themselves, since persistence is more likely when one reports progress to someone else).

3

Recognize Contributions and Successes

Recognition of positive actions is the heart of a *PEACE POWER* culture, whether a family microculture or a larger culture in an organization or community (Sidman, 2001). High levels of recognition can dramatically change the atmosphere in a home, organization, or community. A quantitative behavioral principle indicates that high levels of recognition for prosocial acts will naturally and dramatically reduce the level of antisocial acts (Embry & Flannery, 1999). As Embry and Flannery note, targeted recognition and reinforcement for prosocial behaviors can "foster . . . high levels of intrinsic motivation, giftedness, and world-class talent" (1999, p. 66), as well as social competence.

People act in prosocial or in antisocial ways because doing so gives them personal satisfaction, recognition, opportunities, protection, or, in some cases, tangible rewards. Recognition and other rewarding consequences are, in fact, the closest thing to magic available for dealing with youth *or* adults and behavioral research indicates that significantly increasing the level of such consequences provided can dramatically increase achievement and decrease behavior problems (McDowell, 1988). Effective rewards need not, and often should not, be tangible—acting to improve the lives of other people can be very satisfying in itself for those who have learned to value this outcome, for example.

To the extent possible, reinforcement should also be intrinsic. For example, schoolwork pitched at an appropriate level is often challenging and interesting, and only minimal external reinforcement may be necessary to maintain motivation. For many youth with little experience of success, however, recognition by others is essential to beginning a process of growth. Harnessing the power of reinforcement, particularly for youth who have little experience of such recognition, is a primary prevention strategy for many problems of concern—not only coercion and violence but also substance abuse, high-risk behaviors, vandalism, and many others.

In group settings, reinforcement can also be used to manage problem behavior. Many good teachers, for example, have learned that one way to eliminate minor disruptive behavior is to ignore the child involved and attend to those who are acting appropriately. This tactic needs to be handled carefully—some kinds of behavior should not be ignored but be handled relatively nondisruptively (see chapter 10). Selective attention is ordinarily very useful, however, particularly in settings in which adults have gradually come to pay much more attention to minor problem behavior than to prosocial actions, which paradoxically encourages more problem behavior. Perhaps surprisingly, research consistently indicates that this is a common dynamic in families and classrooms.

Just as each individual values different things, so do different cultures. And within any culture, there is enormous variation. Among many cultural groups in the United States, verbal praise is common and effective—but not all groups. For some Asian American groups, such overt praise may be embarrassing, but private or more subtle nonverbal expressions may be of great value. The smile of a Native American grandmother, her sometimes indirect report ("Oh, she's not too bad a granddaughter") to a third party about a child's actions, or simply being asked to continue to contribute as one has been doing can be powerful recognition in some indigenous cultures. It is essential not to oversimplify a principle that has broad applicability, but only within the cultural context of those involved. Although recognition has great power in all cultures, meaningful forms of recognition for individuals and cultural groups are highly variable, and no single formula will work everywhere. Therefore, those involved should collaborate in designing the forms of recognition used. It is also important to experiment, because myths based on inaccurate assumptions about what will and what will not work in a particular setting are common.

The *PEACE POWER* strategy is designed not only to encourage personal success but also to construct cultures of mutual recognition and respect. For this reason, *PEACE POWER* explicitly emphasizes regular recognition both for personal successes and for contributions to the collective good. A success is a personal achievement, like getting a good grade or being on time for class every day. A contribution is something that benefits others or the whole group. For example, if one young person encourages another to make peace rather than to fight, that is a contribution. If a teacher spends time teaching children how to manage their anger, that is a contribution. If a group of older youth spend time tutoring younger kids, that is a contribution. It is essential to recognize *actions* (e.g., "you produced a lovely piece of work here") rather than attributes (e.g., "you are so talented"); recognizing actions encourages further effort, while recognizing attributes often leads to anxiety about possible loss of the positive label the next time, or to counterproductive egotism.

Recognition is seldom provided at adequate rates without specific programming. Many youth, therefore, experience very low rates of praise, recognition, and reward (Connolly, Dowd, Criste, Nelson, & Tobias, 1995). Disruptive youth, in particular, often experience far more reprimands than recognition events. Daniels (2000) notes that a ratio of recognition events to reprimands and threats of at least four to one in classrooms, families, and organizations leads to achievement and good discipline, while ratios smaller than this are associated with problems (see also Davis, Nelson, & Gauger, 2000). Unfortunately, the data show that ratios in most settings are closer to only one recognition event for every two punishments (one to two). Because it can be difficult to maintain an adequate rate of recognition, even for those who are committed to doing so, the *PEACE POWER* strategy provides a number of concrete tools that can structure this process.

The "Rewards Controversy"

The popular media have addressed the "rewards controversy" at some length. Kohn (1993), in particular, has written about possible problems with the use of any positive consequence, whether it be money, praise, or good grades. As is often the case, media presentations have often distorted scientific findings. The following are crucial points that can be drawn from a very large body of work in this area:

- In practically every study of reinforcement procedures the use of praise and recognition has both increased positive behavior and increased intrinsic motivation (Carton, 1996).

- Applied research in real-world settings consistently demonstrates that recognition produces strong positive effects, with no apparent negative side effects. Similarly, those working in business settings have long been aware of the importance of recognition (Carnegie, 1936; Daniels, 2000).

- In some studies, "tangible" rewards (usually small amounts of money) appear to decrease intrinsic motivation, but the effect appears to be "transient and not likely to occur at all if extrinsic rewards are reinforcing, non-competitive, based on reasonable performance standards, and delivered repetitively" (Dickinson, 1989, p. 1). The transient effects that do appear seem to be the result of experimental conditions. For example, in one experiment, participants receiving small amounts of money for finding words in a puzzle are at some point told that they will no longer receive money. At that point, not surprisingly, they tend to stop working on the puzzle (Carton & Nowicki, 1998). The equivalence of these experiments to salaries, compliments, and other real-world incentives is at best tangential.

The power and importance of recognition is not really in question at this point. The PEACE POWER strategy relies heavily on recognition, because it is a natural consequence of positive action, costs nothing, has no known negative side effects, and is very powerful. Some other forms of reinforcement are often useful as well. Privileges (e.g., opportunities to use a computer after completing a challenging task) have often increased motivation for tasks that are not themselves motivating and have demonstrated no negative effects. Group "rewards" (usually opportunities for group members to collectively earn privileges) and group recognition often produce better results than do individual privileges and recognition; further, they teach collective responsibility. Such group incentives are common in PEACE POWER programs.

All of the forms of reinforcement discussed so far are intangible and relatively noncontroversial, and they can be incorporated very naturally into the cultures in which young people are embedded. But are there ever times when tangible rewards are indicated? In most cases, because such rewards can be costly and are artificial to the setting, PEACE POWER programs do not rely on them. Important research, however, indicates that in some cases, it may be necessary to contract temporarily with very aggressive, coercive youth for such rewards, because these youth have often not yet learned to value social recognition highly (Mattaini, 1999; Patterson, 1976). Such contracting may be appropriate, for example, in intensive *PEACE POWER* work with high-risk youth (see chapter 9), but in general, *PEACE POWER* relies on interlocking, natural incentives, particularly social recognition, to construct a positive culture.

The material that follows identifies a menu of tools for increasing recognition events in collective cultures. Tools for schools and other youth-serving organizations, families, and communities are discussed separately, but many ideas that may be useful at one level can also be adapted for others. Each approach listed also has endless variations, and programs using the *PEACE POWER* strategy are strongly encouraged to use creativity in designing their own packages.

Tools for Increasing Recognition Events in Schools and Organizations

Youth-serving organizations, including schools, recreation programs, and residential programs, are ideally situated to contribute to constructing cultures of nonviolent empowerment for young people, because such organizations provide a nexus for extensive contacts among youth and members of the adult community. These organizations also can often contribute to changes in peer cultures maintained by youth themselves. A variety of tools are available to structure high levels of recognition for successes and contributions (Table 2).

Recognition Notes

Perhaps the tool with the strongest empirical support for increasing recognition is the recognition note (see, e.g., Embry, Flannery, Vazsonyi, Powell, & Atha, 1996; Mayer, Butterworth, Nafpaktitis, & Sulzer-Azaroff, 1983; Mayer, Mitchell, Clementi, Clement-Robertson, Myatt, & Bullara, 1993). Recognition notes are written praise statements, identifying the person and the behavior for which he or she is being recognized, and may be signed by the preparer or completed anonymously (depending on situational factors). See Figure 5 for an example.

Recognition notes can be used often, many times a day, to recognize successes and contributions by anyone. The design of some systems allows teachers, administrators, security staff, students, and everyone

Table 2. Tools for Building Recognition

Tools for Schools and Youth-Serving Organizations
- Recognition notes
- *PEACE POWER* Circles
- *PEACE POWER* Pledge
- Group recognition and incentives
- Group work
- Modeling and rehearsal
- Home recognition notes
- Peer monitoring
- Self-recognition
- Activity sampling
- Poster making and murals
- Celebrations
- Staff self-monitoring and self-management

Tools for Families
- Recognition boards and notes
- *PEACE POWER* Circles
- Monitoring and incentives
- Building of life and leadership skills

Tools for Communities
- Media efforts
- Neighborhood and community recognition processes
- Contributions from the business community
- Recognition posters

else to use them to give recognition to anyone. For example, students can recognize students and teachers, and teachers can recognize lunchroom staff or students. In two of our projects, recognition notes were used first among staff members, then expanded to include youth.

It is important for those in any particular organization to think through and experiment with the best way to use notes. For example, in some schools teachers initially prepare all notes, and as youth learn to use notes appropriately, they earn the privilege. (In a few places, "screening" of notes for propriety may be necessary, at least for a time.) Once notes are prepared, they can be publicly posted on a "recognition board," slipped into individually labeled envelopes hanging on the wall, or read

Figure 5

PEACE POWER!®

- **Recognize Contributions and Successes**

I Recognize: *Josie*

For: *Spending 2 hours*

tutoring Zoey

Sample recognition note.

as part of a *PEACE POWER* circle (see later discussion). The first option, public posting, provides public recognition, and positive actions recognized for one youth can serve as models for others. In several of the projects with which the *PEACE POWER* Working Group has participated, recognition boards were mounted (or existing bulletin boards were claimed) in classrooms, hallways, lunchrooms, and staff rooms (for staff recognition). Staff members may find it useful to read some of the posted notes publicly every day. About once a week or more, depending on the number of notes, staff may count the completed recognition notes to track them for program evaluation (see chapter 7) and may randomly select some of the notes to be announced to the whole organization. Where embarrassment with such public attention is a group or cultural issue, the more private envelope arrangement may be preferable. In one project, teachers also used preprinted, self-adhesive recognition notes, inserting them in student folders and sticking them to student papers.

It is essential, of course, that everyone regularly receive recognition in such systems. Although it is common to hear, "He never does anything positive!" extensive experience indicates that everyone does some things worth recognition. The person who is also involved in high rates of negative actions may never receive recognition for those worthy behaviors, however. All recognition, whether in writing or otherwise, should be genuine, never patronizing. Everyone is different; for some young people, making it to class four times in one week may be a genuine achievement deserving recognition, while for others it is not. Recognition notes permit extensive individualization.

According to G. Roy Mayer (personal communication, May 30, 1999) many young people have learned to discount oral praise, and pairing it with notes increases its valence. In some cases, their skepticism may be because others have used oral praise to manipulate young people. In addition, some of the behavioral research literature suggests that if young people have a history of getting attention for disruptive behavior, attention for positive behavior may "induce" the young person to act in ways previously associated with attention—disruptively (Allen & Warzak, 2000; Balsam & Bondy, 1983)! Written praise, however, is a novel and powerful experience for many young people without such problem associations.

As noted earlier, recognition notes also can serve as a valuable evaluation tool, since they are permanent products that can be counted (Is the number of notes being prepared increasing, decreasing, or remaining stable?) and examined for adequacy (Are the notes recognizing actions rather than attributes?) and breadth of coverage (Are the notes recognizing only personal successes, or are an adequate number of notes directed toward community contributions?).

Given their record of success in many settings, including agency settings where the adult staff use them, recognition notes are a core *PEACE POWER* tool and probably should be used in practically every local program in some way (see note 4). Notes can be photocopied from the template in Figure 6, or local programs can design their own variations.

Figure 6

Recognition note template for duplication. Source: Reprinted with permission from *PEACE POWER* Working Group, 1999. May be freely reprinted.

PEACE POWER Circles

As group activities that have demonstrated great power for many purposes, *circles* are useful for public recognition of successes and contributions. For example, program staff can schedule weekly (or in some cases daily) *PEACE POWER* circles in which members of a group (e.g., classroom, camp cabin, family) provide recognition and express appreciation for things that others have done during the past week. The following are examples of circle contributions:

- "I want to thank Tanika for helping me make it through a hard week."
- "I appreciate Mr. Rogers for being willing to negotiate the math assignment."
- "I recognize Jonathan for volunteering to tutor third graders; this is really an important thing for someone to do."
- "Joan, what I appreciate about you is how cheerful you are, even on hard days . . . ."
- "I want to recognize José for helping Josie and me to settle an argument without losing control."

Although perfect balance is not crucial, it is important that everyone receive some recognition in such circles on a regular basis. The leader may in some cases take responsibility for recognizing those who have been left out, but it is a more effective procedure for the group to discuss the importance of inclusion and, at least occasionally, to monitor their success in this by using a circle diagram (Figure 7).

Recognition provided should be authentic; approximations (e.g., recognition that is not as behaviorally specific as would be ideal) should be encouraged in the beginning, and then gradually refined over time by asking questions to clarify meaning. It may be useful, particularly in the beginning, to have participants complete recognition notes privately, then to read those notes in the circle as a way of priming the activity. In some cases, circles can focus on particular themes (e.g., contributions to improving classroom climate). So long as the agenda includes the recognition function, it is also possible to use the circle for other functions. For example, circles can be used to identify interpersonal events that have made people feel uncomfortable or disrespected, followed by discussion and rehearsal of alternative ways to deal with those exchanges (see chapter 4). Circles can also be used for conflict resolution (see chapter 6). PEACE POWER circles are generally regularly scheduled, for example, at the beginning or end of homeroom periods in schools or during a review of the day in residential programs.

Such circles are a very useful way to embed recognition into group culture and are often considerably more powerful when experienced than one might expect in reading about them. In one camp program, inner-city teens and staff met in circles of persons who had known each other before coming to camp. Each was asked to complete the following statement for everyone else in the circle: "____, what I appreciate about

58

Figure 7

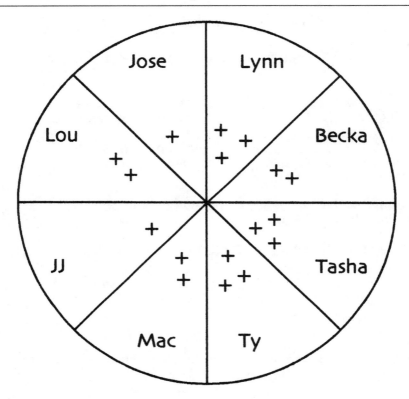

A diagram to track the number of times each member of a group is recognized. Each plus sign represents one recognition event. Source: Adapted from Rose, *Group Therapy: A Behavioral Approach.* Copyright 1978 by Allyn & Bacon. Adapted by permission.

you is _____." One person at a time was the focus of the exercise (a form of "hot seat" technique), with every other member addressing that person in turn. Within less than two minutes in several such circles, everyone was in tears, sometimes even the group leader, because the experience was so new and powerful for those in the circle.

The PEACE POWER Pledge

Designed to be used regularly, such as every morning in classrooms or at camp, or at every meeting of youth groups, the *PEACE POWER* Pledge

Figure 8

The <u>PEACE POWER</u> Pledge:

Today I will <u>Recognize Contributions and Successes</u> of those around me.

Today I will <u>Act with Respect</u>—for myself, others, and the earth, giving up putdowns, threats, and weapons.

Today I will <u>Share Power to Build Community</u>, using my power and recognizing the power of others to contribute to the human web.

Today I will <u>Make Peace</u> by resolving conflicts, and healing broken relationships.

Today I will live <u>PEACE POWER</u>!

The *PEACE POWER* Pledge. Source: Reprinted with permission from *PEACE POWER* Working Group, 1999. May be freely reprinted.

---

incorporates the program's four core practices (Figure 8). For example, the first line of the pledge states, "Today I will *Recognize Contributions and Successes* of those around me," a very simple reminder that recognition needs to be a daily practice directed toward those in one's circle. It is important that *PEACE POWER* language is used often, so it becomes part of the culture of the group. Repeating a pledge is one way to encourage this. In stating the pledge, an individual commits to action consistent with each of the four core *PEACE POWER* practices.

Groups and organizations can either design their own similar pledges or simply adopt the pledge as provided here. A pledge can be mounted on the wall, printed on wallet-sized cards, displayed in meetings, posted on websites—the more ubiquitous it is, the better (see note 5). If used regularly, such pledges not only may serve as simple reminders, but also may introduce dissonance if an individual has not been acting in ways consistent with commitments made. In the latter case, the pledge may act as a motivating antecedent for action. For example, if a young person repeats the words, "Today I will act with respect . . . giving up putdowns" and remembers that she has been involved in teasing a quiet classmate, the associated discomfort may encourage a shift in her treatment of the other girl.

Group Recognition and Incentives

Although individual recognition may be the most common application of the first core practice, there are considerable advantages to the use of group recognition and incentives under many circumstances. Group recognition and incentives can promote positive collective action; group leaders can structure the events to ensure that all group members participate actively, thus encouraging inclusion, and simultaneously move away from egotism. Research suggests that group recognition and incentives are generally at least as powerful as are individual arrangements, and they may be more so in the social arena (Embry & Flannery, 1999; Lloyd, Eberhardt, & Drake, 1996). How group incentives are arranged, however, is often crucial.

For example, in *PEACE POWER* Life and Leadership Skills group sessions that members of the Working Group have conducted with youth involved in the justice system, breaking a larger group into two teams that can earn points for cooperative and creative participation in activities has proven very useful. Teams that earned a certain number of points were eligible for a pizza party once a month; if every team earned enough points, everyone could participate. Although the accumulation of points can earn minor privileges for the group, points themselves are powerful incentives for young people who have been immersed since infancy in a culture of sporting events that produce scores. *PEACE POWER*, however, is not about producing a few winners in conjunction with many (or even a few) losers. As a general rule, therefore, *every* team that reaches an established score (or a higher score than its own previous record) should be able to earn privileges.

It is also crucial to avoid coercive exchanges within teams, for example, threats to those who may be seen as failing to contribute to the team. Such problems can usually be prevented by ensuring that any particular action or lack of it does not produce a major penalty, by establishing a scoring system that depends much more on what is done than on what is not, and by requiring that the team act with respect for each other to earn points. Point systems not associated with privileges may produce fewer problems of these kinds. It is important to maintain a balance; although mild competition may be motivating, cut-throat competition that produces losers who experience embarrassment, humiliation, or a sense of failure is counterproductive. (As noted by Cavanaugh, "From a scientific perspective . . . our evolution fitted us for cooperation, not for cold-blooded competition [though there is room for some degree of competition]" [2000, p. 243].) Particularly in the case of win/lose forms of competition, the experiences of those who lose should be continuously monitored. Systems in which all teams can win have the advantage of avoiding these issues.

It may be particularly effective to use group recognition for increasing community contributions. For example, if members of a youth group are involved as a small working team in a service project, public recognition of the team as a collective (e.g., by giving the team a name like the Intergenerational Task Force or a catchy name selected by the group, by posting photographs of the team, by writing about the team's work in newsletters) teaches a number of important lessons about interdependence and the sharing of power (see chapter 5). Many other group incentives may be useful. Rose (1998) suggests the use of videotape equipment, an approach that health educators in New York found useful with older inner-city youth (Armstrong, 1997); applications may range from opportunities to act as cameraperson during the group session to the development of a group film. He also suggests a range of other rewards, including opportunities to work on junk cars; activities like swimming and cross-country skiing; visits by high-status guests like celebrities and sports figures; dance, makeup, and karate lessons; and many others. Youth can be very creative in identifying and developing group incentives.

Group Work

By adolescence, most young persons are ready to engage in group approaches involving the development of critical consciousness through genuine dialogue (Freire, 1994). Group leadership skills are important for initiating and maintaining such groups, but youth themselves, often with only limited guidance and structuring, can take much of the responsibility for group process. Icebreakers that encourage youth to talk about their perceptions and values can be helpful for beginning such groups. The classic "forced-choice" exercise in which participants step to one side of the room if they agree, step to the other side if they disagree, then discuss the reasons for their choices is one example of such an icebreaker. Statements might include the following:

- Everyone has talents for which her or she can be recognized.
- It's important to tell people if you appreciate what they do.
- Students shouldn't expect to be praised for doing what they are supposed to be doing.
- I would rather be recognized privately than publicly when I do something well.

Many other similar statements can be designed specific to the setting. What is important is that the exercise involves everyone and can open discussions that can be deepened in other ways.

Some of the important themes for group work include developing common understandings of the terms *recognition*, *contributions*, and *successes*, as well as extensive lists of examples to clarify among the group members the many possibilities. Youth often use the word *recognize* (as well as *respect* and other *PEACE POWER* terms) in different ways. One of the goals of *PEACE POWER* is to develop common understandings consistent with nonviolent empowerment. Following are some group approaches that may be useful:

- Breaking the larger group into smaller subgroups to develop definitions of the terms, and later lists of examples, which they can report back to the larger group;
- Asking each subgroup to define just one of the terms and produce a list of examples, which are reported back;
- Giving individuals, dyads, or small groups the assignment of identifying specific contributions and successes that have occurred recently among people they know and merit recognition (even if they have not yet been recognized); and
- Discussing within subgroups why recognition does not occur more frequently.

In each case, general discussion among the whole group should follow.

In many groups within the dominant U.S. culture, participation itself becomes a competition with winners and losers. As a result, some group members attempt to draw attention to themselves and away from others, and some tend to participate at high levels while others remain relatively disengaged and quiet. There are many approaches for dealing with such dynamics (see, e.g., Rose, 1978, 1998). One of the most elegant, the *talking circle*, originated in Native American cultures. A true talking circle involves a spiritual dimension that may go beyond the function of many groups, but the basic way of structuring the process is quite simple and powerful. Traditionally, a talking feather or stick is passed around the circle, with the person holding it being the only one allowed to speak. (The direction in which the feather or stick is passed does not matter, so long as it is consistent.) One common variation we have used extensively is to write the question or issue to be addressed on a card and to pass that card around the circle. The following guidelines apply:

- Only the person holding the card can speak.
- Participants are expected to listen while others speak, rather than plan what they will say when their turn comes.
- People can "pass" when they receive the card, but if they do, they must wait until it comes around again to speak.
- Participants are reminded that the purpose is not for anyone to "perform" and that to be respectful to others, each person should be as brief as possible.

In the beginning, a few respectful reminders may be necessary to help people learn the process. Dialogue tends to deepen if the card goes around the circle more than once and if at least a few members make a real effort to be as honest as they possibly can, because this tends to spur others to do likewise. As a general rule, the more times the card goes around, the more significant the dialogue. With some groups, it is useful to give everyone a minute or two to write down their thoughts before beginning the circle. Among possible topics are the reasons that people do not recognize each other more often, the many different ways that people respond to praise or statements of appreciation, the many kinds of contributions that young people can make in their worlds, and the obstacles that they face in doing so.

Modeling and Rehearsal

Skills training is a primary means for changing behavior. In many cases, young people (and adults) do not know effective ways to deal with challenging situations. Sometimes people have the needed skills in their behavioral repertoires, but may not use them appropriately. For example, many people know how to manage frustration at work, but may not use those skills at home or with peers. In other cases, people genuinely have never learned certain valuable life skills. In our society, recognition skills are often poorly developed, and even when present may not be used. Expressing and responding to appreciation or recognition may be seen as unnecessary, or even embarrassing. Therefore, explicit recognition skills training may be necessary.

Key approaches to skills training are modeling, in which one individual watches others perform the desired behavior, and rehearsal, in which that individual practices the behaviors herself or himself. Such training is often progressive, with participants gradually refining more and more effective approaches in response to group feedback. It can begin, however, with very simple exercises that, in fact, blend into *PEACE POWER* circles. Rose (1998) describes an exercise in which pairs of group members work together, and each writes down one positive behavior that he or she has observed in his or her partner in the group. They then share these observations with the larger group. The exercise continues by changing partners (thus offering additional practice with a different person—which supports generalization) and similarly identifying one positive behavior that person shows outside the group. The exercise is a way to observe and practice recognition skills.

More elaborate modeling and rehearsal exercises often involve role playing of sample situations like those that follow:

- One of two friends just successfully completed a school assignment that has been giving him a lot of trouble. What would his friend say? What would he say in return?
- One of the kids in a special education class just learned that she will be mainstreamed (i.e., was accepted into a school to which she had applied). She is talking to two friends. What would the dialogue be like?
- Two kids are talking on the bus. One of them just talked two younger kids into settling a disagreement peacefully. What would those two friends say to each other?
- A teacher just gave a young woman a very positive job reference, and she got the job. The next time she sees him, what do they say?
- (*Have a student take the role of the teacher.*) Three students planned a special program for their classmates about summer job opportunities, and the program went very well. One of their teachers is speaking to them about the event.

In these exercises, special attention should be paid both to expressing recognition and to acknowledging recognition graciously rather than arrogantly or with false modesty.

Videotaping such exercises is particularly effective. Youth usually enjoy watching themselves, and taping provides an unlimited number of opportunities for them to observe themselves and gradually to refine their skills. Youth should participate extensively in developing scenarios for skills training, as their scenarios tend to be far more realistic. Groups of young people can be split into subgroups, for example, with each group given the assignment of developing a role-played scenario of effective recognition.

Home Recognition Notes

Descriptions of behavior in school sent home to parents have been shown to be useful components of a number of structured behavioral programs in which consequences are provided at home for behavior at school (Ginsburg, 1990). These "home notes" contribute to home–school partnerships that can dramatically change youth behavior. One very simple variation of home notes is the home recognition note. Prepared by staff working with young people in any setting, such notes detail for parents the positive achievements and contributions of the youth in that setting. There are several advantages to the use of these tools. First, many parents' primary contact with schools occurs when their children get into trouble, and "notes home" often are of this critical type. Naturally, repeated experiences of this kind are aversive and tend to produce distance between program and home. By contrast, home recognition notes build bridges and provide parents an opportunity to join school staff in recognizing positive actions.

Examples of the importance of these notes are everywhere. The author vividly remembers a moment when a large, older adolescent girl with a history of school problems very proudly showed a home recognition note she was taking to her care-giving grandmother. The recognition by her teacher and the opportunity for recognition by her grandmother were deeply meaningful to her. In one alternative high school, students preferred recognition certificates that they could take home to prizes like compact discs! The principal of the same school reports that at a wake for one of his students who had died, two things were on display: a photograph of the young man and a framed recognition certificate from the school.

It is easier to identify positive acts by some youth than others, so a commitment to really look is critical. In busy youth-serving organizations and schools, it also is easy for staff members to intend to send home such notes regularly, but not to do so in the press of daily activities. Setting clear goals for oneself (e.g., "I will send home at least 15 notes a week") and incorporating these into a self-management program is often essential for maintenance. In one school, each staff member completed at least two home recognition notes before leaving the room after each weekly staff meeting.

Peer Monitoring

An additional way of increasing the level of recognition is to assign one or two young people as peer monitors. Unlike that of traditional hall monitors, for example, the role of peer monitors is to identify and report *positive* actions that other young people have taken. This approach can be particularly useful for preteens and young teens. The role of monitor may rotate on a regular basis, or interested youth may form an organized "secret society" of monitors. The procedure may work best if the monitoring role is confidential, with designated youth reporting positive actions to a staff member, who then posts the findings without identifying the source. Monitors may observe and report positive actions by staff members and other adults in the setting as well. There is much room for creative adaptation.

Self-Recognition

Exercises in which youth learn to recognize their own successes and contributions in nonegotistical ways may be useful in many settings. These should generally be quiet rather than very public exercises, for example, written assignments in which youth describe positive contributions that they are trying to make to improve life among their peers, in school, or in the community. Very small group discussions may also be workable—once youth learn to recognize their strengths with humility. The following guidelines may be helpful:

- Describe one thing you have done or are doing that you hope will contribute to the community.
- What gifts do you have that you are using in that effort?
- What is going well in that effort?
- What will you do next?

This exercise involves recognizing one's own effort, but not taking credit for talents (which, as both the science of behavior and the understanding of Native America teach us, are gifts, not something for which one deserves praise). Opportunities to discuss in detail how one is achieving success are often reinforcing (Daniels, 2000), so rich description should be the goal in this type of excercise.

Activity Sampling

In some cases, youth have relatively few opportunities in their lives to make contributions and achieve successes. Members of poor and oppressed groups, in particular, often live relatively restricted lives. If such youth encounter opportunities to try new activities, however, they may discover new talents and gifts. In using those talents and gifts, they find new opportunities for recognition by self and others. Enrichment activities offering youth opportunities to experience something very different from their everyday lives, then, can contribute to the level of recognition present in a system.

Poster Making and Murals

Many disease prevention and health promotion efforts have discovered the utility of poster making and poster-making contests for keeping programs at the forefront of people's attention. Commercially prepared posters often capture attention initially, but as they hang in the same place for long periods of time, becoming increasingly faded and tattered, they become invisible. A far better alternative is to hang posters constructed by youth in which they provide their own interpretations of program principles, changing them on a regular basis. In PEACE POWER programs, groups like students in each classroom or residents of each cottage can take responsibility for changing and updating a particular wall, for example, perhaps with prizes for the groups who do best each month. Individual poster-making contests can also be held once a year, perhaps in conjunction with some marker event (e.g., the beginning of a new semester or Martin Luther King, Jr. Day). For either group or individual contests, some of the best work might be duplicated and sent to other community groups or turned into a calendar that can be used as a fundraising tool to obtain resources for other PEACE POWER efforts. The depth of expression that sometimes emerges from such posters can be breathtaking.

An even more ambitious, and very valuable, alternative is the creation of murals, permanent products in public places that serve as reminders to the community. The messages conveyed in words and images can draw public attention to the importance of constructing community cultures of nonviolent power. Mural projects have demonstrated considerable power to involve groups of youth in partnership with adults in a meaningful collective effort; youth often dedicate a great deal of time to the design and construction of these projects (Delgado & Barton, 1998).

Celebrations

When an individual or a group has achieved some sort of noteworthy success, group celebrations can be an effective form of recognition (Daniels, 2000). Such celebrations occur frequently in many well-functioning cultural groups, serving not only to recognize contributions and achievements but also to build a sense of community. Monthly *PEACE POWER* celebrations remind everyone of the program and offer opportunities to read randomly selected recognition notes. A celebration, of course, should include other reinforcers, like refreshments and entertainment, with recognition being only one part of the program.

Staff Self-Monitoring and Self-Management

Embedding many of the tools and activities that have been discussed within an organizational culture requires regular effort. Just as there is a natural process of reinforcer erosion in couple relationships—that is, partners gradually put in less effort, and each notices efforts that are made less and less—the same can happen in an organizational culture—that is, cultural actors may do less and less, and notice what is done less and less as well. It is easy to provide recognition notes or organize *PEACE POWER* circles once, but far more difficult to institutionalize these efforts in one's day, week, and month. Overall organizational self-monitoring, as discussed in chapter 7, can be part of the answer, but individual self-monitoring and self-management by staff can also be essential.

Self-monitoring involves pinpointing the planned actions, setting goals for the frequency of such actions, and keeping records to track actual frequencies. Self-monitoring is a major component of intensive *PEACE POWER* work with youth (chapter 9), but can be just as crucial for staff. The *PEACE POWER* Planner is a tool to structure this process (Figure 9).

Figure 9

 PEACE POWER!
Planner

S	M	T	W	T	F	S

Performance Data

Recognize:	

http://www.bfsr.org/PEACEPOWER.html   © 1999 Walden Fellowship, Inc.

The *PEACE POWER* Planner. Source: Reprinted with permission from *PEACE POWER* Working Group, 1999.

Figure 9 can be duplicated for use each month (see note 6). The calendar area can be completed to plan which activities will be implemented each day; for example, a classroom teacher may note when written assignments about contributions made by historical figures are due, or a recreation program leader may note days when *PEACE POWER* circles will be conducted. As each activity is completed, it can be checked off on the planner. The lower area permits a staff member to make a hash mark for each time some target behavior is performed. Some teachers, for example, make a small mark in this section each time they consciously provide recognition, then enter the daily total in the calendar above, erase the hash marks, and begin again the next day. There are many other ways pinpointed behavior can be tracked, of course (see chapter 7).

Although self-monitoring by itself can be effective for some, successful performances that are not shared with someone else tend to fade over time (Malott, 2000). It is usually preferable, therefore, for persons involved in self-monitoring to share their data with others; the attention and response of others provide social consequences, which expand a self-monitoring program into a self-management program. Many people also find that associating small, self-generated positive consequences for completing a targeted behavior a certain number of times or negative consequences for failing to reach goals is surprisingly useful in keeping their attention focused on the priorities that they have set.

Unfortunately, many readers may agree that self-monitoring and self-management procedures would probably be useful for others, but are also likely to believe that they themselves don't need them. The research is quite clear, however; self-monitoring and self-management can be of critical importance in maintaining a focus on recognition, and performance that is not monitored in some way is likely to fade.

Tools for Increasing Recognition Events in Families

Like organizations and communities, families are cultures; the most effective *PEACE POWER* programs are likely to work with all of these collectives. Any *PEACE POWER* project should ordinarily include workshops for families to introduce the core practices and offer families opportunities to work with each other, youth, and program staff to refine and implement the program. Even if only a small proportion of families whose children attend a school or are involved in a recreation program participate, the contributions of those families are still essential and should not be neglected. Many of the tools and activities described earlier for work with organizations can be adapted for work with families as well. Community organizations, in particular churches, may be in ideal positions to sponsor family enrichment programs that can incorporate some of these tools and activities.

Recognition Boards and Notes

Written recognition can be even more powerful in families than in organizations. In families that are already strong, additional attention to contributions and successes further enhances relationships, and there may be less need for posturing than sometimes occurs in other settings. In families that are struggling, increasing the rate of positive exchange is among the most important and powerful interventions known (Mattaini, 1999). Standard recognition notes and recognition boards as described earlier can be used, but may in some cases seem cumbersome. For this reason, the *PEACE POWER* Working Group developed the home recognition record, illustrated in Figure 10.

The sample shown here or a similar form developed locally can also be duplicated; if this approach is taken, it is important to ensure that families have a supply of forms readily available, or use may fade as soon as the first page is complete (see note 7).

Three components are integrated on the home recognition record. The *PEACE POWER* Wheel appears on the upper left, as a reminder of the core practices. On the upper right is a message board for telephone or other messages; its purpose is partly to increase the likelihood that family members will often look at the board. Finally, the lower portion of the board includes columns in which family members can name the person whom they wish to recognize and the contribution or success being noted. Family members can have a great deal of fun with this tool, while it serves as a consistent reminder of the need for recognition. The home recognition board can be provided during workshops, in which case families can actually practice completing it. If this is not possible, simple instructions should be provided with the board so that family members clearly understand how to use it.

PEACE POWER Circles for Families

Just as regular oral sharing of statements of recognition can be useful in organizations, families can ritualize circles, perhaps informally at din-

Figure 10

PEACE POWER!
Home Record

Week of:_____

Messages:

Recognize
Contributions
& Successes

Make
Peace

PEACE®
POWER!

Act with
Respect

Share Power
to Build
Community

We Recognize:

For:

http://www.bfsr.org/PEACEPOWER.html

© 1999 Walden Fellowship, Inc.

Home Recognition Record. Source: Reprinted with permission from *PEACE POWER* Working Group, 1999.

ner or breakfast every day (if there is a meal in which all or most family members are present) and more formally once a week at a predictable time. This can be called a *PEACE POWER* circle, a circle of appreciation, Appreciation Day, or whatever makes most sense to the particular family. Different cultural groups are likely to handle *PEACE POWER* circles in different ways, which is as it should be. For some cultures, the theme of these family rituals may be, "what we have to be grateful for this week"— including not only personal successes, but also other events and opportunities that have enriched the lives of the family. Such an emphasis on gratitude may be especially appropriate for certain more collective (as opposed to individualistic) cultures, including some African American, Latino, and Native American families. It is always crucial, however, not to overgeneralize; family cultures within larger ethnic cultures are enormously variable. In other families (e.g., some Asian American families), explicit recognition of what each family member has contributed to the family may be the primary emphasis. Families that are particularly interested in raising children who are committed to social and community welfare may emphasize service activities, both within the family and in the larger community. The variations are infinite, and communities and families should be encouraged to develop approaches that really fit them.

Monitoring and Incentives

Not all families require monitoring and incentives; in many cases, however, youth and their families have goals that are difficult to accomplish. For example, a teen who has missed a great deal of school may require substantial support to begin attending regularly. Family members and professionals working with the family may need to advocate for the young person with the school or other systems (Mattaini, 1999). At the same time, parental monitoring, sometimes including explicit consequences for truancy, may be important. Schools often do not have as much impact and influence on youth as do families, and the message that what the young person does really is important to the family can be crucial to changing behavior.

It is essential in this kind of effort that attention (and temporary incentives, if necessary) focus primarily on successes, rather than on failures. Some forms of "contracts" are simply statements of the punishment that youth will experience if they do not do what adults want. Such contracts are generally ineffective. By contrast, contracts that (a) emphasize positive consequences for desired behavior and (b) result from negotiations in which the young people involved fully participated tend to produce excellent results (Mattaini, 1999).

The utility of structured incentives and their appropriate forms also appear to vary among cultures. Recent work indicates that directive, strategic interventions of particular kinds may be particularly effective with Latino families (Robbins & Szapocznik, 2000), while for traditional Native American families, entirely different approaches that involve modeling by older persons and teaching through stories may be much more appropriate.

Building of Life and Leadership Skills

Families are among the most powerful teachers of life and leadership skills (see chapter 8). Two sets of skills are particularly useful for indirectly increasing the levels of recognition that young people experience, and workshops that discuss these skills may be helpful to families with strong interest. First, youth who experience a great deal of satisfaction and success are those who are able to identify activities that they really care about; in other words, they "find a passion." Parents, other caregivers, and older siblings can be key players in helping and encouraging youth to search out such activities. The key behaviors in this instance are actively searching and experimenting with new possibilities.

The second set of key skills involves "envisioning a path." Research has demonstrated that youth who are skilled in identifying the steps needed to reach a goal and then following those steps experience substantially more success than those who lack those skills (Shure, 1999). These youth are also at lower risk for involvement in antisocial behavior. Less successful youth often have goals, but lack skills for identifying and taking the intermediate steps needed to reach their goals. Family members, through regular dialogue, can help youth to learn these skills.

Community Recognition Tools and Activities

Some of the most powerful interventions to prevent violence among youth may occur at a neighborhood or even broader community level, because these interventions can include school, organization, and family components within a larger collective commitment to nonviolent empowerment. Naturally, community level initiatives are more challenging to mount. As Embry and Flannery (1999) note, considerable research indicates that neighborhood and community factors, ranging from high levels of unemployment and mobility to high levels of exposure to violence, contribute significantly to poor social and academic outcomes for youth; research and theory suggest that the following steps, among others, may be useful:

- "Minimize focus on fear and threat stimuli and increase focus on activities that create a sense of orderliness and even beauty" (Embry & Flannery, 1999, p. 57).
- "Engage in frequent public displays of the positive community-wide norm. Public events help create a climate of belonging and acceptable standards of behavior. . . . Whenever possible, the children in the neighborhood need to work alongside the adults. In Chicago, the Neighborhood Authority, a self-help group, gives weekly awards to members of the community who have helped make the neighborhood more peaceful" (Embry & Flannery, 1999, p. 58).
- "In general, an effective neighborhood program to prevent youth violence would provide extensive positive models instead of negative models, provide high rates of positive feedback for imitation, and offer many cues, prompts, and tools that facilitate generalization" (Embry & Flannery, 1999, p. 59).

These strategic directions build over the long term, rather than emphasize short-term enforcement approaches (although these have their place). Embry and Flannery note that the experimental evidence for what works at a community level is thin, but there are some tools and activities that appear promising.

Media Efforts

There is general acceptance in our culture that the media play a major role in behavior change; this is the basis of much of the marketing and advertising materials that bombard everyone. Media clearly can encourage positive behavior among youth not only by providing healthy role models, but also by providing regular recognition for positive contributions to the community. Young people look for "heroes," people to look up to, and the media are in a strong position to provide such models. It is important that these efforts be professionally prepared, however, because they must compete for attention.

In some communities with a PeaceBuilders program, for example, television news shows have highlighted a "PeaceBuilder of the Week," someone who has made a real contribution to the community. Ideally, such an effort should highlight some children, some adults, some famous persons, some older adults, some African Americans, some Asian Americans, some gay and lesbian persons, some who have significant financial resources, and others who have practically none. Consistent with its European roots (Martin, 1999), U.S. culture often emphasizes that the world is a dangerous place, not to be trusted. A different message, that many people are acting all the time to enhance an already strong community, needs to be communicated.

Neighborhood and Community Recognition Processes

Like the media, neighborhood and community groups such as the Neighborhood Authority in Chicago mentioned above can develop regular recognition processes to honor members of the community who have made contributions, neighborhood "heroes" who have used their talents well. They can work with schools and youth-serving organizations to ensure that successful role models, often people who came from the local community, have frequent contact with youth. Such contacts should not happen only occasionally, but rather regularly. If, as an example, young African American students in a generally poor and stressed neighborhood have the opportunity to see successful African American professionals and to offer those individuals recognition—by giving them an opportunity to "tell their stories"—everyone benefits.

Contributions from the Business Community

Businesses can contribute to a culture of recognition in the community in many ways. They can, for example, sponsor media efforts to recognize community contributions. Embry and Flannery (1999) report that businesses willing to display student artwork related to violence prevention experienced declines in vandalism and petty crime. Businesses can provide goods and services as prizes for persons who improve the community. In a number of places, businesses have contributed prizes as incentives, particularly for youth who struggle to attend school or to achieve successes there. Businesses and individual contributors can sponsor advertising for community violence prevention programs, as well as provide promotional materials for those programs. And of course, individual business owners and employees in the community can volunteer their time to many kinds of programs (see chapter 5).

Recognition Posters

Community groups can regularly produce posters that recognize particular contributions of groups and individuals in the community. These can be especially powerful, because the people who see the posters know, live with, work with, and go to church with the people recognized. Posters like this can now be produced relatively inexpensively and can serve as changing displays to remind people of the strengths of their communities and the individuals in them. Such posters can be distributed to organizations, churches, health centers, government offices, post offices, and businesses on a regular basis, keeping the notion of recognizing contributions alive in the community.

Conclusion

Nothing is more important for preventing violence and other forms of antisocial behavior than developing cultures of recognition. Many other approaches and strategic options can contribute to reducing violence and increasing nonviolent power among youth and their communities, but the critical importance of recognition cannot be overlooked. Recognition is a long-term rather than a short-term strategy, and our society often tends to overlook such approaches. Along with sharing power (see chapter 5), which is in many ways another facet of the same dynamic, however, constructing cultures that recognize and honor contributions and positive actions without encouraging egotism is the single most powerful means available for reducing violence and coercion.

Act with Respect

The second line of the *PEACE POWER* Pledge reads, "Today I will *Act with Respect*—for myself, others, and the earth, giving up putdowns, threats, and weapons." Acting with respect encompasses a wide range of behavior, encouraging positive actions and discouraging aversive behaviors. Problem behaviors tend to occur at higher rates when a person experiences high levels of coercion and threat, as discussed in chapter 2. Respectful action, by definition, is noncoercive. Although many adults associated with programs and organizations believe that both youth and adults in their programs experience high levels of respect, the results of anonymous surveys are often surprising. In fact, developing and implementing a *respect survey* in which participants are asked to evaluate the extent to which different groups in the organization act with respect and act with disrespect, and to give examples of each, can be an eye-opening experience. Such surveys in several *PEACE POWER* projects have produced disappointing results for some program participants, who find that the level of disrespect experienced is much higher than they had expected. This information can be useful both generally as a motivating factor to support programming and specifically as guidance for collective action. Planning and conducting such a survey can itself be an example of shared power (see chapter 5), as youth and adults can participate in all phases of the work. The question format suggested in chapter 7 can be adapted for such surveys. Respect surveys can also be repeated to monitor progress over time.

Respect and *disrespect* are common words among youth, although their definitions and uses are quite variable. Clarifying definitions is often an important first step in moving to increase respectful action. In fact, acting with respect for oneself, acting with respect for others, and acting with respect for the environment are all deeply interconnected. Einstein described individual autonomy from a scientific perspective as a delusion and indicated that "the individual is what he is and has the significance that he has not so much in virtue of his individuality, but rather as a member of a great human society, which directs his material and spiritual existence from the cradle to the grave" (n.d., p. 8). Native American cultures (*The Way of the Spirit*, 1997) and contemporary biological science (Goodenough, 1998) teach that humans can have no independent existence apart from the human and nonhuman environment. In a profound and very literal way, we are all connected.

Acting with respect for oneself involves not only giving up self-punishment but also recognizing one's value and talents, and avoiding actions likely to damage oneself. Acting with respect for others means avoiding coercive strategies (e.g., threats, punishment, needless hurt), while honoring the value of the other. Appropriate assertion is respectful and is a reflection of noncoercive power. Speaking truth is also respectful, though it may sometimes require real courage. By contrast, acting to preserve a false image of oneself or others is dishonest and ultimately disrespectful to those whose perceptions are targeted. Similarly, acting with respect for the environment requires avoiding actions that damage it in either the short or the long run, while acting in ways that help to maintain and restore balance.

All of these actions can be difficult in contemporary society, and encouraging respectful action is deeply challenging. Dominant society relies on coercive strategies in most spheres, from the family to education to the "justice" system—despite the costs. Sidman (2001) indicates, "Coercive control permeates our lives. . . . Coercive interactions threaten our well-being and even our survival as a species" (p. 245). From within this system, it is hard to even imagine alternatives, but such do exist. For example, acting with *harmony* and *compassion*, two of the cardinal virtues (*Ma'at*; O'Donnell & Karanja, 2000) characterizing certain traditional African societies, is highly consistent with cultures of respect. In fact, respect for the value of every person and for the Earth, recognition of interconnectedness, and action consistent with these perspectives characterizes the Pueblo, Navajo, Anishinaabe, Haudenosaunee, and many other indigenous worldviews in this hemisphere. Those alongside whom we have lived for so long are in a position to help U.S. society see alternative cultural possibilities, and the *PEACE POWER* strategy has emerged in part from these.

Certain coercive and potentially damaging social exchanges are very common in the lives of youth in the United States; their seriousness is often not recognized, but their cumulative effect is powerful. If one simply listens to contemporary children and youth in informal situations, for example, the rate of subtle or not-so-subtle criticisms of appearance, family, behavior, and capacities is often astonishingly high. These "putdowns" are often framed as humorous, and some good-spirited teasing, if limited, may not be damaging. In many cases, however, these aversive exchanges actually function to establish dominance, to punish variations from the norm, and frankly to hurt. In addition, most young people in the United States regularly experience threats of various kinds, ranging from the bullying experienced by the vast majority of U.S. youth at some point to subtle threats by peers to withdraw their acceptance. Although youth who fear for their safety often carry weapons for self-protection, the very presence of weapons increases the level of threat in an environment. For this reason, *PEACE POWER* programs ask both youth and adults to proactively give up putdowns, threats, and reliance on weapons for the good of the collective—often a request with which people find it difficult to comply. Overt violence—which, of course, people also must give up—is not as common as these other related aggressive and coercive acts, but tends to emerge from the coercive matrix that they construct. *PEACE POWER* programs help youth learn to communicate with each other and with adults in ways that respect everyone involved—one of the best definitions of "assertiveness" (see Rakos, 1991, for more specificity). On a broader level, teaching tolerance and respect for those different from oneself and activities to protect and heal the environment are also part of the class of respectful actions.

Some of the tools and approaches suggested in this chapter explicitly address the challenge of helping people see their own behavior "objectively." Like those described in the previous chapter, the tools offered here have either some (in some cases, considerable) empirical support or are consistent with well-supported theory. Local programs should, as always, use these suggestions as starting points for developing programs that fit local conditions, values, and cultures.

Tools and Activities for Increasing Respectful Action in Schools and Other Organizations

Many tools and activities may be used and combined in various ways to increase the level of respectful action in schools, youth programs, and

Table 3. Tools for Building Respectful Action

Tools for Schools and Youth-Serving Organizations
- The *PEACE POWER* Pledge, "Respect" buttons, and related reminders
- "Putups, not putdowns"
- Critical dialogue
- Improvisation and theater
- Respectful discipline procedures
- Teaching sportsmanship
- Cooperative games and sports
- Bullying prevention
- Teaching of tolerance
- Communication skills training
- Empathy education
- Role-played practice of challenging situations
- Environmental education and action

Tools for Families
- Family self-monitoring
- Parent/caregiver interviews as homework modules
- Family participation in gap-bridging and multicultural activities

Tools for Communities
- Presentations by high-visibility figures
- Movie making
- Pledge campaigns
- Police–youth dialogues

residential settings, as well as in systems involving primarily adults (Table 3). There are numerous opportunities to open discussions of respect in organizations. For example, disrespect and challenging behavior are often very common in schools, when substitute teachers are covering classrooms. As suggested by the developers of PeaceBuilders (Embry, Flannery, Vazsonyi, Powell, & Atha, 1996), establishing a norm in which students regard substitute teachers as "guest teachers" and treat them respectfully as guests can be a meaningful and educational shift in organizational culture that bridges the gap between adults and youth. In addition to targeting organizational cultures, programs implemented in such settings may also influence practices among peer networks, powerful cultural environments for contemporary youth.

The PEACE POWER Pledge and Related Reminders

The *PEACE POWER* Pledge (see Figure 8), or something like it, can remind everyone involved, every day, of the importance of acting with respect, of making a personal decision to forego opportunities to hurt and threaten others, and of taking the sometimes courageous decision not to carry or use weapons, thus reducing the general level of threat in the environment. Rather like a 12-step "one day at a time" commitment, the pledge does not ask for a once and for all decision. Instead, it asks each person to recommit daily to respectful action.

Other reminders may also be useful. After the Columbine High School tragedy in which over a dozen youths died, young people in Colorado began wearing small patches reading "Respect." Some *PEACE POWER* programs have adapted the idea, using very small lapel buttons that read simply, "Respect." It is difficult in today's youth culture to act with respect for persons who are different—for gay and lesbian youth, for those with physical differences, for those with cognitive delays, or for those of other racial and ethnic groups. Wearing such a button is a way of publicly committing to doing so and may also induce dissonance if one acts disrespectfully while wearing a "Respect" button. Local programs may be able to develop other creative reminders like posters, street theater, or dramatic presentations that keep the practice of respectful action at the forefront of attention.

"Putups, Not Putdowns"

A number of programs, particularly PeaceBuilders (see note 1), emphasize the importance of giving up putdowns, and some emphasize the need for increasing "putups" (recognition, in *PEACE POWER* terms) as well. "Putups, not putdowns" must be more than a slogan, however, if organizational and peer cultures are to change. The first step is to clarify definitions of each and to explain the reasons why the shift is important, which can occur through Socratic discussions led by a staff member (e.g., "What are some examples of putdowns? Why are they sometimes a problem?"). More intense group dialogue can be more powerful, but simple discussions are a useful place to begin.

Once the meaning of respectful action is clear, it is sometimes useful to "challenge" the group; for example, "Can we as a class make it through social studies without a single [with no more than two, with no more than three, etc.] putdown(s)?" The length of such putdown-free intervals can be gradually extended (even by using a timer, if desired), and after reaching a predetermined goal, the group may receive some kind of reward or privilege. This kind of procedure, called differential reinforcement of (any) other behavior (DRO), can be handled lightly and with humor. This can be a useful way to operationalize what may otherwise be experienced as just a "nice idea." There are many variations, including teacher monitoring, student monitoring, and videotaping a segment of student discussion and having each participant keep track of the number of putdowns that occur.

Critical Dialogue

Although some of the techniques used, like DRO, involve a light touch, the basic principle of acting with respect is, of course, very serious. It is one of the areas in which critical dialogue and the development of critical consciousness are essential. The youth involved tend to emulate the seriousness with which the staff person or leaders present discuss the issues. Before large group discussions take place, small groups and talking circles can address questions like the following:

- What are the real meanings of "respect" and "disrespect"? What are some important examples of acting respectfully or disrespectfully that you have observed at school, with peers, at home?
- Why do people so often act disrespectfully?
- Using an example of disrespectful behavior that you have observed, what are the ways the person being treated in that way could react? How could others present react? Which of these ways are best?
- What kinds of people, and what kinds of behavior, are hard to respect? Should you still act with respect under those circumstances?
- Many people act disrespectfully toward people different from themselves (e.g., gay and lesbian youth, persons with physical or mental disabilities, people of different races). Why do you think this is, and how serious a problem is it?
- How would things be different if everyone here always acted with respect?
- Do we as a group have a responsibility to promote respect?
- What are some of the ways children learn to act disrespectfully?

- In what ways do the media (e.g., movies, television, music) encourage acting with respect or acting disrespectfully? (This is a particularly important discussion, given the intense levels of coercion and violence modeled in and supported by contemporary media, often targeted specifically toward a youth market. Entire class projects can emerge from such dialogue to explore these media influences.)

These questions, of course, should be adapted and expanded to fit each situation in which they are used. It is often possible to use events occurring in the news or in the lives of well-known persons as examples.

Improvisation and Theater

There are many ways to engage the creative potential of youth in *PEACE POWER* programs; theater and improvisation are among these. Youth involved in a theater or film-making group or class, for example, can prepare presentations related to coercive behavior and alternatives that they can present within the organization and throughout the community. They will probably need some support through drama coaches, teachers, and technical experts, but youth can do most of the work themselves. In several places in the United States, such acting companies have become very well-known and successful. The presentations of one program for adolescents sponsored by a hospital in New York City are in high demand in elementary and high schools, and at community events and workshops, for instance. The process of developing and making presentations offers strong opportunities for the youth involved to grapple with the issues; the modeling presented is also valuable for those who observe the presentation. Live performance may be the most powerful, but there is also tremendous power in film.

Improvisation, by contrast, involves acting out situations spontaneously. It is very similar to role playing, but may have a less didactic feel. In addition, in skills training using role play, there is heavy emphasis on discussion; in improvisation, some discussion is useful, but much of the time is devoted to the theatrical action. The basic process is very simple, although leadership that is encouraging, very creative, and prepared is essential. It may be helpful to have a grounding in semistructured improvisational techniques (Thompson, 1999) or to simply begin with a book of improvisational openings (e.g., Bernardi, 1992), always bearing in mind that procedures should be creatively modified for the group. Basically, the leader begins by having one or more scenarios in mind, asks for volunteers to take on roles, explains to each person what his or her role is, and has the group play out the scene.

Because the purpose of the exercise is learning, brief discussion, particularly about alternatives, and an opportunity to "try a different way" should follow the scene. As soon as the group members exhaust the energy in one scene, they move to a new scenario. Very quickly, the process should move from leader-initiated scenes to youth-initiated scenes. The leader's role here is critical; she or he needs not only to establish that the purpose of the activity is to experiment with the *PEACE POWER* practices, but also to gently keep the focus there throughout the process in ways that are consistent with the flow. For example, role plays of coercive behaviors should always be followed by discussion and, usually, role plays of prosocial alternatives. After each scenario, very brief discussion by those involved about what they experienced, and by the audience of what they observed, can help to clarify the lessons.

Respectful Discipline Procedures

In all settings where youth are served, there will at some point be discipline problems. High rates of recognition and consistently respectful behavior will substantially reduce such problems, but will not eliminate them. The manner in which discipline problems are handled will determine whether problem behavior is a minor disruption or escalates into a major organizational issue. The responses of others in the young person's environment are among the primary determinants of outcome (Wood & Long, 1991).

In the face of a behavior problem, respect is even more important than under other circumstances. Unfortunately, it is common at those times for staff, parents, and others to become highly punitive and coercive. Our consultants have observed even highly trained professionals with advanced degrees become enraged, swear, and physically threaten young people at such moments. These approaches are ultimately ineffective, but most important for our purposes here, they damage the culture of respect. Rules can and should be collectively reassessed periodically and very consistently enforced. At the same time, these efforts can and should be completely respectful.

A central role not only for adults but also for peers is to teach young people the skills they need to succeed and contribute to the common welfare. A young person who achieves a success or makes a contribution, of course, deserves recognition. Behavior that is not consistent with the well-being of the individual and the group calls for teaching. Some of the best developed and empirically supported work in this area has come out of Boys Town (see, e.g., Connolly, Dowd, Criste, Nelson, & Tobias, 1995). While it is very useful to examine the complete Boys Town model through their literature and training programs, two specific, very straightforward procedures that can be applied in most settings working with youth are *guided self-correction* and *crisis teaching* (Davis, Nelson, & Gauger, 2000). These procedures are discussed in detail in chapter 10.

Teaching Sportsmanship

Research suggests that persons teaching or coaching sports and physical education are in particularly good positions to teach respect under pressure (Sharpe, Brown, & Crider, 1995). In their work with elementary school–aged children, Sharpe et al. discovered that directly and explicitly teaching sportsmanship can result in large increases in student leadership behaviors and teacher-independent conflict resolution when engaged in sports activities. Even more impressively, this training can also reduce off-task behavior by about three-quarters, triple student leadership behaviors, and quadruple teacher-independent conflict resolution in other classes as much as a day later. Although there have been no reports on similar research with older youth, given the respect that coaches and physical education teachers often carry, teaching sportsmanship with teens is also likely to produce excellent results. Theory also suggests that it may be useful with some groups of kids to use a sportsmanship metaphor in settings outside schools, because sports play so large a part in the lives of many contemporary youth.

The procedures used in teaching sportsmanship behaviors include the following (Sharpe et al., 1995):

- A brief talk by the physical education teacher each day at the beginning of the period about one or more of the sportsmanship repertoires listed below,
- Teacher scoring of positive and negative behaviors performed by each team,
- Verbal teacher feedback at the end of each period and public posting of results.

With more challenged student populations, the use of group rewards is likely to produce the best results.

The behaviors emphasized by Sharpe and colleagues (1995) included the following:

1. Being good winners
   - Positive and supportive feedback to opposing team
   - Absence of bragging, taunting
2. Being good losers
   - Congratulatory behavior
   - Absence of accusations, blame
3. Demonstrating peer respect
   - Supportive behavior toward peer leaders and peer referees
   - Absence of negative interactions with peer leaders and peer referees
4. Showing enthusiasm
   - Peer encouragement and positive feedback
   - Absence of negative comments to peers
5. Participating actively
   - On-task participation
   - Absence of bystander behavior
6. Resolving conflicts
   - Teacher-independent resolution of game conflicts
7. Helping peers and the organization
   - Peer instruction and support
   - Activity organizing

Training for these procedures is quite straightforward, and variations for youth recreation programs can easily be designed.

Cooperative Games and Sports

Children and youth learn how to act socially partly through play and games. There is considerable evidence that children and youth engaged in cooperative games learn skills that generalize to other situations, including the classroom; similarly, those who engage in highly aggressive, competitive games learn aggressive ways of behaving that generalize to other settings (see Bay-Hinitz, Peterson, & Quilitch, 1994, for a brief review). Creative, cooperative games, therefore, are often preferable. If organized with an eye to sportsmanship, however, competitive games can also contribute to cultures of respect.

Cooperative games are characteristic of many cultures (Orlick, 1982); not surprisingly, they are much less common in U.S. society, in which adversarial, win–lose practices are so widespread. Resources are available, however, that can guide efforts to expand cooperative activities among youth (e.g., Luvmour & Luvmour, n.d.; Orlick, 1978, 1982). Many existing sports and games can be adapted, games from other cultures can be imported, and youth and adults can also creatively develop their own. Although adults may wonder if children and youth will really accept noncompetitive alternatives, experience in many settings indicates that they do. In fact, Orlick (1982) notes that in his research, youth consistently expressed a wish to play in ways that reduce their fear of failure (and injury). A few possibilities (summarized and adapted from Luvmour and Luvmour, and Orlick) are summarized here:

- *Three strikes and you're in.* In this variation of baseball, "if the pitcher from the opposite team is not able to deliver the ball in a manner that enables the batter to hit it within three throws, the hitter automatically goes to first base" (Orlick, 1982, p. 80).
- *Connecting eyes.* Beginning with a group in a circle, individuals attempt to "connect" with someone else in the circle by making and holding eye contact. When contact is made, those who are connected exchange places without losing eye contact. Players attempt to include everyone, and many pairs swap positions at the same time.
- *All score basketball.* A team wins a round when each member of the team has scored one basket. (This involves an element of competition between teams, but with multiple rounds and a commitment to sportsmanship, such hybrids can work well.)
- *Rotational volleyball.* Although played like regular volleyball, one person rotates to the other team with each rotation! No score is kept. A variation is to begin with two equal teams, but each time one side scores a point, the other team gives them a player. The game ends when all players are on one side.
- *Malaysian bucket brigade* (adapted from Orlick, 1982). An outdoor game for use at programs like camps, this activity begins with a large container of water. Teams of six, each with a bucket, form lines radiating from the large container and attempt to move as much water from the center to separate barrels a distance away. The exercise is timed; for each round, the score is the total number of inches of water in all the outside barrels. In the next round,

the entire group attempts to better their collective score. Moving large quantities of water quickly, of course, leads to all kinds of social transactions!

- *Group obstacle course.* Players complete an obstacle course while tied together as pairs or in groups of four or five who link hands throughout.
- *No-touch football.* Touch football, except that only the person carrying the ball can be touched. If any two other players touch each other, they freeze for the play. (After a few tries, people generally tire of being frozen out of the action.)

Orlick (1982) also suggests activities with ecological themes; for example, having one team lay a nondamaging trail (using, e.g., downed sticks or flour) that a second team tries to follow or "silent appreciation" hikes in which a small group takes a hike without speaking, paying real attention to their surroundings and reporting to the group afterward what they saw and heard. Orlick suggests that note taking for later discussion and reflection and nonverbal communication may be acceptable during the hike. The crucial point in all of these activities is that they move groups of young people out of adversarial and into cooperative experiences. The best cooperative activities may well be those that the youth involved adapt for themselves.

Bullying Prevention

Bullying is very common among youth in the United States. The research indicates that more than three-quarters of high school students and even higher proportions of younger students have been bullied in school; rates in this country are substantially higher than those in Europe (Walker, Colvin, & Ramsey, 1995). Most youth probably have also at some point participated in bullying. Mean-spirited teasing (i.e., "putdowns") is often a precursor of bullying, which in turn is often a precursor of violence. Over 150,000 students in the United States skip school each day because of their fear of bullying (Lee, 1993), and many students carry weapons out of their fear of bullying. Youth with disabilities, unusual physical attributes, gay and lesbian youth, and others who may be in some way "different" are at especially high risk. An atmosphere of bullying creates fear and scanning for threat in the environment, and thus it interferes with learning and relationships. Such an atmosphere is directly contrary to the kind of environment that *PEACE POWER* is designed to construct.

Bullying is not an individual problem of the victim and (often multiple) perpetrators. It is a community problem, for which all (staff, youth, parents, police, the larger community) share responsibility, both individually and collectively. Well-developed and detailed programs for bullying prevention are available (e.g., Olweus, 1993; Walker et al., 1995). The following basic principles underlie effective programs of this type:

- Bullying is not normal youthful behavior; rather it is damaging behavior, sometimes severely so. In some cases, bullying can lead to depression and even suicide attempts, and in all cases, bullying teaches those involved directly and those who observe it that coercion is acceptable and fun. Such coercion, according to the research, rapidly expands and reverberates throughout peer exchanges in the setting (Sidman, 2001).
- "Adults should act as responsible authorities" (Walker et al., p. 191). Adults are responsible for protecting young people and teaching them that disrespect, threats, and injury are unacceptable.
- Everyone in the network, particularly adults, is responsible for monitoring organizational and community settings. In most cases, areas where bullying is likely to happen can be identified and observed or secured.
- The program developed by Olweus (1993) includes strategies for the entire organization (e.g., school conference day on bullying, parent circles to discuss responses to the bullying problem), strategies for use in subgroups like classrooms (e.g., clear, enforced rules; group contingencies), and strategies for individual work with the youth involved (e.g., serious talks with both bullies and victims, help from neutral students). Everyone can have a place in these activities.
- Periods of unmonitored activity are high-risk times for older youth, particularly if the peer group does not strongly support respectful behavior. Similarly, for younger students, recess provides a common occasion for bullying. The research suggests that structured activities rather than free play, in conjunction with a time-out procedure, can dramatically reduce aggression during recess (Murphy, Hutchison, & Bailey, 1983). A more complex program targeting aggressive youth also produces strong effects (Walker et al., 1995).

Rather than focusing only on bullying, *PEACE POWER* projects should focus on constructing an environment of respect. Bullying prevention efforts should be defined as just one part of this effort, without minimizing their importance.

Teaching of Tolerance

Many violent and coercive incidents occur across racial, ethnic, socio-economic, differences of physical or mental ability, religious, and other lines and variations. Through most of its history, U.S. society not only has tolerated, but also has actively promoted intolerance and oppression. Photographs of entire communities celebrating while bodies of lynched African Americans hang among them, with young girls gaily waving pieces of clothing ripped from those bodies as keepsakes, are powerful reminders of this all-pervasive issue. Detention (really concentration) camps for Japanese Americans in World War II, alternating policies of cultural destruction and genocide directed toward Native Americans over centuries, bias murders of gay and transsexual individuals, and many other such events large and small have characterized the U.S. experience from the beginning.

Such oppression, which continues into the present, is maintained by social reinforcement and modeling in families and social networks, as well as by structural factors in economic, educational, and governmental institutions (Briggs & Paulson, 1996). Even in contemporary higher education, according to recent work by the Southern Poverty Law Center (2000), bias and intolerance are common among both students and faculty. Bias and associated behaviors damage everyone—victim, perpetrator, and the social networks of each, as well as the larger community. Violence and related coercive and oppressive behaviors are also likely to generalize within groups, perpetuating a culture of oppression.

There are no easy ways to deal with these issues, but they clearly are an important facet of constructing cultures of respect. Unfortunately, they are also among the most difficult issues to address in programming, because both adults and youth tend to feel unprepared to resolve these problems and fearful of the possible consequences (both internally and in the larger community) of trying to do so. There are two sides to this coin, which usually must be addressed separately. One is increasing the general appreciation for the richness and resources of multiple cultural groups; the other, directly addressing oppression. The first is generally easier, as there are many multicultural education programs available that can be seamlessly incorporated into *PEACE POWER* projects.

It is essential to teach about oppression and elicit commitments to challenge it. The *Teaching Tolerance* materials prepared by the Southern Poverty Law Center, which include videos, written materials, and sample assignments, are one excellent place to begin (see note 8). They have been carefully designed to be both accurate and accessible, documenting the extent and depth of bias and hate in ways that support moving toward action. Once the issues have been raised, it may be very helpful to bring in spokespersons from multiple communities to discuss their own experiences. These and related activities can help both youth and adults elaborate their own responses to local challenges and facilitate the passage from acting with respect to sharing power to build community (the third core *PEACE POWER* practice, discussed in chapter 5).

Communication Skills Training

Programs that incorporate life and leadership skills training (chapter 8) have opportunities to teach a wide range of social skills. Certain very basic communication skills can be easily taught throughout youth programs, for example. Those core repertoires can increase the level of respectful action and also can be enormously helpful to those who learn them in all spheres of life. In simplest terms, the two key sets of skills required for communication are listening skills and expressive skills (see Mattaini, 1999, for detailed discussion of these repertoires).

Perhaps the most common barrier to communication is the failure to really listen. The simplest and most important level of listening is simply being quiet and paying attention, without thinking about the best way to "answer" what someone else is saying or the effect of what that person is saying on oneself. Nonverbal listening skills are relatively easy to practice. A group is first split into pairs. One member of each pair listens without speaking, trying to nonverbally communicate interest as the other speaks. The speaker can first talk for two minutes about something really important to himself or herself. If the listener manages to pay attention without interrupting, a more challenging exercise follows. This time, the speaker talks about something that the listener is unlikely to want to hear, usually about something that is not actually true, but would be hard to hear about if it were (e.g., "I've decided I don't want to go out with you on Friday, because I am concerned that you will be drinking").There is room for a great deal of creativity here; it is important, however, that the message communicated not be hurtful.

Once participants have learned to listen in this way, training can move to two higher levels. In the first, the listener may ask informational questions, but not leading questions that actually express an opinion, and "furthering" expressions. Examples of such questions and expressions include "I see . . .," "Tell me more . . .," "And then what happened?" "Um-huh . . .," and other similar statements. The most difficult level involves reflecting feelings, for example, "It sounds like you were pretty irritated when she said that" and "You must have been thrilled!" (Note that communication should involve both positive and negative experiences.) Training at this level may also increase empathy, a response incompatible with aggression (Goldstein, Glick, & Gibbs, 1998).

Communication can also be enhanced if the person speaking learns to express herself or himself in ways that are most likely to be heard. One simple approach for this is the use of "I" statements (Gordon, 1970). Such statements are phrased in terms of what the speaker thinks, feels, or believes, rather than in terms of absolute truth or "you" statements that may be experienced as blaming and, therefore, may elicit defensiveness ("You don't care about anyone but yourself"). Examples of "I" statements include the following:

- I really appreciate your help with this [a recognition statement].
- You certainly should make your own call on that, but I am worried that you may get into trouble if you go ahead.
- I would appreciate it if you don't tell anyone else about this, because I am embarrassed about it.

The following are not, however, clean "I" statements:

- I am angry because you are such a jerk [really a "you" statement].
- I am concerned that you would do something so stupid [a judgmental and, therefore, disrespectful statement].

Once these skills have been introduced, there are many opportunities for "incidental teaching" in the course of regular programming, at times when communication either is going well (with recognition) or is not (a chance for guided self-correction).

Empathy Education

Goldstein and associates (1998) indicate that empathy and aggression are incompatible responses. If one person is able to affectively reverberate with another's emotions, to take the other's emotional perspective, a level of understanding and relationship is likely to develop that precludes threat and attack. Empathy is not a part of the emotional repertoire that receives much emphasis in most spheres of life, however, so specific attention to developing empathic responding through group discussions is an additional step toward the prevention of youth violence. One approach is to offer a series of examples, tailored to the youth involved, like the following:

- A family member of a famous person dies.
- A classmate's grandparent gets sick.
- A sports figure is having a record-breaking season, which is suddenly ruined by a strike.
- Your brother or sister breaks an arm.
- A friend is suddenly dropped by a girlfriend or boyfriend.
- Someone in your class fails an examination.

In each situation, ask the group to answer the following questions as well as they can:

- What is that person feeling?
- How strong is the feeling?
- What could you say to that person that might help?

As an alternative, subgroups can also answer these questions and then compare answers.

It can also be useful to ask the youth to imagine themselves in similar situations and to answer the following questions:

- What are you feeling?
- How strong is the feeling?
- What could someone say to you that might help?

In addition to formal, planned discussions, there are often opportunities for "incidental teaching," such as when an emotion-laden situation comes up in discussion. When this happens, the group leader should try to ask the same questions that have previously been used in discussions:

- What is that person feeling?
- How strong is the feeling?
- What could you say to that person that might help?

In that way, youth have additional opportunities to practice being empathic.

Role-Played Practice of Challenging Situations

In teaching young people to deal respectfully with challenging situations, role-played practice may be useful in many settings. Although role playing may be pursued more intensively in life and leadership skills training (chapter 8), there may be times when it is useful to do some skills training "on the fly" in the natural environment. For example, if students in a classroom have frequently struggled to deal with someone who is angry at them or to deal respectfully with receiving corrective feedback, it may be useful to focus particularly on these issues. The general procedure is as follows:

1. Role-play a sample situation that is either a real event or is very much like a real event. Include the exchanges in which respect is not adequately demonstrated.
2. Discuss with those present where the process broke down and what might have been said instead.
3. Role-play one or more alternative ways to deal with the situation.
4. Have those involved rate (on a scale of 1 to 10) how effective the new approach is.
5. Discuss, role-play, and rate possible further improvements.

Embry and his colleagues (1996) call this process "new-way replays," using instant replays in sports as an analogy. Communication skills (listening and expressive skills as discussed earlier) can make it easier to develop effective strategies for dealing with challenging situations. There are no simple rules for dealing with such situations that always apply, which can be frustrating in the beginning, but in fact, the process in which participants rate the role-played response based on their global "gut reactions" has been demonstrated to be more effective than skills training that relies on instructions to perform specific behaviors (Hayes, Kohlenberg, & Melancon, 1989).

Environmental Education and Action

Young people entering the 21st century are more environmentally aware than ever before, increasingly recognizing that the environment is us and we are the environment. This embeddedness is seen by many as spiritual in nature, but is also clarified by ecological and biological science (Capra, 1996; Goodenough, 1998). Cultures of respect encourage respect for the Earth and all life. Through environmental education and action, youth can contribute to the collective and earn recognition in new ways. Environmental action can, therefore, be explicitly linked to *PEACE POWER* programs. Often, biology teachers can provide major assistance in expanding environmental activities in schools; other organizations may want to invite representatives of environmental organizations to offer presentations and lead discussions to raise interest.

Partnerships between youth-serving organizations and established environmental organizations can be particularly effective, because youth may be able to move quickly into ongoing projects. The Internet is an incredible and expanding resource for education and connections with action possibilities, with both large, established organizations (e.g., the Sierra Club) and small, grassroots activist organizations well represented (see note 9).

Family Tools and Activities to Support Acting with Respect

As with the first core practice, families can pursue many of the types of activities that organizations can sponsor. Families are key to forming values and, therefore, are central to increasing respectful action and discouraging disrespectful action. The ideas listed in this section are purely a beginning; *PEACE POWER* programs should partner with groups of parents to expand on these ideas and develop additional ones that can promote cultures of respect within families, as well as family contributions to cultures of respect in the larger community. For example, families can take steps to limit access to firearms in the home, participate in community initiatives to reduce such access, and seriously discuss alternatives for dealing with threat.

Family Self-Monitoring

Giving up putdowns is at least as important in homes as in schools and other organizations. A family whose members share a vision of themselves as a *PEACE POWER* family, in which people act respectfully and refuse to put each other or others down (no matter how tempting it may sometimes be), shapes the behavior of children and youth in profoundly important ways. Acting with respect does not mean approving of problem behavior, but rather dealing with even problem behavior in ways that respect the person. The first step in a family's effort to end putdowns is to discuss together why the family wants to do so, how challenging giving up putdowns and acting respectfully may be, and making a collective commitment.

Just as for individuals, a collective resolution may rapidly fade unless there is a structured way to track its implementation. Some form of self-monitoring, therefore, is usually necessary. Although families should be creative in finding individual approaches that work for them, they should all begin by determining how often putdowns occur. One way is to put a chart on the refrigerator, for a brief period, three days to one week, and each family member puts a mark on the chart any time that he or she experiences a putdown. Then the family members establish a goal that is half or less of the current rate and decide on some sort of reward that they together can enjoy (perhaps a movie or a special meal) if no more than that goal level of putdowns occurs in a consecutive block of three days to a week. (Discussion about the importance of honestly reporting times one feels put down may be important. "Cheating"—for example, colluding so everyone gets to go to the movie—would obviously be self-defeating.) This structured self-monitoring with family rewards might be done for about two weeks, just to raise awareness. After that time, continuing use of the chart, with weekly discussion of how well the family is doing, perhaps at Sunday dinner, may be useful for maintenance.

Parent/Caregiver Interviews as Homework Modules

Biglan (1995) and his team at the Oregon Research Institute discovered that families became aware of programs originating in schools much more often if young people were given class assignments that required them to interview parental figures than if the schools carried out media campaigns or sent flyers home with youth. Therefore, homework modules may be a superior way to extend awareness of *PEACE POWER* into homes and may also be useful for encouraging discussion of important issues that otherwise may not arise in the home. Modules related to "Acting with Respect" may be particularly valuable, because respectful action is closely tied to values that develop in significant part in the home.

A suggested homework module would include a *PEACE POWER* information packet containing a short summary of the local program written on organizational letterhead and signed by the administrator, a *PEACE POWER* pocket card, a *PEACE POWER* home recognition record, and the assignment. The length and complexity of the assignment could vary, in some cases involving audiotaped or even videotaped interviews, but simplicity is probably best for most youth. Therefore, a single sheet listing three or four questions for them to ask their parent figures, with space for summarizing answers, may often be about right. Completed sheets are then returned and used in small group discussions as a follow-up. Questions can be selected from the following, or be tailored for the setting:

- Is it really important not to criticize or put down other people? Why or why not?
- Why is it sometimes challenging to respect someone of a different race or culture?
- What is your opinion of young people carrying weapons?
- What kind of people is it hard to respect? Should a person still act respectfully to people like that? Why or why not?
- What can families do to increase respect between children and adults?

Either as part of the written assignment or as part of the follow-up discussion, young people should have an opportunity to respond to what they heard—do they agree or disagree with parts of what the adults that they interviewed said, and why?

Family Participation in Gap-Bridging and Multicultural Activities

As noted earlier, the divides between and among racial, ethnic, class, age, and other groups and the biases associated with those divisions can make acting with respect more difficult. Individual families as well as groups of families, (e.g., parent organizations connected with schools and youth programs) can help to increase respect not only by discussing diversity, multiculturalism, bias, oppression, and the ways that society maintains those problems, but also by taking action. At a minimum, families can attend multicultural events, demonstrating interest and curiosity in the events and the values that they reflect. Parents can plan to attend festivals and performances with their children, and they can organize more ambitious trips with their children, exposing them to new experiences. Just as important is helping children to make sense of what they see, while recognizing and accepting the limits of understanding that are always present for the outsider.

Families can also participate in and even organize multicultural events; they can build multigroup coalitions (see, e.g., Wilson, 1999), modeling interest in diversity and concern about larger social issues. In general, the goal should be not so much multicultural events to which people from different groups are invited, but rather ethnoconscious activities in which multiple groups participate from the beginning, having major voices in planning, organizing, and evaluating the program (Gutierrez, 1997). This kind of organizing is much more likely to produce events that truly reflect diversity. For example, it is common for members of the dominant society to organize festivals in which diverse ethnic foods and costumes are the theme; many people of color, however, may view such festivals as superficial efforts that ignore or submerge real community issues. The ethnoconscious planning and organizing that can prevent such insensitivity are likely to be based in schools, neighborhood organizations, political groups, churches, or other networks in the larger community. Those networks can also contribute in many other ways to constructing cultures of respect.

Tools and Activities to Shape
and Support Communities of Respect

In addition to the activities that can be carried out in individual organizations and families to build cultures of respect, there are many actions that can be taken in the larger community (usually sponsored by one or more organizations that have taken on the challenge to increase constructive, nonviolent empowerment). The following are just a few possibilities that have been used in some places; data regarding which may be most effective are limited, however. It is very likely that any activity that increases the visibility of PEACE POWER programs, provides positive models, and encourages community members to relate in noncoercive and respectful ways will contribute to positive collective outcomes.

Presentations by High-Visibility Figures

There are many areas in which sports figures, entertainers, police officers, and media figures can contribute to community programs. The
modeling research indicates that people are likely to imitate the behavior of highly respected figures, particularly persons with whom they
can identify. If, therefore, high-visibility models who are of the same
racial, cultural, or socioeconomic groups make presentations encouraging respect across groups and action to address oppression, they are
likely to be heard. Such presentations can be incorporated into community forums around race and culture, speaker series in schools, or semi-
nars for businesses. One or two businesses or community groups may
organize such presentations, but it is often useful to seek sponsorship
from multiple sectors, thus engaging a variety of groups in the project.
Of course, it is essential to market such presentations well and to design
them to be interesting to the audience. One approach is to include in-
spirational speakers and entertainment in a single event, with giveaways,
refreshments, and other features to make it as reinforcing as possible.

Movie Making

Young people find movie making very engaging, and the technology for
making quite sophisticated films has become widely available and inexpensive. Youth, either working with adults or working independently,
can now plan, film, edit, and present theme-oriented films. The process
of doing the film can be an enormously useful learning experience, and
the ultimate product can itself be a contribution. Such films can focus
narrowly on building respect between groups (e.g., perspectives on how
multiple cultures can live together in peace) or can have other themes
(e.g., the history of the neighborhood), but by drawing on the multiple
perspectives of community groups from several sectors, the films can indirectly build respect. Films may include interview segments, as well as
action sequences that clarify "how things are done around here." Given
the extent to which contemporary youth are immersed in a video culture,
they are often well-prepared to take on such a challenge. Almost any group
can sponsor film-making activities, but as with many other *PEACE POWER*
activities, the more community sectors involved, the greater the impact
on community culture. Media, businesses, and youth programs can form
partnerships for planning, preparing, and distributing the work.

Pledge Campaigns

Although there is little direct empirical evidence that pledge campaigns will increase desirable actions (e.g., attending school) and reduce undesirable ones (e.g., carrying weapons), there is certainly theoretical support for their possible utility under certain conditions. For example, Jesse Jackson's Rainbow Coalition at one time organized a "Back to School" pledge campaign, in which youth pledged, among other things, to attend school, avoid carrying weapons, and do homework (Mattaini, 1996). Parents pledged to meet with teachers, turn off the television for three hours each evening so youth could do homework in a quiet setting, and take other actions consistent with the goals of violence reduction and academic success. Although there may have been some gaps in the program, it was a major advantage that churches, schools, and families all participated in the pledge campaign. These groups provided interlocking supports, so signing a pledge was not an isolated act, but rather one step in a community effort to provide social support for the actions described in the pledge. A current pledge campaign that may be of use in PEACE POWER projects is the Student Pledge Against Gun Violence (see note 10).

Knowledge of behavioral science and experience suggest that effective pledge campaigns are likely to have the following characteristics:

- Pledges, whether oral or written, are made publicly.
- Pledge campaigns are sponsored by multiple community sectors.
- Those taking the pledge commit to positive actions that will be taken (e.g., "I will act to make peace among my peers."), although they may also commit to actions that will not be taken (e.g., "I will not carry weapons.").
- Highly respected models (again) publicly support the pledge.
- Some form of regular follow-up occurs, so the pledge is not a one-shot behavior.

Follow-ups might include media interviews in which respondents talk about the challenges that they have had in keeping the commitments made or discussion groups in which those who took the pledge a month earlier examine how well they have been able to do.

Police–Youth Dialogues

In many communities, the relationships between youth and law enforcement personnel are highly conflicted and characterized by mutual dis-

trust. In some cases, there has been substantial history of serious oppression; some residents of inner cities report that they see the police
more as an occupying force than as a resource to turn to for protection.
Commonly, youth have minimal contact with police officers except under stressful conditions, and many police officers have very little contact with anyone but family and other officers except in the course of
their work. These factors result in two separate cultures with very limited authentic exchange, empathy, or understanding. Dialogues between
the groups will not magically resolve long-standing problems grounded
in institutional racism, homophobia, and other deeply held biases. They
can, however, begin to heal divisions and, in some cases, can enhance
respect between the groups. It is crucial that the officers selected to
participate in these dialogues be genuinely interested in reaching out to
youth and not be attending just because they have been told to, but in
most localities, there are many such officers. Once some have had good
experiences, other officers may also be willing to become involved.

One initial approach that has been useful in some places is simple
"survival training" for minority youth, offered by police officers. Because minority youth are at particular risk for dangerous interactions
with the police, the purpose of these workshops is to teach young people
how to speak and act in ways that reduce their risk. Some attention to
the potential for collective advocacy by police officers, youth, and community members to address systemic inequities like racial profiling may
also be incorporated into such programs. Minority police officers are
often ideal trainers (e.g., the "100 Black Men" in the New York area),
because they may be in the best position, at least to some degree, to
understand both of the cultures involved. Such workshops include discussion as well as opportunities to role play realistic transactions like
traffic stops and confrontations on the street.

Constructing deeper exchange requires a more intensive approach.
The process is crucial in these dialogues. The "rules" should be clear in
the beginning. There must be a commitment by at least some of the
parties, and as much as possible by all, to really listen—even to things
that they find very aversive to hear. There must also be a commitment
to truth and honesty. When participants are unwilling to share the truth,
they must feel free simply to say so, and the person facilitating the dialogue needs to ensure that these feelings are respected. For example,
youth are unlikely to be willing to talk specifically about crimes that
they and their peers have been involved in, and officers are unlikely to
be willing to talk about specific racist actions that they have observed

by their peers. Each, however, can acknowledge that such things some-times happen and move to the effects on individuals and communities. Although representatives of each side should plan the specifics of pro-grams of dialogue, they may include topics like the following:

- If I think about the police/youth in this community, the first words that come to mind are . . .
- Some of the reasons youth and police find it hard to trust and respect each other might be . . .
- The best, and worst, experiences I have had with the police/youth are . . .
- The biggest differences I see between youth and police in this com-munity are . . .

As they near the end of the dialogue, participants should address some-thing like the following:

- One way that police and youth could work together to increase respect in this community is . . .

Finally, dialogues should end with expressions of appreciation for hon-esty and with a period of informal "breaking bread together"—refresh-ments and casual conversation to build personal bridges. Such conversation may follow up on what was discussed, but may also shift to sports or other topics that establish commonalities.

There are other creative approaches to establishing police–youth con-nections. There is a long history of connections around sports leagues (e.g., Police Athletic Leagues). In one Chicago suburb, an alternative that may allow more opportunity for deeper sharing is being developed: a theater improvisation program for police officers and young people. Many other possibilities are likely to emerge from creative, co-constructive planning.

Conclusion

The practice of acting with respect may at first glance appear very simple, and in some cultures, it probably is or has been. Contemporary culture, however, relies on coercive control and on competition, both personal and group, which requires someone to lose. Both of these practices tend to be inconsistent with maintaining respect for self and others, much less respect for the larger human and natural environment. Commentators constantly remark on the loss of civility in contemporary society. Coercion and competition that emphasize ensuring that others lose (as opposed to competing with oneself to do as well as possible, and encouraging others to do the same) both promote incivility. In addition, the larger that cultural networks become (e.g., huge cities, schools with thousands of students), the less face-to-face contact that individuals have with particular others over a long period of time and, therefore, the less powerful those diluted contacts.

High levels of recognition and mutual respect will benefit everyone over the long term, but are unlikely to increase merely through exhortation. No doubt there are many other creative approaches to promote those goals, if opportunities for communities to elaborate them are arranged. Everyone has a part to play in constructing communities of recognition and respect. The process of sharing power, as discussed in the next chapter, provides a strategy for engaging multiple voices and sectors in those efforts.

5

Share Power to Build Community

Mark A. Mattaini and Christine T. Lowery

"What would happen if society viewed young people as competent community builders? This question is not trivial, for the dominant view of youths in any society will affect the beliefs and behaviors of adults and of youths themselves" (Finn & Checkoway, 1998, p. 335). Viewing *both* youth and adults as competent community builders, as bearers of gifts from which they can contribute, as individuals bound by mutual obligation to contribute from those gifts, and as groups collectively responsible for the outcomes is the core of shared power in *PEACE POWER* programs. In the examples that they provide, Finn and Checkoway demonstrate the profound difference between regarding youth as valued contributors and regarding them as developmental problems to be solved, or as victims. Youth carry enormous power that can contribute to community building; it is essential that society honor this power, rather than attempt to impede it. In fact, youth potential is usually dramatically underestimated. Few would expect that youth members of a joint task force would be the ones who would continue to gather and work over time until reaching a meaningful community goal, while adult members dropped out (Ross & Coleman, 2000). Also, who would imagine that junior high school–aged children living in deep poverty in Haiti could nearly independently operate a radio station over an extended period? And yet they do (Aristide, 2000).

The concept of sharing power, as used in this volume, is a gift from Native America; its basis is in traditional Pueblo thought, but other indigenous nations have contributed as well (Lowery & Mattaini, 1999). Sharing power involves collective action to which all contribute from their gifts (powers). Each explicitly recognizes the essential importance of the others' contributions, genuinely values the voices of the others, and understands that all are individually and collectively responsible for outcomes. From this perspective, power is not limited or hydraulic; an increase in power for one does not entail a decrease for another; in natural and social systems, winners do not require losers. Power does not consist, in this framework, of what one can coerce another to do (A over B), but rather of what one can contribute to the construction of an improved reality. This is constructive rather than coercive power, and it is very foreign to many ways of operating in dominant society.

This approach is considerably different from that of many discussions of empowerment, in which, for example, the professional is exhorted to "give up" some of his or her power so the client can have more (Lowery & Mattaini, 2001). In a shared power arrangement, *both* professionals and program participants have critical contributions to make; their contributions are different, and neither is more important than the other. If clients or program participants bring all the gifts, talents, and powers that they have to the table, and professionals do so as well, aggregate power increases, and no one need lose. There is no need for competition if there is a recognition that strong power is constructive, whereas adversarial power is ultimately limited and weak—although in the short run this may not be obvious. Sharing power supports the development of empowerment cultures. Cultures of shared power are naturally grounded in recognition and respect; in fact, the multiple segments of the *PEACE POWER* wheel are, ultimately, integral to each other.

Although sharing power sounds very attractive, many people question whether it is realistic. Two sets of data indicate that the answer is yes. First, there are centuries of experience of Native American and many other indigenous cultures; the Iroquois (Haudenosaunee) League, which was a model for the U.S. Constitution, is one example. Unfortunately, the framers of the Constitution omitted certain central Iroquois practices that assured both women and men, and persons from all sectors of society, essential voices. Second, the basic practices of sharing power are highly consistent with the findings of contemporary behavioral science (Lowery & Mattaini, 1999).

Shared power does not mean "equal power"—a meaningless concept from this perspective. If power lies in contributions from one's gifts and everyone has different gifts, equality is not an issue. In most cases, participants also carry different responsibilities; for example, a high school principal has different responsibilities than does a student. Recognizing that everyone has something critical to contribute and genuinely re-specting the gifts of each, rather than blocking contributions to main-tain what feels like some control, turn out to be much more difficult than it may sound, however. A desire to protect one's image of being "in charge" and an inability to give up the only form of power one knows (coercive control) are serious obstacles to shared power. Persons who are deeply embedded in cultures of coercive and adversarial control, therefore, often find sharing power difficult to understand and imple-ment. Often, they cannot see the obstacles that they introduce. As a result, the sharing of power requires a shaping process through succes-sive approximations and a willingness to really listen to feedback. What is generally required is a small group who have a genuine commitment to sharing power, who support each other, and who are able to establish "islands" of shared power from which the practices can spread. Shared power can be contagious, but needs first to be well-established some-where in the system.

Two clusters of practices characterize shared power cultures within families, organizations, and communities. The first cluster involves en-couraging contributions from actors' and groups' unique repertoires, gifts, and powers; the second involves increasing sensitivity to long-term collective outcomes (Lowery & Mattaini, 1999). Practices and scenes of the first type include the following:

- The incidence of recognition events is relatively high, while that of coercive events is relatively low.
- Participants actively seek alternative voices.
- Cultural actors privately and publicly question the motivations for their own actions, with an eye toward reducing rates of behav-ior that produce rewards only for themselves rather than for the collective that includes them.

The second cluster of practices is likely to enhance responsiveness to aggregate outcomes; the following are a few examples:

- Participants honestly explore long-term consequences of decisions taken; in the Haudenosaunee tradition, for example, consequences out to the seventh generation are considered.
- Cultural actors specifically identify any and all negative conse-quences, to anyone, of actions taken or proposed and attempt to minimize those consequences to the extent possible.

- "Stakeholder satisfaction" is a primary determinant of the need for changes in cultural practices; for example, the levels of satisfaction of administrators, professionals, parents, and youth are all taken seriously in decision making.

Identifying shared power practices is the first step toward collective power. The second, crucial step is the construction of cultures that shape and maintain such practices—the "co-construction of empowerment cultures" in which scenes of shared power occur often, while scenes involving adversarial power occur infrequently. The tools and activities described in this chapter can contribute to that effort.

By definition, a culture of shared power emphasizes inclusion and belonging, which not only is an important goal developmentally for young people, but also is incompatible with the isolation sometimes associated with violence. In discussing ways to discourage gang involvement, Flannery and Huff (1999) indicate that it is essential to offer "activities and incentives for prosocial activities that meet the needs of young people, the same needs that are currently attracting them to gangs (belonging to a peer group and having a sense of 'family' and a sense of 'protection'— though the latter is illusory because . . . a child's risk of victimization, death, and incarceration increases substantially with gang involvement)" (p. 304). Hagedorn (1998) notes that increasing gang involvement and violence in recent decades also has economic dimensions.

Similarly, feminist scholars examining possible approaches for intervening in the increasing violence among young women indicate the importance of dealing with and reconceptualizing power, seeking communal solutions, valuing both solidarity and diversity, valuing multiple perspectives, and moving toward social change (Potter, 1999). Although not all feminist conceptualizations of power are entirely consistent with the approach outlined here, the emphasis on shared power, multiple voices, and collective solutions blends well in the PEACE POWER strategy. Feminist theory, Pueblo philosophy, and the science of behavior (very distinct paradigms) all suggest similar strategies, indicating that something quite basic is involved.

Some of the tools and activities suggested in the following discussion are also consistent with the emphasis on *cooperation training* that is included in recent iterations of aggression replacement training (Goldstein, 1999). Goldstein comments, "By using shared materials, interdependent tasks, group rewards, and similar features, these methods . . . have

110

consistently yielded numerous interpersonal, cooperation-enhancing, group, and individual benefits" (p. 267). Although Goldstein's approach tends to emphasize advantages for the individual youth and sometimes the small group, a shared power perspective expands the focus to include the larger community. Teaching both youth and adults the skills of sharing power to enhance the collective web produces positive outcomes for both individual and community. In fact, pushed to the most basic level, a shared power perspective views individual and collective good as the same thing, though one need not accept this epistemic perspective to use the tools outlined. One additional skill area from Goldstein's (1999) program has direct application for sharing power, namely, teaching youth to understand and use group process. Goldstein's group process course addresses the importance of learning to recognize and resist group pressure and other process problems, as well as skills for leading and working cooperatively in groups, which are clearly essential to collaboration and sharing power for constructive purposes.

As with recognition and respect, there are a number of tools available that may increase the skills required in sharing power and encourage their use within organizational programs, peer groups, families, and communities (Table 4).

Table 4. Tools for Increasing Shared Power

Tools for Schools and Youth-Serving Organizations
- Group work: Recognizing different kinds of power
- Councils, task forces, and working groups
- Service learning and service projects
- Participation in governance

Tools for Families
- Family goals
- Family–school–community partnerships
- Families and Schools Together (FAST)
- Family community service

Tools for Communities
- Community organization
- Councils and working groups
- Community coalition building

Organizational Tools and Activities Supporting Shared Power

Most organizations (and many families and informal networks as well) are organized in a hierarchical model; some participants are viewed as more important than others, and some gifts and powers are highly valued while others are not. Typically, such organizations rely heavily on coercive control, particularly the negative reinforcement process whereby people act in ways that allow them to escape or avoid unpleasant consequences (Daniels, 2000). Such arrangements, however, produce only as much of the desired behavior as is required to avoid negative consequences and are very fragile, requiring constant surveillance to maintain even that minimal level of action. It is also unpleasant to live and work within such organizations. The following tools and activities, in conjunction with the other core *PEACE POWER* practices, may be useful for moving away from such arrangements and toward shared power.

Group Work: Recognizing Power

Crucial to shared power is all participants' recognition of the power that they themselves carry, as well as the powers of others. In a culture of shared power, I see you in your power, and you see me in mine. Many youth (and adults), however, do not know what they can do to contribute to the collective good—do not know their own power. Young people may not yet have discovered all of their gifts and talents, nor have used those gifts and talents to create their unique power; collective arrangements can help them to achieve those crucial developmental cusps. Those who do not see their own power often perceive the powers that others carry as a threat—something to resist and block. Exercises to help participants recognize their own power, as well as that of others, can be an important first step in creating a culture of shared power.

Group work is an excellent strategy for this process, because peers often can see talents and gifts more clearly than individuals themselves. There are many group approaches for this work. One approach, when people know each other relatively well, is to ask dyads to identify each other's gifts and talents, and then to share those with the group. Another is "strengths bombardment" in which one person sits in the center of the circle, and others honestly discuss that person's strengths, talents, and gifts. Yet another approach is a variation of the talking circle, which can lead to particularly thoughtful responses.

A talking circle for identifying power should begin with an introduction to what is meant by "power." The following points are valuable for establishing a context for work:

- Real "power" is what one does to contribute to the group.
- My power is what I do. Power is acting. It is not an attribute like being good-looking or smart.
- Many people do not recognize that they have power, but everyone does.
- Everyone's power is unique in some way.
- My power is a gift, not something I can take credit for (may require discussion of natural talents and opportunities life has offered).
- People do not always use their power, sometimes because they do not think it will be appreciated, sometimes because they do not know they have it.

These points may be posted on the wall as reminders throughout the process of learning to share power, because it is easy for discussion to lose focus and move toward identifying attributes or toward adversarial power and competition. The points can be presented and briefly discussed, but extended discussion should wait until after the talking circle is completed. As noted in previous chapters, only the person holding the discussion card (or other item selected by the leader or group) can speak during the actual talking circle, and others cannot respond until their own turns come or until a general discussion after the circle has been completed one or more times. Neither interruptions nor immediate responses are allowed, because they interfere with really hearing what others are saying.

The first discussion point to be passed around the talking circle should be something like the following: "One power that _____ (the person to my right) carries is . . . ." In many cases, it is best to have those in the circle first write down what they will say (no more than a minute is required). Each participant, in turn, then reads what he or she wrote and explains it very briefly. A second round in which each person discusses the power of a different person follows. Finally, in a third round, the assignment is to discuss one's own power. This discussion should begin with a reminder that one's power is a gift and, therefore, not something that should cause conceit. The discussion point can be phrased something like the following: "One power I can contribute to the group is . . . ." As usual, each person should be given an opportunity to speak in turn. If some individuals either pass or indicate that they do not know of any power that they carry, the leader should lead a discussion with the group as a whole, after the circle is completed, to assist those individuals unable to recognize their own power.

Councils, Task Forces, and Working Groups

Sharing power is a skill, and like any other skill, people need practice to refine it. Organizations that wish to increase the level of shared power present and to assist young people in learning to recognize and refine the constructive power that they carry, therefore, need to provide multiple opportunities for collaborative, constructive action. Councils, task forces, and working groups offer many possibilities for this work. (Notice that these labels suggest action, which the term *committee* often does not.) The ideal forum for shared power is a group situation that includes both youth and adults, all working toward a common goal. For example, a school may establish a working group to improve "school climate." A group for this purpose should probably include youth and representatives of staff groups (e.g., teachers, administrators, support staff). To demonstrate organizational commitment and willingness to value the work done, the school may give the working group a modest amount of financial resources for the task. The group then defines its focus, develops a plan, and implements that plan.

In a housing project, a possibility for practice in shared power is a violence prevention task force with representatives of youth, families, the housing authority, police, youth programs, the elderly, and religious groups with significant representation in the project. It may be particularly valuable to have a critical mass of youth involved in such an arrangement, because one or two youth representatives alone may find large numbers of adults intimidating. Organizations may also establish a task force or working group around an issue that concerns many youth, say, environmental protection and action, perhaps in partnership with an environmental group that may provide ongoing education and consultation in return for the energy that youth can bring to the effort.

Task groups like those mentioned provide opportunities to practice recognizing and respecting multiple contributions, but in many cases should also involve explicit training in collaborative work. There are excellent resources available that can guide this training (e.g., Tropman,

1996). Research indicates that training in just three relatively simple skills can considerably enhance the effectiveness of working groups. Briscoe, Hoffman, and Bailey (1975) found that training members to carry out the following three steps led to improved group process and decision making:

1. Identifying and isolating the problem to be addressed:
   • "The problem is . . ."
   • "I think the issue is . . ."
   • "The main problem is . . ."
2. Stating and evaluating alternative solutions:
   • "I think one solution is . . ."
   • "One way to solve it is . . ."
   • "Could you solve that by . . ."
3. Selecting a solution and making an implementation plan:
   • "What action are we going to take?"
   • "Who will do it?"
   • "When will it be done?"

Briscoe and his colleagues found that actually having people practice these skills in role-played situations increased their use of the skills in real meetings. It may also be useful to post these steps on the wall and to remind working group members about them at the beginning of meetings on occasion to support maintenance over time.

Service Learning and Service Projects

Sharing power is a noncoercive strategy by which young people and those who are collectively entwined with them can influence their world. The emerging emphasis on service learning (e.g., Waterman, 1997) can support this effort. *Service learning* refers to programs in which youth participate in community service activities as part of a program, usually for school credit, that includes both service and discussions of the experience to clarify learning; it is, therefore, usually structured as a formal class. A number of positive outcomes seem to arise from the structured involvement of youth in community service activities, including increased self-confidence, increases in moral reasoning, improved academic performance, and decreases in disciplinary problems (Waterman). Interestingly, the advantages for "youth at risk" may be particularly strong (Blyth, Saito, & Berkas, 1997). In their article on viewing youth as competent community builders, Finn and Checkoway (1998) describe a number of projects involving community service in which youth take on significant organizational roles. Youth can also participate in larger efforts like Habitat for Humanity. All of these opportunities for community service support movement toward shared power.

Participation in Governance

Another avenue for shared power in organizations is the involvement of all stakeholders in governance. This prospect is often much more threatening than many of the others, because the idea of sharing power in governance implies to many people that someone must "give up" power. For persons whose understanding of power is limited to adversarial and competitive power, the value of sharing power in making decisions about organizational priorities, directions, and allocation of resources is often not at all obvious. In organizations where the sharing of power does occur, the additional perspectives that emerge can clearly be useful.

Although educational and service organizations exist to serve participants, members, or consumers, traditional organizations may offer very little room for the voices of those stakeholders to emerge. Democratic values under these circumstances are not very deeply rooted, in part because it is in the nature of professions to attempt to control the services that they provide. Thus, token participation by parent or community members on boards and councils is common, but organizational processes are often structured to minimize real influence by limiting the number of such members, selecting members who tend to have views very much like those of the professional staff, or limiting the amount of information available to community members. Youth are often excluded altogether.

New participatory possibilities that go far beyond token involvement emerge within shared power processes. Participants respect and solicit different voices, without hearing other opinions as threatening. An administrator with budget authority, for example, would not need to give up that responsibility and put all decisions to a vote—that would not be consistent with her obligations. In a shared power culture, she would have a real interest in the ideas of multiple stakeholders, because she would recognize that they may be able to provide her with information needed for better decisions or to help the organization identify additional sources of resources. The administrator would make different decisions, not because doing so avoids conflict but because the additional information leads to different conclusions. If outcomes are monitored with feedback shared among all participants (see chapter 7), such processes can be self-correcting.

So long as the contributions of all are recognized and honored, working from common goals in partnership is far less likely to lead to conflict than is an arrangement in which the interests of multiple groups are in competition. Because this is a dramatically different approach from the ordinary in this society, it may be necessary to introduce it gradually. In organizations that have been traditionally structured, the introduction of shared power in a small number of areas, followed by its gradual expansion as people learn the skills and become comfortable with the process, may be the best approach. A group of people whose experience of organizations is as adversarial systems will not, without models and experiences, be good at sharing power. As Daniels (2000) indicates in discussing empowerment, "As in all performance change initiatives, the strategy that must be used for maximum effectiveness is shaping"(p. 141). Sharing power requires shaping through successive approximations, skills training, and a commitment to go beyond ego and be guided by the data in making decisions.

Family Tools and Activities Supporting Shared Power

Shared power in the family? Of course. Does this mean that everyone has "equal power" in the family? Of course not. As emphasized in the initial definition of shared power—everyone can act to contribute to the family, everyone shares responsibility for family life, and everyone's voice is important. This does not mean that children are "in charge" or that a family is a democracy. It means that *for a family whose life together is characterized by recognition, respect, and an emphasis on contribution from the power of each, such questions are far less central than they are for families that rely on coercion.* Patterson (1976), in his early and important research on families, found that aggressive and hostile children lived in families in which the rate of coercion, punishment, and threat was much higher than in families of nonproblem children. Similarly, Alexander (1973) found that family processes among the families of delinquents were predictably different from those among nondistressed families. In the latter, there was a more equal distribution of talk time among family members, as well as higher levels of supportive talk. In the families of delinquent youth, verbal participation was less evenly distributed and significantly more defensive. One of the key procedures in Alexander's functional family therapy, therefore, is to help families of delinquents act more like nondistressed families (Barton & Alexander, 1991).

Families in which there is a struggle for control typically find themselves in an escalating pattern of coercion (Patterson, 1976). In nondistressed families, parents can set limits without a major struggle, because there is a pattern of recognition, respect, and participation. Shared power in the family does not mean that the members give up the authority that they need to meet their responsibilities; rather it means that much more effort goes into recognition and contribution. The key question for each individual is, "What can I do (contribute) to make this family a rewarding place to be?" When a problem arises, family members work together to construct a solution, and everyone takes responsibility for this solution. Parents have the responsibility to make some ultimate decisions and take that seriously, but the question of who is in control is not the axis around which the family revolves. In families in which there is significant sharing of power, people talk about each other's strengths and think in terms of contributions. The following are a few ways to encourage such exchange.

Family Goals

Some families find it useful to talk about a small number of family goals, things that everyone cares about, and then to plan and work together to achieve them. Very simple places to begin include planning a vacation together or even an enjoyable evening together, perhaps once a month. Planning community service activities together is another possibility. Such discussions can be structured according to a very few simple "rules":

- Everyone can give his or her opinions.
- Everyone will listen to each other.
- Everyone makes statements like "I could ____," identifying what he or she could do to make the plan work—making calls, collecting information, riding quietly in the car . . . something!

An exercise like this reinforces a concern with positive outcomes for everyone, emphasizes the contributions that everyone can make, and provides additional practice in respectful communication. (Note that the first two items in the list involve practice in listening and expressive skills, as discussed in the previous chapter.)

Similar procedures, of course, can be used when the family faces a problem. Family members who are developmentally old enough to understand the issue can discuss the problem (e.g., a reduction in income, one child in trouble with the law), communicate their feelings and thoughts about the issue, then identify possible ways that each could contribute to a solution. This kind of communication may require a certain amount of skills training, modeling, and practice; such training could be incorporated into communication skills training programs for families sponsored by youth-serving organizations.

Family–School–Community Partnerships

In recent years, it has become clear that programs to strengthen partnerships between families and schools, and between families and other community networks, produce positive outcomes in many domains. Although such programs have often been conceptualized in remedial terms, it may be even more useful to think of them in terms of shared power—bringing the resources of family, school, and community together to reach a common goal: the development of healthy, successful children who can, in turn, contribute to the community. Behavioral science has learned a great deal about what is necessary to reach this goal, and widespread partnerships across many community sectors are clearly necessary (Biglan, Metzler, & Ary, 1994).

While parenting education is often useful, recent research indicates that outcomes are even better when the focus of programs is expanded from simply improving parenting skills to "broader goals of strengthening parents' social support and increasing their school and community involvement" (Webster-Stratton, 1997, p. 156). According to a study by Comer and Fraser (1998), effective family support programs treat clients as colleagues or partners in the work rather than as patients who need to be repaired. The process that they describe is one approximating shared power; parents, community professionals, and educators work together toward a common goal, with each bringing their own unique strengths and resources to the process. There is, again, no "giving up" of power involved; teachers do not give up acting based on their professional skills, for example, but rather honor the unique contributions that parents bring.

Families and Schools Together

Bringing at-risk children and their families together into partnerships with schools to improve child outcomes, the Families and Schools Together (FAST) program has been widely applied with elementary and middle school students, with outstanding outcome data across many replications in different settings (McDonald & Frey, 1999). As currently implemented, it typically targets younger ages than does the *PEACE POWER* strategy, but several of the principles that underlie FAST are almost certain to be valuable in family–school partnerships that include teens as well (note that there is less emphasis on enhancing the power of children in FAST, given the different developmental capacities of younger children):

- "The FAST process utilizes the existing strengths of families, schools, and communities in creative partnerships." (McDonald & Frey, p. 2)
- "The team structure ensures that parents are included as partners." (p. 2)
- "Half of the activity-based program takes place at a family table, which means the parents 'deliver services' to their own children." (p. 6)
- "FAST activities are structured to increase the power of each parent systematically." (p. 4)
- FAST program activities are designed to apply behavioral research to "building community" (pp. 8–9), which is the primary intermediate goal tracked in the program.
- After the family completes initial training through a series of multifamily groups, they graduate into a program called FASTWORKS in which parents determine agendas, receive a small budget, and get support from the school. This progression from empowerment training toward participation in independent collective decision making and activity is an outstanding model for many programs. In FASTWORKS, as described by the developers, "an association of parents begins to express its own unique agenda with the school and community, with a positive unified voice and informal social support" (p. 9)—an outstanding example of movement toward shared power.

Leaders of *PEACE POWER* programs can adapt any of the FAST principles and procedures, and groups sponsoring *PEACE POWER* programs may also wish to sponsor a FAST program for families of younger children. More information can be obtained from the FAST Research Project at the Wisconsin Center for Education Research at the University of Wisconsin–Madison (see note 11).

Family Community Service

One approach to building a community through shared power that has not been adequately explored is community service in which all, or at least several, family members work together. Many religious groups and nonprofit organizations offer a wide range of volunteer activities, in which people most often participate individually. Families could take part in many of these activities, however. For example, family members could volunteer at a homeless shelter one day every month or two, participate in wildlife counts, or tutor children who need help in reading. Such action can establish a family tradition of using one's gifts in community service and provide many opportunities for recognition. In an era in which volunteerism is declining in many areas, such community action can bring families together in ways that simple recreation cannot. It is certainly possible to construct new family traditions; for example, on the first weekend in August every year or on the Martin Luther King, Jr., holiday, a family may plan to do some kind of community service. *PEACE POWER* organizations may also consider sponsoring parent–child or family service projects.

Community Tools and Activities Supporting Shared Power

Youth can be central players in a wide range of community activities that offer them opportunities to use their power in constructive ways. The rewards for such involvement compete directly with the rewards for antisocial behavior and, given the potentially high levels of recognition, are often of much higher quality. Although practically all young people will sometimes test limits and participate in activities that are inconsistent with community norms, those who are quite invested as participants in the community typically exhibit much less of this behavior.

Community Organization

Young people, over and over again, have demonstrated that they can make substantive and meaningful contributions through community organizations. Finn and Checkoway (1998) completed a study of nearly 200 projects across the nation in which young people participated substantially in planning and implementing community level activities. They report on a small number of exemplary programs, each of which demonstrates the enormous potential of offering youth opportunities to use their power in constructive ways. Among the programs they describe are The City, Inc., in Minneapolis, Minnesota, a complex organization that began as a drop-in center and now operates a variety of service activities, ranging from an alternative school and legal advocacy to a center for action research. The project relies heavily on traditional Ojibway practices regarding healing, growth, and advocacy, while youth and adults share power at all levels, including the board of directors. Another program studied by Finn and Checkoway is Youth as Resources in Indianapolis, Indiana, which provides modest grants for youth-developed community initiatives. Again, youth make up a substantial portion of the board, structuring a reciprocal learning process between adults and youth.

Youth are one of the two groups in U.S. society that have substantial time and energy available, but are commonly overlooked in community planning. (The other is the elderly.) Given opportunity, these resources can be channeled into valuable contributions. Ross and Coleman (2000) report on a project in Worchester, Massachusetts, in which the Oak Hill Community Development Corporation sponsored a Youth Working Group as part of a larger community-building agenda. The working group initially consisted of service providers, parents, and youth. As the project developed, however, the participation of adult members faded because of their other commitments, while youth members continued to attend regularly. In fact, over a two-year period, the young people implemented a comprehensive community organization project grounded in the Urban Community Action Planning model (Ross & Coleman), which moved from gathering and organizing information to establishing priorities, mobilizing resources, and implementing action plans.

In this project, a diverse group of mostly 11- to 16-year-olds took major responsibility for an effort that ultimately resulted in the reconstruction of a dilapidated and dangerous park. Based on extensive community input, their activity was part of a process that engaged short-, medium-, and long-range goals. The case study demonstrates, once again, not only that youth have the potential and resources to complete such a project successfully, but also that it can have a significant impact on the youth themselves and the community, who came to see the capacities of youth in new ways.

Colby (1997) reports on another way to involve youth in community organization activities. As part of the Fort Worth, Texas, Neighborhood Mentors Project, young people aged 13 to 18 were hired as interviewers for a community needs assessment (in addition to their participation at other levels in a neighborhood mobilization effort). This project specifically recognized that "a critical error often occurs when local leaders and community groups neglect the ideas and energy of youth. . . . Their strengths for the most part are not recognized while the weight of adult-based stereotypes encourages their exclusion in program planning, development, and implementation. Yet youth, too, are members of a community" (Colby, 1997, p. 7). An audit demonstrated a high level of accuracy in the surveys completed. Other results should not, given everything discussed so far, be surprising:

> In general, neighbors accepted the youth as interviewers; very few youth reported being denied interviews and there were no reported complaints to the project's office regarding the youths' behavior. Through informal neighborhood communication channels, word spread about the project and the youths' involvement; neighbors seemed to be looking for the interviewers, wanting to participate in the project. . . .Youth too responded in a very positive fashion to the experience. Overall, their grades and school attendance improved during their participation; their contacts with the police declined dramatically, and, most important, the youth began to feel a sense of membership in their neighborhoods. (Colby, 1997, p. 9)

The messages here are clear. Youth have the capacity to contribute effectively in community-building efforts, and doing so links them to the larger community, increases their opportunities for recognition for prosocial behavior, and decreases their antisocial behavior. All of this is consistent with the predictions of the science of behavior, with data from many other projects, and with the understanding of collective connection that emerges from a Native American perspective on shared power.

Councils and Working Groups

Both youth and adults may participate in the development of councils or working groups around issues of importance to the community. For example, intergroup relations, particularly among racial groups, are a serious problem in nearly all communities, in part because of "racial ideology" among individuals and groups, in part because of structural factors that maintain racial divisions (Wilson, 1999). There are many ways that communities can address such issues, ranging from structuring increased personal contact to the development of broad-ranging multiracial coalitions. "Communities" as aggregates do not behave, but individuals in the community can act collectively if structures are established to plan and organize such action.

Similarly, community working groups on the environment, violence prevention, neighborhood beautification, and many other issues and goals are possible (as the community organizing and community psychology literatures detail). Such activities provide many opportunities for youth and adults to work together to have an impact on the community, which can benefit both the community and the individuals involved. Broadly based neighborhood organizations with multiple goals produce a wide range of positive outcomes, subjective and objective.

Existing organizations—including private businesses—can include youth representatives in their decision-making processes (e.g., as full members of boards of directors) and can also sponsor youth advisory boards. Such a group can benefit everyone, since youth can provide insights about emerging interests in the local community, which can be valuable for marketing; can advise on pending organizational decisions; and can learn about the formal operations of organizations while they experience being heard by adult society. Having a voice in such operations is a validating experience; it is essential, however, that youth advisory groups have a real and clear role. Although advisory groups by definition give advice, they should be viewed as decision-making groups; they are making collective decisions about the specific advice to send forward (Tropman, 1996). Advisory groups should not be viewed as merely places for open-ended discussion, some of which may in some vague way, at some indeterminate point, affect organizational operations. Lack of a clear process that allows them to offer specific advice is typically very frustrating to group members, who feel (with justification) that their input is not taken seriously. (A portion of advisory group meetings can, however, be dedicated to less structured discussion that may later lead to specific advice.)

Community Coalition Building

There are many ways that sharing power in community coalitions can have an impact on violence prevention and many ways that youth can have active voices in such operations. One very promising coalition strategy is the Boston Plan, a collaboration between local police, clergy, and social service organizations. In this project, young people who are at high risk for perpetrating serious crime (usually those who have already had significant legal problems) receive intensive attention from police, clergy, and service providers—all at the same time. Representatives of multiple sectors (e.g., a minister and a police officer) may together visit the young person in his or her home, making clear not only that help is available, but also that the community has a substantial interest in ensuring that the young person stays within the law. An important consideration, recognized by other communities looking at replicating and extending this approach, is that young people themselves, including some who have a history of legal involvement but who are now in productive roles in the community, may have something valuable to contribute to such efforts as well.

Finally, youth and their families can participate in the construction of broad, multiracial, progressive political coalitions that can address issues of social and economic justice. Wilson (1999) has argued that despite the enormous challenges that personal and structural racism place in the way of such efforts, the underlying common interests of those left behind as the economy moves forward may make such coalitions possible. Given their successes in many other areas, young people potentially could play a major role in these coalitions. Young people at many points in history have been able to entertain and construct new visions that elude their elders.

Conclusion

Shared power, in the long run, can have stronger effects than does adversarial, coercive power, but the construction of a shared power culture is seldom an easy process. Nonviolent resistance like that practiced by Gandhi and Martin Luther King, Jr., can profoundly change sociocultural networks, but there are costs. The same is true of shared power dynamics in organizations and communities; simply suggesting shared power does not make it happen. Real and persistent effort is required. Those involved need to provide each other with mutual support, but also with honest feedback, because people raised in coercive systems often cannot see their own participation in coercive processes.

There are important cost–benefit considerations associated with shared power. The use of adversarial power involves enormous costs, because it is necessary to maintain constant surveillance and readiness to threaten and punish (Lowery & Mattaini, 2001). The benefits for individuals can be quick and real (which is why coercion persists), but are always at risk. There also are significant long-term costs, including costs to the community; consider, for example the many costs associated with incarcerating large numbers of young African American men—cost to families, neighborhoods, and the economy, among others. Shared power, on the other hand, relying as it does on recognition and respect, may take longer to produce its effects, but those effects tend to be long-lasting and to produce benefits for both individual and community. Scientifically, the choice is between (1) a culture of positive reinforcement for actions that support collective well-being and (2) a culture of negative reinforcement and punishment that protects narrow individual interests, but ultimately proves damaging even for the individuals who initially appeared to benefit.

6

Make Peace

Many "conflict resolution" and peer mediation programs have been developed and implemented around the United States (e.g., Aber, Brown, Chaudry, Jones, & Samples, 1996; Bosworth, Espelage, DuBay, Dahlberg, & Daytner, 1996; Kaplan, 1997). Those that have been evaluated have often demonstrated some utility, but usually at a modest level. This is understandable, as many coercive and violent episodes do not emerge primarily from narrowly defined conflicts (or from lack of anger management skills, another useful focus that is not a panacea). Still, there are many conflicts in contemporary society, in part because of low levels of recognition and power sharing, and high levels of threat and disrespect. Approaches to making peace when conflict does emerge are, therefore, useful components of a comprehensive strategy to prevent violence among youth, even though not a complete answer in themselves.

There is a serious concern that extensive attention to conflict may be iatrogenic. Embry and Flannery (1999) suggest that for young people who are not very involved in antisocial behavior, conflict resolution programs may be of some help. For youth whose problem behavior is more extensive, however, the attention that they receive during conflicts and efforts to resolve those conflicts may be an issue, because those young people may not receive social attention for much else. This is an additional reason that conflict resolution programs should be implemented as components of an overall strategy that emphasizes the other core *PEACE POWER* practices, such as ensuring that every young person receives significant recognition.

Within a *PEACE POWER* perspective, the primary goal in making peace is not simply finding a solution to the immediate problem, but rather healing the relationships damaged by the behavior of one or more of those involved. Indigenous cultures from many places in the world, including the Maori of New Zealand and many native cultures in the Western Hemisphere, have elaborated this view best. The Diné (Navajo), for example, have instituted a Peacemaker Court based on traditional practices rather than on adversarial European justice models. Ross (1996) describes a Canadian First Nations' perspective on punishment and incarceration as seen by community leaders assembled to deal with serious interpersonal crimes:

> [P]romoting incarceration was based on, and motivated by, a mixture of feelings of anger, revenge, guilt, and shame on our part, and around our personal victimization issues, rather than in the healthy resolution of the victimization we were trying to address. Incarceration . . . actually works against the healing process, because "an already unbalanced person is moved further out of balance." . . . [T]he threat of incarceration prevents people from coming forward and taking responsibility for the hurt they are causing. It reinforces the silence, and therefore promotes rather than breaks, the cycle of violence that exists. (p. 38)

From this cultural perspective, what is needed is some mix of teaching and healing, not punishment, with the ultimate goal being broader healing of the web of relationships damaged by crime or conflict. In fact, the more serious the conflict or offense, the more important healing rather than punitive approaches may be. Ross reports that among the Ojibway Nation in Canada, some crimes are viewed as "too serious for jail" (p. 37). Within this worldview, so profoundly different from that of European societies, healing both relationships and the community are the critical objectives for making peace and achieving justice at all levels.

The Haudenosaunee, under the guidance of an individual known as the Peacemaker, constituted the Iroquois League (sometimes called "the first United Nations") centuries ago after reaching a cultural crisis in which individuals and communities had come to live in fear of threat and attack. The Great Law of Peace was based on the belief that "human beings whose minds are healthy always desire peace, and humans have minds which enable them to achieve peaceful resolutions of their conflicts" (*Akwesasne Notes*, 1978, p. 10). Further, "peace was to be defined not as the simple absence of war and strife, but as the active striving of humans for the purpose of establishing universal justice. Peace was defined as the product of a society which strives to establish concepts which correlate to the English words Power, Reason and Righteousness" (*Akwesasne Notes*, pp. 10–11). In a modest way, this is also the spirit of a well-implemented *PEACE POWER* strategy.

In recent years, a multipronged movement toward *restorative justice* (McCold, 1997) has spread into the justice system, schools, treatment of sexual abusers, and a wide range of other community-healing efforts (O'Connell, Wachtel, & Wachtel, 1999; Ross, 1996). The core concept of restorative justice is healing. Restorative justice is not grounded in an artificial dichotomy, or even continuum, between punishment and permissiveness; it begins from a different point and operates within a different set of dimensions. Tools and activities that support restorative justice take into account the fact that many conflicts affect not only the relationship between individuals who are immediately in conflict, but also other individuals and social networks connected to those individuals. Conflict and hurt tend to propagate and reverberate through social networks, in some cases escalating in the process. For example, if two members of a youth peer group are in conflict, others may feel pressured to choose between them or may find their enjoyment of group activities spoiled. Similarly, if one spouse or partner is arrested for assaulting the other, not only are both partners and their relationship affected, but it is likely that their friends and family, people in both their work sites, children in the neighborhood who observe the arrest, the police officers involved in the arrest, the spouses or partners of those officers, and often many others will be affected as well. Because everyone is connected, the entire web of relationships in the community has been damaged in multiple obvious and subtle ways. In some cases, many relational fibers of this web may need attention in the process of healing. In other cases, early intervention can prevent wide propagation of the conflict.

The basic processes involved in making peace are relatively straightforward, and generally scale up and down among large and small social systems well. In the material that follows, the basic strategies of (a) structured problem-solving communication, (b) conferencing and circles, and (c) mediation are discussed for use in organizations, families, and the larger community (Table 5).

School and Organizational Tools and Activities for Making Peace

Youth-serving organizations are in an ideal position to help young people, as well as the adults they associate with, learn new peacemaking skills

Table 5. Tools for Making Peace

Tools for Schools and Youth-Serving Organizations
- The making peace tool
- Conferencing
- Mediation
- Recognition for peacemaking

Tools for Families
- The family conference
- The making peace tool in the home
- Family mediation

Tools for Communities
- Conferencing
- Circles
- Healing circles
- Community mediation programs
- Public recognition of those contributing to community healing.

and practice them in real-life situations. This is a win–win process: youth learn skills that they can use not only in organizational activities but also elsewhere, and schools or other youth-serving organizations become more peaceful, less threatening systems in the process.

The Making Peace Tool

When there is a conflict of interests or values between people, it is commonly necessary to make peace. That conflict is a problem, and nearly all conflict resolution approaches rely on some kind of "problem-solving" model to resolve the situation. Although there is some variation among theorists (e.g., Goldfried & Davison, 1994; Reid, 1985), they generally agree that the basic steps are something like the following:

1. Establish a problem-solving set.
2. Define the problem.
3. Generate alternatives.
4. Decide among alternatives.
5. Implement the decision.
6. Evaluate the outcome.

This process is generally viewed as an iterative one through which those involved in the conflict may need to cycle more than once before achieving a solution. Professionals who work with family and other interpersonal conflicts have long recommended a similar process that also incorporates listening and expressive ("I" statement) skills (e.g., Gordon, 1970; Mattaini, 1999).

The most common problem with the interpersonal problem-solving process is that people do not actually use it when circumstances call for it—even if they have learned to apply the skills in training. In their research, Serna, Schumaker, Sherman, and Sheldon (1991) found that family members who had received extensive training in problem-solving communication and related skills did not use those skills spontaneously despite intensive training, home visits, practice in the home, and other procedures that are very common and usually regarded as adequate. Jointly completing a written card that guided the family though a problem-solving process step by step did work, however. Based on this and other research indicating the problems with generalization from training to real life (Stokes & Baer, 1977), our working group developed the *PEACE POWER* making peace tool to structure interpersonal conflict resolution and healing (Figure 11).

Designed to be used in any interpersonal setting, including youth-serving organizations, schools, and families, the making peace tool draws on very simple problem-solving models (e.g., Briscoe, Hoffman, & Bailey, 1975; Gordon, 1970; Reid, 1985). Until the process becomes second nature to participants, the tool should be used regularly. The more practice, the better (so long as there is also a high level of recognition for other behavior so that conflict does not become the main opportunity for positive interaction with adults). The tool can be incorporated into youth-to-youth, youth-to-adult, and adult-to-adult conflicts.

It is probably essential that the tool actually be completed in writing during the process. The "quality" of what is written may not be nearly as crucial as the process of writing, which ensures an orderly process and offers many prompts for positive behavior (see Stuart & Lott, 1972, for research suggesting a similar conclusion about contracting with youth).

Consistent with general problem-solving models, the first step on the tool is to define the issue clearly, to "name" it—which involves making "I" statements and accepting that different participants may see the issue somewhat differently. What is written is a brief indication of what

Figure 11

Make Peace

Step 1: Name the Issue
(For example, "I am concerned about . . .")

Step 2: Listen Respectfully to Everyone's Experience
(For example, "How did this event affect you . . .?")

Step 3: List Choices for Repairing the Harm Done
(For example, "One choice would be . . .")

Step 4: Make an Agreement
(For example, "So, you would be willing to commit to . . .")

Step 5: Recognize Contributions to Healing
(For example, "Thank you for listening and . . .")

http://www.bfsr.org/PEACEPOWER.html   © 1999 Walden Fellowship, Inc.

The Making Peace tool. Source: Reprinted with permission from *PEACE POWER* Working Group, 1999.

those involved see as the issue, with some attempt to state it broadly enough for some agreement. The second step involves practice in respectful listening (see chapter 4), with the person recording the peacemaking session asking for and repeating each person's perspective on the issue (e.g., "What's your take on this?") and summarizing the response verbally and in writing. The third step involves specific elaboration of choices, which should be listed, with some discussion of each that moves toward an agreement (Step 4). The agreement is written, and those participating in the session are asked to recognize or thank each other for whatever steps they took to resolve the issue and heal relationships. The last step, recognition for contributions to healing, moves at least modestly beyond simply reaching a narrow agreement and toward addressing the damage resulting from the conflict.

The making peace tool is available at cost in pads of 50 sheets and can be freely copied from this book (see note 12). The same tool can be used with families. In fact, there are major advantages to using the same tool in the multiple spheres in which youth live their lives, since this increases opportunities to practice the procedures and generalize positive actions between settings.

Conferencing

One very important segment of the restorative justice movement has been the development, particularly over the past decade, of the processes of *conferencing* and *circles*. In conferencing, all participants in a conflict come together in a structured manner that builds empathy, rebuilds connections, develops plans to repair damage, and restores balance for individuals and the collective. It is critical that not only the parties to a dispute, but also representatives of the larger social networks in which they are embedded, participate in the conference. For example, a conference related to a serious conflict between two or more youth in school includes the youth involved, their parents or other family representatives, and representatives of the school. Conferences to address criminal acts include the perpetrator and his or her supporters, the victim and his or her supporters, and representatives of the community (often police or probation officers).

There are many related approaches to conferencing and the use of community or healing circles (see Ross, 1996, for some examples). The specific process presented here emerged from *family group conferencing*, a very straightforward and powerful approach that originated in New

Zealand as an adaptation of traditional Maori practices, then spread to Australia, Canada, the United States, and elsewhere. There are parallels in traditional Navajo practice and elsewhere as well. Outstanding outcome data support this approach. In New Zealand, for example, when conferencing was applied to nearly all youth offenders between the ages of 14 and 16, the results were stunning. The number of young people admitted to youth custody facilities dropped by about two-thirds, and half of those facilities were subsequently closed (Ross, 1996). There was also a substantial reduction in the number of youth prosecuted for later offenses.

In addition to extensive and growing use of conferencing in the justice system, schools, neighborhoods, youth-serving organizations, and community dispute resolution centers are also increasingly turning to the process and report strong success (see note 13). Real Justice is an organization based in Pennsylvania that has been involved for several years in developing tools to facilitate effective conferencing. They have developed a highly structured script (available on the Real Justice website) that the facilitator (e.g., probation officer, police officer, school official, social worker) of a conference can follow to structure the process effectively. The key components of the family group conferencing process are listed in Table 6.

From their now extensive experience, the Real Justice developers strongly encourage facilitators to carefully follow the script, because it has been designed and tested to prevent common problems that are likely to emerge in a less structured process, including focus on the assignment of blame, avoidance of discussions of affect, or uneven participation. Real Justice also offers books, videos, and training sessions

Table 6. Components of the Family Group Conferencing Process

- Welcoming and introduction to the process
- The offender(s) describe the incident and its effects
- The victim(s) describe the effects of the incident
- The victim(s)' supporters describe how they see and were affected
- The offender(s)' supporters describe how they have been affected
- The offender(s) are given an opportunity to respond to what's been said
- All present work toward a restorative agreement
- The conference is formally closed, followed by refreshments and informal contact

for persons interested in establishing conferencing programs. As a next step for problems and conflicts that cannot be handled through simple application of the *PEACE POWER* making peace tool, conferencing can be an enormously useful tool, one that, because of its structure, can be implemented even by persons without extensive professional training in conflict resolution.

Mediation

An increasingly popular approach for "making peace" in organizations and communities (Kruk, 1997), mediation is a structured approach to problem resolution; it uses a process that is different from those generally used by professionals like attorneys and social workers. As a result, mediation requires specialized training and, in many cases, certification. Most mediators are volunteers, which, of course, reduces the costs involved. Mediation has proven useful in many settings; it often is more effective and less expensive than court procedures for conflicts ranging from divorce settlements to neighborhood disputes, for example. At the same time, standard mediation procedures are grounded in European American values like "open communication" and the central importance of individual interests over the collective, potentially resulting in culture-bound arrangements that in some cases may also "privatiz[e] social conflict" (Kruk, p. 9). Although culturally specific approaches and transformative rather than settlement-driven approaches can expand the applicability of mediation, it is clearly not the answer to all conflict. Still, it has a valuable place as one tool for conflict resolution.

Mediation programs, in particular peer mediation programs, have become common in schools over the past two decades. Although the evidence for their effectiveness in reducing violence is limited, a number of studies support the utility of the approach (reviewed in Kaplan, 1997), and mediation programs can be one useful component of an overall strategy for making peace and supporting respect. Effective peer mediation programs require initial and ongoing support from school administrators and teachers, essentially ensuring that respectful conflict resolution becomes part of the school culture. Unfortunately, at least some evidence indicates that white students are more satisfied with the process than are students of color (Kaplan), which again probably indicates the need for cultural consultation in the development of mediation programs. Mediation is probably most effective with those who are involved in relatively few conflicts. Still, mediation is a next step that can be used when the conflict calls for more than the making peace tool and when organizational staff have training or a strong interest in developing a mediation program. At the same time, unless the other core *PEACE POWER* practices become part of that culture as well, mediation will have at best a modest effect and may work best with lower risk youth.

Recognition for Peacemaking

Whatever specific programs and structures may be in place to structure peacemaking, positive practices will continue only if their use is recognized on a regular basis. For example, if institutional staff have opportunities to discuss their successes in using the making peace tool, if youth who attempt to prevent and heal breaches among their peers are recognized, if staff members who plan and implement a system of conferencing receive peer recognition for their effort, then such practices are likely to be maintained and extended. If, on the other hand, these positive actions receive no attention (even if the lack of attention is entirely inadvertent), they will fade over time (Daniels, 2000). It is essential, therefore, to structure monitoring and recognition systems into programs that are developed. (See chapter 7 for further detail.) Recognition of those who contribute to community healing can similarly be a useful component of programming for the larger community.

Family Peacemaking Tools and Activities

As cultural networks, families can also adopt procedures for peacemaking, and structured tools can help them to do so. In fact, some of the tools discussed earlier for use with other systems emerged from work with families.

The Family Conference

The small, but important, study by Serna and associates (1991) provides important hints about what it may take to actually help families learn to resolve conflicts and solve problems. There are many skills training programs that teach problem-solving communication, and it is clear that families can learn new skills in this area and use them when they are with a family educator or counselor. An important question, how-ever, is whether the family can use their newly learned skills spontane-ously when they face new problems on their own. In a relatively rigorous single case study with three families, Serna and colleagues found that the families did not do so until an additional component was added.

The study began with about 24 hours of skills training and super-vised practice for all family members, using the ASSET social skills train-ing package (Hazel, Schumaker, Sherman, & Sheldon-Wildgen, 1981) in an agency setting. Twice a month skill reviews in the home took place over another 6 to 11 months. Family members learned the skills and were able to use them reliably when directed by a counselor in the home. When simply audiotaped without supervision or guidance, however, family members usually did not use the skills that they had learned. These were, of course, discouraging results. At that point, the counse-lors implemented a new procedure, which they called the *family confer-ence*. This was a structured process of weekly family meetings, in which the family practiced resolving issues that family members had previ-ously listed on cards. Parents learned to "moderate" these sessions, us-ing a checklist that included the following steps:

- Preparation. Family members complete cards for issues to be discussed.
- Initiation. The conference begins with the collection of cards and the exchange of positive comments among family members.
- Problem clarification. The moderator selects one issue card and has the person who completed it describe the issue.
- Selection of skill. From the list of ASSET skills, the family member with the issue identifies the skill needed to resolve the issue.
- Problem resolution. Family members attempt to resolve the issue using the skill identified. This and the previous two steps are re-peated for additional issues.
- Evaluation. Family members rate the effectiveness of their prob-lem solving, identifying areas of success and additional steps that could improve effectiveness.
- Positive exchange. To end the conference, family members again exchange positive comments among themselves.

Implementation of this procedure produced a reliable and large im-provement in spontaneous effective communication in undirected ex-changes, as rated by the participants themselves, by independent judges, and by moment-by-moment analysis of audiotapes by trained raters (Serna et al., 1991). These promising results suggest that some sort of structured process may be important in helping families learn to resolve problems on their own. Family counselors often provide the structure when working with families; the structured conference format may help families learn to do so themselves. The family conference approach, therefore, or something very much like it, may be a valuable approach for those working intensively with families.

Although systematic replication of this study is necessary to determine, for example, whether families need the full ASSET program or whether basic communication skills training would be adequate, it seems likely that training in core skills, in conjunction with a device for structuring their use, may be valuable. Implementation of an approach like this would require less time and training, so this kind of simple structuring tool may be most realistic for widespread application in *PEACE POWER* programs. Very simple behavioral tools have proven powerful in many areas; the making peace tool has produced good results in preliminary tests with a few families in regular agency practice (see Figure 11).

The Making Peace Tool for Families

An important principle for *PEACE POWER* programs is to apply the same language and technology as consistently and frequently as possible across all settings. Therefore, the identical tool used in organizations can be used with families. Although the data are only suggestive at this point, it appears that training and encouraging family members to use this tool may be the single most effective, most widely applicable step for positively shifting the way that families with teens handle conflicts. It is much simpler than either the family conference or mediation, much less therapy, and can be presented as an enhancement tool for typical families, with no need for family members or professionals to label them as dysfunctional. Rather, it just provides families with opportunities to practice useful skills.

The skills structured by the making peace tool are expressing one's feelings through clear "I" statements regarding issues, listening respectfully, generating alternative solutions, negotiating solutions acceptable to all, and recognizing family members' efforts to work together to resolve issues. These are, perhaps, the most crucial skills in effective communication in families that include adolescents (Mattaini, 1999). More could certainly be added; the ASSET program, for example, which was used in the family conference research discussed earlier, targeted seven skills for youth and eight skills for parents, with some overlap. For widespread application, however, simpler is probably better.

The *PEACE POWER* making peace tool can be used in many ways, but the ideal arrangement is probably to model its use, provide opportunities for parents and youth to practice using it in family workshops, then ask people to experiment with it at home by using it with one or more issues that are not necessarily very challenging, and then report back to the group in a follow-up. Families could then be strongly and sincerely encouraged to actually use the tool several times (perhaps once a week on a scheduled basis for a month) and to use it when more challenging issues arise. It may be helpful to give family members opportunities to practice asking to use the tool as well. Most families will probably not use the structured tool forever, but the research by Serna and colleagues (1991) suggests that, after a period of such structured practice, the skills may be maintained without the structure. For families with more serious conflicts, for example, those in situations that warrant intensive *PEACE POWER* services, much more practice using the tool in training and at home may be required.

Family Mediation

Some families generally function adequately or even very well, but at some point an issue arises that they are unable to sort out for themselves. Research into family (especially parent–child) mediation suggests that in such cases, mediation can be very effective both in resolving the immediate issue and in changing the ways that families address problems in the future (Umbreit & Kruk, 1997). A number of issues remain unresolved, including the extent to which standard mediation processes are appropriate or effective with diverse families. Still, mediation programs appear to be valuable as one of multiple components in a package of peacemaking processes.

Family mediation is a structured process that is generally limited to a prespecified number of meetings (often one to four); either a single mediator or a team of two mediators (in some cases, an adult and a teen) guide the family through a series of relatively standardized steps. (The steps used generally are quite similar to those of the standard problem-solving model discussed previously.) Family mediation is appropriate when a family cannot resolve an issue (e.g., even after trying to use the making peace tool), but does not have a history of severe and long-lasting conflict. Families with such a history usually require more intensive family services and counseling. Mediation is emphatically different from "treatment," because it specifically eschews any emphasis on family dynamics and focuses tightly on the immediate issue. As was true for organizationally based mediation programs, trained and often certified mediators, in most cases volunteers (both professional and nonprofessional) in community programs, conduct family mediation. In many cases, *PEACE POWER* programs partner with family mediation programs already available in the community.

Community Tools and Activities for Making Peace

Conferencing

As noted earlier in relation to organizational peacemaking procedures, conferencing appears to have wide applicability within communities. O'Connell and associates (1999), for example, describe programs in the juvenile justice system, the criminal justice system (including quality-of-life crimes, but also variations for quite serious crimes), neighborhood organizations, schools (e.g., "peer conferencing"), community dispute resolution centers, police departments, and work places. There are many other related programs as well (see McCold, 1997), all of which are viewed as restorative in nature and many of which rely on conferences that include representatives of the multiple parties and systems that may be involved in a dispute.

The data suggest that conferencing procedures can be very, very powerful. In the vast majority of conferences involving youth in schools and the justice system, outcomes satisfactory to all are identified, and agreements made are kept. This success makes sense, because persons important to the youth (including parents or other caretakers and siblings) are involved, representatives from all of the networks that have an interest in the outcome participate, and resolution and healing benefit everyone. Even "skeptics" are often won over to the process once they observe it. Conferencing has even played a role in working through the aftermath of serious crimes, including murder, although in a different way. In those cases, conferencing occurs after trial and during imprisonment, as a means of allowing survivors (usually relatives of the victim), the perpetrator, the perpetrator's family, and community representatives to deal with what happened and to move at least some distance toward personal and collective healing.

Like the family conference and the making peace tool, conferencing is based on a simple, structured process; therefore, persons with only a modicum of specialized training can effectively implement the process. So long as the standard script as described above is used within an atmosphere committed to honesty, it is possible for resolution, restoration, and healing to occur. Brief training sessions are easily accessible (see note 14) and organizations and community groups can send one or two representatives to such training, who can then train others.

In addition, beyond formal conferencing, "there are an infinite number of opportunities for restorative interventions" (O'Connell et al., 1999, p. 84). Other more flexible processes that bring together those affected by an incident, so long as they incorporate certain basic practices, can promote healing. The basic practices suggested are as follows:

- Fostering awareness of how others are affected;
- Avoiding scolding and lecturing;
- Involving offenders in active ways, for example, by asking them to speak and including them in decision making about repairing damage;
- Accepting ambiguity, in particular about who is responsible for what, since full agreement may not always be possible;
- "Separat[ing] the deed from the doer" (O'Connell et al., 1999, p. 85)—focusing on the behavior, but respecting the person, and, when possible, recognizing positive actions on his or her part; and
- "See[ing] every instance of wrongdoing and conflict as an opportunity for learning" (O'Connell et al., 1999, p. 85).

There are extensive connections between these practices and many dimensions of the *PEACE POWER* strategy. Although requiring some effort to establish, conferencing programs are not terribly difficult to organize in many community settings and networks. An even more intensive process, *healing circles*, requires a much heavier investment of time and commitment, but may have potential for collective community healing that goes beyond anything discussed thus far.

Circles

A broad term, *circles* cover a range of practices, all of which involve the sharing of power as groups address problems, construct solutions, or engage in authentic dialogue, generally in ways that place primary emphasis on the welfare of the collective (and the individuals involved *as part of that collective*). There are many varieties of such practices, ranging from conferencing and modifications of traditional Native American talking circles (discussed earlier), to sentencing circles used as alternatives to standard court procedures, to healing circles for the community treatment of sexual abuse. All of these practices involve groups, usually with at least some members representing the larger community. All involve efforts to encourage real honesty and listening, and critically, all ultimately are constructional (Goldiamond, 1974)—they aim primarily to build something rather than to punish behavior (or, worse, to punish people).

A few paragraphs will not prepare anyone to design intensive circle programs, of course. In fact, First Nations people who developed the healing circle approach described have found that it is not even very effective for a group of them to go to another community and tell people how to establish a program of healing circles. Rather, they now ask people to come to them and participate in ongoing circles, because observation, modeling, and practice elaborate dimensions that cannot simply be described. (Effective use of circles, in other words, is not governed by rules, but shaped by experiences.) Nevertheless, simple descriptions may establish interest in pursuing these directions. The best available source about intensive circles is Ross (1996).

The *sentencing circle* in First Nations communities in Canada is one relatively widespread approach that has many variations and is used to resolve problems associated with a crime. Participants in sentencing circles are seen as representing the community, which includes the victim and the offender. In contrast, the Western, adversarial view is defined in terms of "the state versus" the alleged perpetrator; the victim, the networks connected to the victim and offender, and the community have no real place. In sentencing circles, however, participants include the victim, those working with him or her, and his or her family; the offender and his or her support people and family; court personnel; representatives of the larger community; and other members of the community who wish to participate. All sit in a circle, and after certain preparatory rituals (including, in the Hollow Water Ojibway community, for example, smoking of the pipe, smudging, and prayer), participate in several rounds during which each participant speaks in turn. Each round has a different purpose, such as speaking to the victim, speaking to the offender, and making recommendations for sentencing. Not surprisingly, this very different process leads to very different sentences, often involving specific steps toward healing the damage done, continued involvement in healing circles, and participation in learning activities that the community believes the offender to need.

Healing Circles

Even more complex than sentencing circles are *healing circles*, an indigenous alternative to "treatment" that emphasizes healing and learning through a collective group process. As might be expected, there is no single, universally applicable approach to such circles, and, of all the processes discussed in this book, healing circles are the least possible to implement merely from a written description. At the same time, they are also among the most powerful. Ross (1996) again provides an exceptionally strong example, the Community Holistic Circle Healing Program at Hollow Water, in Manitoba, Canada.

At Hollow Water, healing circles are part of a larger process involving a team of indigenous providers and professionals working with victims, offenders, families, and others affected by abuse and family violence, sexual abuse in particular. The process is communal and spiritual, and it requires a very challenging level of shared power. In the process of building the team, histories of abuse in the families and close networks of team members were addressed. Dealing with these issues required a depth of emotional, interpersonal, and spiritual sharing and commitment that went far beyond simple training and collaboration, and these histories came to play important parts in the work done later.

The basic strategy developed in this community for healing after sexual abuse is described by Ross (1996):

> The community strategy the team developed involves a detailed protocol leading all the participants through a number of steps or stages. They include the initial disclosure of abuse, protecting the child, confronting the victimizer, assisting the (nonoffending) spouse, assisting the families of all concerned, coordinating the

team approach, assisting the victimizer to admit and accept responsibility, preparing the victim, victimizer and families for the Special Gathering, guiding the Special Gathering through the creation of a Healing Contract, implementation of the Healing Contract and, finally, holding a Cleansing Ceremony designed, in their words, to mark "the completion of the Healing Contract, the restoration of balance to the victimizer, and a new beginning for all involved." (pp. 32–33)

Months of time in weekly or more frequent healing circles, a central part of the Healing Contract, are required to reach a satisfactory outcome, in part because the goals of the intervention are so ambitious. Follow-up circles every six months are also mandated over the long term. Almost no recidivism occurs with the use of this process, and—surprising to those accustomed to the dominant society's ways of dealing with sexual abuse—in some cases, offenders have come forward on their own to disclose their abuse and ask to participate in the healing process.

Community Mediation Programs

Just as in organizations and in families, mediation is an increasingly popular community level service. Not only can mediation significantly reduce costs, compared with handling conflicts through the justice system, but also it usually produces outcomes satisfactory to participants. *PEACE POWER* programs can easily link to existing community dispute resolution and mediation services, and where such programs are not available, community leaders may wish to advocate to establish them. Mediation has been useful in the following situations, among others: divorce, postdivorce parenting, disputes among neighbors, child protection, step parenting, adoption, issues related to the elderly, care planning in physical and mental health settings, and juvenile and criminal justice (Kruk, 1997).

Some programs use face-to-face mediation almost exclusively; some rely on extensive "shuttle diplomacy," bringing the parties together when an agreement is close; and others use the two approaches flexibly. There is still debate in the mediation field as to whether the goal of mediation should be exclusively reaching a settlement or whether the primary emphasis should be on healing and restoring balance. Programs valuing the latter may be of most use in *PEACE POWER* collaborations.

Another debated issue is the extent to which mediation can be effective in situations of multiple, multicultural realities (LeBaron, 1997). Certainly, mediation-like processes designed by different cultures sometimes look different. In many of the dominant society's mediation programs, there is a heavy emphasis on keeping the mediator an entirely disinterested party whose role is to ensure equal participation in a context of relatively equal power. (See chapter 5 for a discussion of why "equal power" may be an illusory and, in fact, problematic goal.) In one contrasting example, the Navajo Peacemaker Court uses a strategy that is sometimes labeled "mediation," but in fact, is something quite different from what has been described so far. In this process, the central figure is the *naat'aanii*, usually a respected elder, whose role is to counsel and guide the parties to the resolution of a dispute in ways that are consistent with traditional and community values. Thus, the *naat'aanii* does a considerable amount of teaching, and there is no effort to make the process value neutral. Moving toward *ho'zho'*, roughly "harmony in the universe," is the goal, one that has little or nothing in common with reaching a signed settlement on paper. The process is not viewed as hierarchical; those involved in establishing the Peacemaker Court describe it, not surprisingly, as a circle, in which everyone's part is critical. Recognizing the probable limitations of any single mediation program for all types of disputes among diverse persons and groups, persons involved in constructing *PEACE POWER* cultures and programs should view other types of programs as useful partners. The more seriously mediation programs take multicultural realities, the more broadly helpful they may be in personal and community healing and peacemaking.

Conclusion

Respectful, collective processes for making peace that go beyond simply making agreements, aiming to achieve healing as well, round out the core set of *PEACE POWER* practices. Simple conflict resolution programs, by themselves, are weak interventions. Healing programs are much more powerful. And healing programs in the context of high levels of recognition, respect, and shared power are more powerful yet.

The four practices are deeply interwoven, and it is often difficult to determine where one ends and another begins; they are, at their core, an integral whole. Assuming that a cultural network, be it an organization, family, community, business, school, or whatever group decides to seriously engage in building *PEACE POWER*, the next step is to determine how they will know that they are actually succeeding in doing so.

Monitoring and Evaluating *PEACE POWER* Programs

Change that is not monitored will not last. Though program developers may wish it were not so, this statement has proven consistently true. Good intentions do not change cultural practices. When individuals decide to change their behavior (e.g., through New Year's resolutions), they often find it very difficult to make lasting changes. Cultural change is even more difficult, because it involves coordinated, interlocking changes among multiple individuals. Cultural systems, like all other systems, are structured to maintain homeostasis except under extraordinary circumstances. A monitoring system, one of the most powerful ways of establishing and maintaining motivation over time, can create such extraordinary conditions. In addition, because the substantial constructive change built on the core *PEACE POWER* practices usually occurs gradually, it can be difficult to notice unless a system for structured tracking is in place. (Funders increasingly demand accountability and evaluation as well, of course; this is an additional, but not the primary, reason to monitor.)

Evaluation often seems at first glance to be complicated and technical, but the most effective monitoring systems are usually very simple and involve only modest additional effort. As a general practice, the best monitoring and evaluation strategy is one that those involved design collaboratively to answer the basic questions:

1. Are the actions that we planned actually happening?
   - How can we be sure of that?

2. Are collective outcomes (positive and negative) changing over time?
- How can we be sure of that?

Both levels of monitoring are usually important: process monitoring to track whether planned actions are being taken, outcome monitoring to determine whether those actions are producing the desired effects. An example of process monitoring is, How often are we using the making peace tool? Examples of outcome monitoring are, Is the rate of fights and arguments changing? and, Is attendance improving? In some cases, it is also possible to determine whether changes in outcomes are directly related to changes in program activities, although this requires a level of testing rigor that may be neither realistic nor necessary for community programs.

Monitoring Methods

The participants developing a monitoring system have a number of options regarding just what events and conditions to track, as well as how to track them. The most reliable and valid information usually comes from direct observation, but such data are usually very difficult to collect in everyday settings. For example, it would be very useful to actually observe and count the recognition events that occur in a residential setting or recreation program, and then to track changes over time. It would also be helpful to be able to observe the number of antisocial actions that occur within a peer group, and then correlate those with recognition events and other directly observed program activities. In most youth-serving organizations, however, such observation is unrealistic. Videotaped time samples can be used (and the *PEACE POWER* Working Group will assist groups wishing to develop such a system), but videotaping can also be quite demanding in terms of time and resources. For this reason, simpler measures are usually better choices.

Several such options are outlined in the following discussion, but organizations should feel free to creatively develop their own monitoring systems. In developing such a system, organizations often begin with overly ambitious plans; although it would be wonderful to collect many types of information, staff in most programs can consistently collect at most a handful of data items. A realistic plan may include counts of one or two permanent products over time, incidence data on three or four kinds of events, and one measure of social validity. Research programs may be able to collect more.

Permanent Products and Self-Monitoring Data

Perhaps the most valid data that can be easily collected are from *permanent products*, that is, written or other tangible pieces of information that are produced naturally in implementing a program. For example, those in programs that use recognition notes can collect completed notes periodically (once a week, once a month), count the number prepared during that period, and chart levels and trends in number of notes prepared. If the trend is upward, or the level is high and stable, no change is necessary in the program, and people involved can and should receive recognition for their efforts. If there is a descending trend, if the level is low and stable, or if the rate is variable and unstable, changes in the way the program is being implemented may be necessary.

Permanent products can also be examined for quality, either immediately or later. For example, if a program is using the making peace tool, the number of forms collected can be tracked as the recognition notes were tracked, but forms can also be checked to determine the percentage on which every step has been completed and which steps are most commonly not adequately addressed. These data will suggest types of program enhancements that may be useful.

If self-monitoring is a procedure already in use (see chapters 3 and 9 for extended discussions of self-monitoring by staff and youth, respectively), it may be relatively easy to collect and evaluate self-monitoring data. For staff members who are keeping track of the number of home recognition notes that they send to parents each week, typing those numbers into a spreadsheet to produce a graph or simply graphing them by hand is a natural next step that provides information both for self-management and for program evaluation.

Archival Records and Existing Data

Many systems already collect data that can be incorporated into monitoring systems. For example, well implemented *PEACE POWER* projects should produce changes in the incidence of such events as fights, suspensions, vandalism costs, achievement, and attendance. Table 7 lists some types of existing data that may be included in monitoring systems.

It is important that data items selected make sense in context; data that appear comparable may have quite different meanings in different systems. For example, some violence prevention programs in elementary schools have reduced the number of nurses' office visits, because

Table 7. Existing Data That May Be Included in Monitoring Systems

- Disciplinary records
- Incident reports
- Number of violent incidents
- Number of weapons incidents
- Attendance
- Number of disciplinary referrals (e.g., to the vice-principal)
- Number of students sent out of classroom for timeout or calming down
- Number of suspensions
- Bus reports
- Indices of academic performance (e.g., standardized tests)
- Vandalism costs
- Number of nurse referrals (or referrals for fight-induced injuries)
- Number of arrests
- Grade point averages
- Complaints filed by teachers and staff with administration or unions
- Sick days taken by staff
- Measures of parent satisfaction
- Number of parent visits

Note: Not all systems will keep all data items reliably.

they reduced the number of fight-related injuries. In one high school program, however, *increasing* numbers of nurses' office visits was a program goal, because in that school, such visits were primarily preventive in nature.

There are often problems of accessibility, reliability, and validity with existing data that must be considered. Sometimes, counts of fights and disciplinary referrals are not kept reliably or are regarded as confidential information, because public disclosure can be embarrassing for a program. Existing data that are not regularly reviewed are often not accurately recorded, even when administrators believe that they are. For example, in one school, administrators were certain that one accurate measure was daily attendance—the school's funding, by legislative requirement, depended directly on daily census. Review of these data, however, revealed numerous instances in which children recorded as absent had grades recorded for that day and vice versa, incorrect totals, and other anomalies. It is easy under these circumstances to suggest that there are no really useful data available, but this is usually an over-reaction. Even somewhat "dirty" data are often accurate enough to reflect really meaningful levels of change.

Just as persons living and working with youth often pay much more attention to negative behavior than to positive behavior, it is sometimes tempting to look only at data regarding incidence of negative behaviors. It is useful and motivating to include counts and rates of positive actions as well—for example, number of recognition notes or events, numbers of students involved in community service, positive changes in attendance rates—not just such data as numbers of fights, numbers of suspensions, and vandalism costs.

Social Validity and Survey Data

Although less rigorous than some other kinds of data, there is much to be said for regularly collecting data about participants' opinions of programs. There are two reasons that this can be important. First, once they are clear about concept definitions, respondents often can report reasonably accurately on whether, for example, people in the program treat each other with respect or have opportunities for sharing power in a setting; trying to gather more precise data may be unrealistic. Second, people will actively and consistently participate only in programs that they believe are useful and consistent with their needs or values. If a project lacks such *social validity*, it is certain to fail (Wolf, 1978).

An example of a social validity and subjective evaluation questionnaire that the *PEACE POWER* Working Group has used is shown in Figure 12.

This instrument asks two questions for each core *PEACE POWER* practice: (1) How important do you think this practice is here (social validity), and (2) How often do people carry out this practice here (a subjective rating of incidence)? In addition, the instrument asks the respondent to identify program activity that is going particularly well and one possibility for further action that might be taken. In one school project, the *PEACE POWER* Working Group is asking staff to complete this instrument once a month for a period of two years. The questionnaire was completed for the first time immediately after an initial half-day workshop; periodic consultation was then provided related to one core practice at a time. Data for the first year show that the staff continue in a stable way to regard each of the core *PEACE POWER* practices

Figure 12

Today's Date: _____

PEACE POWER Feedback

How important is each of the following for constructing the kind of culture you value in this organization?

1. Recognizing Contributions and Successes . . .

☐ Not important   ☐ A little important   ☐ Important   ☐ Very important

2. Acting with Respect . . .

☐ Not important   ☐ A little important   ☐ Important   ☐ Very important

3. Sharing Power to Build Community . . .

☐ Not important   ☐ A little important   ☐ Important   ☐ Very important

4. Making Peace . . .

☐ Not important   ☐ A little important   ☐ Important   ☐ Very important

Thinking about the entire organization (not just yourself), how often does each of these practices occur here?

5. Recognizing Contributions and Successes . . .

☐ Seldom or Never   ☐ Occasionally   ☐ Often   ☐ Very Often

6. Acting with Respect . . .

☐ Seldom or Never   ☐ Occasionally   ☐ Often   ☐ Very Often

7. Sharing Power to Build Community . . .

☐ Seldom or Never   ☐ Occasionally   ☐ Often   ☐ Very Often

8. Making Peace . . .

☐ Seldom or Never   ☐ Occasionally   ☐ Often   ☐ Very Often

9. What is the most useful step this organization is taking to support these practices?

10. What one additional step could be taken to increase the frequency of these practices here?

Social validity questionnaire.

at higher than 3.9 on the 4-point scale. The extent to which staff see each core practice as actually present in their organization has gradually increased from month to month, with those that received additional consultation reaching higher levels. These results are extremely encouraging and suggest that the project in this school is maintaining high levels of social validity and is having meaningful effects.

Each project's staff, of course, should design questionnaires and other data-gathering approaches in ways that fit the language(s), values, and reading levels of project participants. Programs may need to use somewhat different instruments for youth, parents, and staff, for example. Interviews and focus groups are other, often very powerful, ways to track social validity, program exposure, and effectiveness.

Although less specific to a particular project and more distal from the general *PEACE POWER* objective of behavior change, some standardized measures may be usefully incorporated into monitoring systems. Most of these actually measure attitudes and beliefs rather than behavior, but there is likely to be at least some correlation. The U.S. Centers for Disease Control and Prevention has published a useful compendium of such measures (Dahlberg, Toal, & Behrens, 1998). The Working Group has used the *Beliefs Supporting Aggression, Violent Intentions—Teen Conflict Survey,* and *Social Responsibility* scales from that volume in some projects, for example, and they appear to be sensitive to change with the populations participating in those projects. The first measure relates to values and beliefs about violence and coercion; the second, to expectations about future behavior; and the third, to values related to contribution, respect, and responsibility. Programs that successfully increase the incidence of *PEACE POWER* practices should have at least some effect in each of these areas.

Design Considerations

Once reasonable and realistic measures have been selected for monitoring, the next necessary decisions involve when to collect those data—decisions about what researchers call *experimental design*. Issues related to design for most community programs are actually quite straightforward, however, and require very little formal knowledge or training in research. For such programs, there are two basic designs for collecting data that are realistic: pre-post and time-series designs. In a few cases, certain contrast group designs may also be possible.

Pre-Post Designs

In pre-post evaluation designs, one form of group "quasi-experimental" designs, the basic structure is (a) to measure some attribute or condition among a group of participants before beginning a program, (b) to implement the program, then (c) to remeasure and see if there is a change. Standardized instruments like those mentioned earlier are often used in this procedure. Pre-post designs are weak as "proof" of effectiveness, because there are many possible reasons (discussed in the research literature as threats to internal validity) for changes found. Among these are practice/testing effects that result from taking the same test more than once, the possibility that other events have affected the scores (technically called *history* effects), and instability of measurements. Also, in some cases, changes in average scores may be statistically significant, but so small as to be practically meaningless. Still, the occurrence of relatively large changes suggests that the program is having some effect, and when other, more rigorous evaluations are not possible, pre-post evaluations are much better than none at all.

A stronger quasi-experimental design involves the use of contrast groups. In this type of design, other, somewhat comparable groups of students or staff who are not participating in the project complete the pre-tests and post-tests at the same times as project participants, and the levels of change between the groups compared (see Mayer, Butterworth, Nafpaktitis, & Sulzer-Azaroff, 1983, for an example). Generally, such contrast group evaluations require more resources than community programs can muster, but they can provide quite persuasive evidence of effectiveness (see Rossi, Freeman, & Lipsey, 1999). In most cases, however, time-series designs are the most realistic, relatively rigorous evaluation designs that are practical in community settings (Biglan, 1995).

Time-Series Designs

The core of time-series designs is to measure the same variable repeatedly in search of possible relationships between program activities and targeted objectives (Kazi, 1998). Because such designs can often be much more rigorous than pre-post designs, their results can be more persuasive. In technical terms, this is because they provide protection against at least some threats to internal validity; in everyday language, they can convincingly trace relationships between a program and its outcomes.

In addition, time-series designs are usually the only approach for tracking process variables over time; for example, tracking the numbers of PEACE POWER circles conducted over a period of months indicates whether this program component is being implemented consistently or whether use of such circles is fading over time. Crucially, and unlike pre-post or other group designs, time-series designs allow program changes to be made as needed, based on the data obtained. A program component associated with positive change can be continued; a component that does not appear useful can be eliminated or modified without destroying the integrity of the design.

The basic time-series design process is as follows: Data on a variable of interest (e.g., number of fights, attendance rate, or number of recognition notes prepared) are collected regularly (e.g., every week or every month) and then are graphed to make it possible to identify and analyze changes in level, trend, or variability. For instance, data on the number of physical and verbal altercations in a group home might be collected every week for three months (baseline data). A *PEACE POWER* program could then be introduced, and data collected for another three months (intervention data). This design is sometimes called an *A-B design*, in which *A* refers to baseline data and *B* refers to intervention data. See Figure 13 for an example.

In some ways, an *A-B* evaluation is similar to a pre-post evaluation; in an *A-B* evaluation, however, data are collected multiple times both before and after intervention. If the number of altercations in this example is relatively stable and high before the program, a stable downward trend after intervention is reasonable evidence that the program may be having an effect (though it does not "prove" the program's effectiveness—logically, there still could be other reasons for the change). It is often possible to collect baseline data retrospectively, if good records have been kept.

The simplest time-series design, which is often used for process evaluation, is a so-called *B design*, in which there is no baseline (*A*) phase; data are simply collected on the same variable over time. For example, if a program administrator wishes to determine whether home recognition notes are being used regularly, staff can keep a running count on a weekly basis of the number of notes sent home (Figure 14).

There is no need for baseline data here; the purpose of data collection is simply to determine frequency of a program activity. *B* designs can also be used to track number of disciplinary referrals. Even without

Figure 13

Number of Altercations

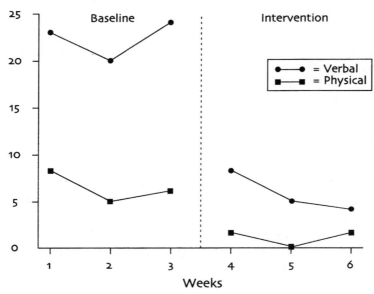

A baseline-intervention (*A-B*) monitoring design to examine the effect of intervention on the number of altercations.

baseline data, a clear trend line showing fewer and fewer referrals over time can be reasonably persuasive evidence of successful interventions.

Even stronger time-series designs can sometimes be helpful. For example, if an organization operates at multiple sites, an *AB* design can be used in each; multiple replications showing similar levels of change as a result of intervention are more persuasive than only one. If program staff begin to collect baseline data in several sites at the same time, introduce *PEACE POWER* activities in one site while continuing to collect data in all, then progressively introduce program activities in additional sites, the evaluation design becomes a *multiple baseline design* (Figure 15).

Another alternative, the *changing criterion* design, can be used when program staff plan to gradually and systematically increase objectives in some area. For example, in Figure 16, staff planned to gradually in-

Figure 14

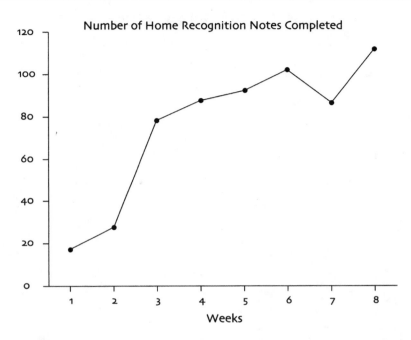

Number of Home Recognition Notes Completed

An intervention-only (*B*) monitoring design, tracking the number of home recognition notes completed on a weekly basis in one program.

crease the number of recognition notes completed in a school over the course of two months, setting progressively more challenging goals each week.

In this figure, the goal level set was reached or exceeded in all but one week.

Regardless of the specific design, data in time-series evaluation designs (sometimes called interrupted time-series or single-system designs) are usually graphed to allow visual analysis. In such analysis, the evaluator is looking for distinct, unambiguous changes that occur or begin to occur when the program is introduced. Such changes are evident in both Figure 13 and Figure 15. If there are enough data points (generally eight or more), there are statistical tools that can be used to analyze time-series data (e.g., Kazdin, 1984; Tryon, 1982), but visual analysis usually is adequate for determining whether socially meaningful change

Figure 15

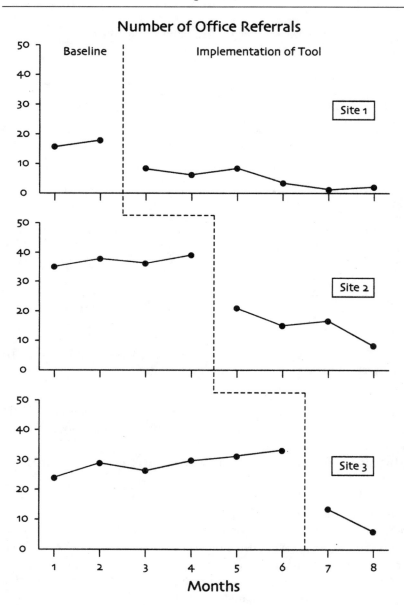

Number of Office Referrals

A multiple baseline-monitoring design, tracking number of office referrals before and after regular use of the making peace tool, when implemented at each of three program sites.

Figure 16

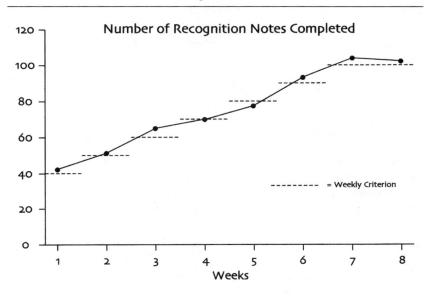

A changing-criterion monitoring record of recognition notes completed.

has taken place. More technical detail regarding time-series evaluations can be found in Biglan (1995), and Bloom, Fischer, and Orme (1999).

Construction and Implementation of a Monitoring Plan

With the material presented so far in this chapter as a foundation, it is possible for program staff to construct and implement their own unique monitoring plan. This need not be technical or complex, and the some- times nonintuitive language of evaluation should not scare staff mem- bers away from monitoring. A program that is not monitored in some way probably will not be effective. Monitoring will, in fact, strengthen program effects, because the research clarifies that the feedback pro- vided by monitoring can be highly motivating. Complicated evalua- tions are usually prohibitively difficult to carry out consistently and often meaningless to those who are interested in the program, but simple ones can be powerful. The information provided should be pre- sented in ways useful to all stakeholders (i.e., staff, youth, parents, the larger community); the only reliable way to ensure this is to include members of all stakeholder groups in designing the monitoring plan—of course, another example of shared power. In most cases, program staff will want to examine at least to some extent both process data (Is the program being implemented and how well?), and outcome data (Is the program "working"?). In both cases, a key question is, What do we really need to know about?

Tracking Program Implementation (Process)

Many programs that have apparently "failed," in fact, were never implemented. Having a plan on paper and even providing staff training do not always result in meaningful behavior change. A school staff agreement to set up recognition boards and to conduct circles regularly does not mean that they will actually do so, often despite the best of intentions. Their neglect of the program does not usually reflect deception or lack of commitment. Rather, staff need to respond to many competing demands, and they often simply put off new initiatives that are not monitored, particularly activities that produce delayed, cumulative effects instead of immediate large effects (Malott, 2000; Malott, Whaley, & Malott, 1997), because they can always conduct these activities "later." Self-monitoring data, shared with others on a regular basis, establishes deadlines. People respond to deadlines because of the immediate, certain consequences.

For this reason, if all participating teachers report data on the number of recognition notes posted in their classrooms, and there is a display of both individual and aggregate data, say, in the teachers' lounge, it is much more likely that teachers will remember to follow through. Such procedures should not be imposed; people should be given opportunities to participate to help them avoid the New Year's resolution phenomenon. In some cases, particularly if the existing level of trust is low, posting only aggregate data for an entire program may be more acceptable; staff, youth, and others can then engage in dialogues to examine and respond to any problems in level (i.e., how many notes are being prepared) or trend (i.e., if the number being prepared is declining over time).

A key technique for monitoring process is the "chart on the wall"—publicly displaying data over time. In some cases, this may involve an actual chart on an actual wall; in other cases, a program "report card" may become part of every issue of a newsletter or handouts provided to a community advisory board at every meeting. What is important is that a small number of key indicators be measured and reported regularly in ways that immediately communicate with those who need to know how well the program is doing. Figure 17 shows a monitoring chart tracking several variables for an after-school program as percentages of monthly goals: (1) attendance rate over six months, (2) number of *PEACE POWER* circles, (3) number of making peace sessions, and (4) rate of youth passing all courses.

Some data on charts like that in Figure 17 are self-explanatory; others, like the number of peacemaking sessions, may require interpretation—Is the number of sessions declining because there are fewer conflicts, or because conflicts are not being addressed? There will always be some complexities like this to deal with, but the basic approach of charting clarifies the questions that need to be pursued.

Tracking Outcomes

Procedurally, tracking outcomes is similar to tracking process. The first step is to collectively answer the questions, "How will program staff know if the program is working? Who will be doing what, when, and how often?" The next step is to determine what data to collect, and when, to determine whether the desired outcomes are occurring. A few key indicators should not be difficult to identify. In schools, numbers of incident reports, measures of attendance, and measures of achievement may be adequate. In recreation programs, monthly ratings by youth of the extent to which they feel safe and respected while attending the program, consistency of attendance, level of parent satisfaction, and numbers of fights requiring staff intervention may be useful indicators.

Given that time-series data provide the most useful programmatic information, a plan for ensuring that outcome data really are collected and graphed regularly is a necessity. This will occur only if the administrator, supervisor, or senior staff person involved in the program monitors this process and demonstrates a high level of interest by, for example, including program participation and data collection skills in personnel evaluations; requesting data from staff on a regular, structured basis; and reporting results regularly to staff, youth, and other stakeholders. In other words, to be effective, monitoring itself must be monitored. Data that no one requests or pays attention to will not be collected and reported reliably, despite good intentions.

Figure 17

Percentage of Goals Achieved

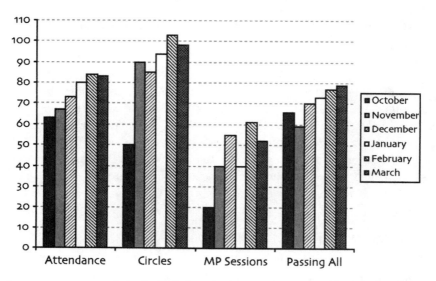

A summary program monitoring feedback chart, showing progress toward goal levels for attendance, *PEACE POWER* circles conducted, making peace (MP) sessions conducted, and rate of students passing all courses.

Time-series data are tremendously communicative, because they enable stakeholders to track changes over time and to identify both short-term trends associated with particular program activities and long-term, aggregate effects. These procedures permit rapid program adjustments and modifications that group quasi-experiments (e.g., pre-post evaluations) with their few measurement points do not. In addition, viewing time-series data can be tremendously motivating, providing opportunities to recognize progress and to respond to results that are disappointing. Therefore, every *PEACE POWER* program staff would be wise to collect time-series data, and to present them graphically on some type of regular programmatic report card or chart on the wall.

Programs and people are complicated, so other forms of outcome evaluation may also be important. For example, focus groups or individual interviews with youth, parents, and staff may bring to the forefront unrecognized problems and constructive program ideas that no one involved in developing the original monitoring plan may have considered. Another useful strategy is to consult outside observers. Persons who are associated with similar programs, who have particular expertise in work with youth, or who simply represent the community in some way can regularly be invited to visit a program and asked for their observations and feedback. This can be done informally, or a structured instrument for soliciting feedback can be developed. Another possibility that dramatically expands the potential pool of external reviewers is to videotape samples of program activities and ask persons not associated with the project to identify strengths in the videotapes and to suggest ways that the program might be strengthened.

Conclusion

Plans for tracking process and outcomes of *PEACE POWER* programs should include clear identification of what data need to be collected, a feasible plan for actually collecting those data (e.g., who will do it, when), and an effective reporting plan to ensure that monitoring actually happens. Although this may seem counterintuitive, a strong monitoring process may be more important than the specific details of a program— monitoring will detect any problems and clarify what is working, what can be improved, and what can be eliminated. Over time, therefore, well-monitored programs will tend to increase in strength. Funders, therefore, should probably pay more attention to the effectiveness of the monitoring program and the extent to which results are feeding back into efforts to enhance the program, rather than focusing primarily on immediate, short-term results.

PEACE POWER and Beyond: Extensions of the *PEACE POWER* Strategy

The material presented so far, if well used, can produce dramatic changes in the incidence of coercive and violent actions, while significantly improving the social webs within which youth and those around them live their lives. Other supporting activities and structural arrangements, some of which are described in this third section, can extend and enhance *PEACE POWER* outcomes. There is a danger here, however. Programs that selectively rely on only some of these adjunctive activities, without paying systematic attention to organizational and community culture, are likely to have only modest success. In an organization in which youth receive limited recognition and respect, in which they have little voice or power to affect events, and in which conflicts fester, training in life skills or attention to the physical environment is likely to produce at best marginal changes. The key to *PEACE POWER* programs is systematic support for the core cultural practices presented in Section II. For programs in which such support is present, adjunct procedures may be useful.

Chapter 8 examines structured small-group education in life and leadership skills for youth. Skills training focused only on youth is different from working toward cultural change systemwide, as considered in the previous section. The purpose of life and leadership skills groups is to enrich the repertoires of individuals. There are many skills that can be useful as young people live through the developmental processes associated with adolescence and adulthood; Goldstein, Glick, and Gibbs (1998) list 50 behavioral skills, in addition to moral reasoning and anger management skills. Chapter 8 focuses on only eight skill areas, selected because most have strong empirical support specifically for reducing aggression, coercion, or violence, and each relates closely to one of the core *PEACE POWER* practices. For example, skill in envisioning a path to success leads to more opportunities for recognition; honoring diversity increases mutual respect; knowing one's power (recognizing one's gifts and talents) is essential to sharing power; and defusing anger is necessary for participation in peacemaking. The eight skill areas discussed are, therefore, highly consistent with strengthening *PEACE POWER* cultures. More skills could certainly be added, but fewer can be more, in that too extensive a list may result in inadequate attention to any area.

Chapter 9 addresses the fact that in many groups, a small number of young people demonstrate particularly high levels of coercive and aggressive behavior. It is common, for example, even in a large high school, for a group of perhaps 20 or 30 youth to be involved in a very large percentage of disciplinary incidents. There is no doubt that these youth require special attention. There is little doubt that such attention, if provided in ways consistent with currently available data, is likely to produce excellent results. There is one additional step that scientific theory and practical wisdom suggest may further strengthen such results: providing assistance to these young people in ways that move toward normalization through a reliance on intensifying procedures used with all youth rather than on approaches that define this group in pathological terms. The four core *PEACE POWER* practices are still the key. There is not, in other words, one program for the "good kids" and a different one for the "bad kids"—the same procedures are used, simply at different levels of intensity ("dose levels"), depending on need.

Chapter 10 turns to other organizational procedures and structures that can be useful as part of an overall *PEACE POWER* strategy. These include disciplinary procedures, attention to the physical environment, and staff skills for dealing with residual threatening and coercive behavior incidents. It is no accident that these issues are considered only near the end of this book, even though they are among the areas that first receive attention in many programs. Within a comprehensive *PEACE POWER* culture, the adjunct procedures discussed in chapter 10 can produce meaningful outcome increments, but they are far less crucial than they are in programs enmeshed in cultures of threat, punishment, and disrespect. It is useful for staff to know how to de-escalate an incident at risk of spiraling out of control, but much more useful to prevent such incidents from occurring at all—the goal of the *PEACE POWER* strategy.

8

Life and Leadership
Skills Groups

In a *PEACE POWER* culture, youth learn not only to avoid violent or aggressive behavior, but also to construct positive alternatives that genuinely empower them to influence their world, to share power in meaningful ways, to contribute and lead others toward contribution as well. This is a far better approach than one that relies on coercive, aggressive power to have an impact, but it requires skills that many youth have not had opportunities to learn. Contextual, cultural supports are essential for maintaining change, but skills are also essential: people can do only what they know how to do. People learn skills, whether driving a car or learning to be assertive, through observation, practice, shaping, and consequences. Small-group skills education is a vehicle for such learning.

Learning to use the core *PEACE POWER* practices is a first critical level of skills training, but there are a number of other skills that can enhance and extend those practices. Within an overall *PEACE POWER* project, a social worker, school counselor, or other professional may wish to lead particular groups of young people as a way of intensifying learning for them. This chapter focuses on structured, small-group exercises for skills building. This is a different emphasis than that of changing overall cultural practices systemwide, but can enhance those efforts. This chapter, then, is intended as a relatively stand-alone manual for those leading such groups, although it assumes familiarity with what has gone before. In some cases, content in this chapter overlaps that presented earlier, but it is handled here in a different way, to guide a different kind of process. Young people can learn life skills and skills that enable them to act as catalysts for positive action by others—leadership skills. Although this chapter focuses on eight basic life and leadership skill areas, there are many other useful skills, of course. For example, Goldstein's skill streaming for adolescents (Goldstein, Glick, & Gibbs, 1998) targets behaviors ranging from asking a question, to dealing with an accusation, to guiding oneself step-by-step through a challenging situation. There is a large literature devoted to social skills, life skills, assertiveness, and leadership skills training for youth (e.g., Forman, 1993; LeCroy, 1994; several chapters in Alberti, 1977); program designers may wish to expand training to incorporate still other dimensions.

Many of the family and peer groups among whom youth live out their lives support behavior repertoires that conflict with those to be learned as part of the *PEACE POWER* program, and group leaders should acknowledge this openly. Often, it is necessary not only to discuss, model, and practice each of the new skills in role plays, but also explicitly to reward the young people socially and otherwise if they are to use and maintain those skills in their lives.

Life and Leadership Skills Education as Group Work

Social skills education is a form of group work, and those leading such groups need training in basic group work skills (Rose, 1978, 1998). Group work is a powerful modality; in skilled hands, it can be among the most effective interventions available. On the other hand, poorly managed groups can do damage. For example, group members who feel humiliated in the group; pressured into uncomfortable self-disclosure; or unprotected, betrayed, or discouraged by the leader tend to have negative group experiences (Smokowski, Rose, Todar, & Reardon, 1999). These findings are consistent, of course, with all that has been said here about the problems associated with punitive, threatening, and coercive social environments. In many ways, the role of the leader in these groups is similar to that of a coach—a very energetic hands-on guide who also helps the group work as a mutually respectful team. Assuming that the leader has basic group work skills, a number of other considerations related to group structure and process are important to achieving powerful effects (i.e., offering a program that actually changes behavior).

Group Composition and Timing

The size and composition of life and leadership skills education groups vary depending on the population being served and on practical constraints. For example, in a special education setting for teens with a history of serious behavior problems, groups of four to six work better than larger groups, because of the need for considerable management within the group. For more typical teens, groups of 8 to 10 are very workable. In one program, funding constraints required the leaders to work with groups of 11 or 12; in this case, it was often useful to split the group into two subgroups that worked independently during portions of the meetings.

Either single-sex or mixed groups are workable, although they may play out in different ways. In mixed groups, leaders need to be prepared to manage a higher level of sexual testing and teasing, but such groups offer excellent forums for work on respect between the sexes, which is often a major issue with adolescents. Single-sex groups sometimes produce a bit more horseplay (mixed genders at least occasionally have a mildly "civilizing" effect). There are advantages to mixing youth who are less advanced in terms of social development with others who are more so, because the presence of more mature youth tends to raise the level of interaction even for those who are less mature.

Although twice a week meetings may be ideal, weekly meetings may fit more practically into ongoing organizational scheduling and are usually adequate. It is most common for group meetings to continue about 8 to 16 weeks, again because they tend to fit into quarterly or school semester schedules around which many young people's lives are at least somewhat structured. It is usually preferable that a cohort move through an entire series of group meetings, but in some settings (for example, short-term shelters or detention centers) group membership can be left open so that participants can attend when they are in the setting. Each session must stand alone in that case, beginning with a clear statement of group purpose and rules, and emphasizing one skill area without relying on knowledge from previous meetings.

Group Culture and Activities

Clear group purpose and rules, and careful planning for structured group activities, can be very helpful in minimizing problems in group process.

The purpose of the group must be stated clearly and honestly. It is usually relatively easy to collaboratively establish rules that everyone treats everyone else with respect, physical fighting is not permissible, and only one person speaks at a time. If the participants clearly state this minimal set of rules in the beginning and immediately deal with any violations as a group problem, they can usually construct a culture of respect. If this begins to deteriorate at some point, the group may again need to turn its attention to rules and group climate.

Group sessions should ordinarily be quite structured; later in a series of sessions, and in some cases, later in a particular session, more open-ended discussions can be realistic and useful. In early stages, however, a relatively tight plan should be prepared, as it can be very difficult to manage a group of youth who are bored and not sure what they are supposed to be doing. Such a plan can always be modified. Group sessions should be highly reinforcing, with high levels of recognition and other incentives for positive contributions and participation; a mix of entertaining, but educational, activities; a high degree of physical comfort; refreshments, if possible; and attention to making the experience one that people can really enjoy while they are learning.

Several key teaching/learning strategies and activities are valuable for structuring effective skills education, including the following:

- *Beginning sessions with warm-up activities* which may include classic group icebreakers like name games, values clarification exercises, or cooperative games as discussed in chapter 4. These activities need not be extremely complicated; they simply serve as a way of starting communication among members.
- The use of a *progressive skills education sequence.* Leaders should usually demonstrate a skill before asking youth to try it; in groups with multiple leaders, the first example may be role-played between leaders. Youth are usually eager to join in after observing this.
- *Involvement of models* who the youth see as like themselves in some way, but whom they also respect. Sports figures, entertainers, police officers, and respected older youth have been useful in some programs. These individuals may make brief presentations, answer questions, and participate in skills training exercises.
- *Realism.* Most examples used should be drawn from the setting in which training is being conducted or from the lives of the youth participating. Although considerable joking and a light touch are

important and always present in effective skills groups, it is important that the situations being role-played are as realistic as possible. Leaders should model taking the content of the group seriously, while enjoying the process.

- *Learners as teachers.* A really effective skills training program functions as a learning collective, in which everyone both learns and teaches. The leaders will also learn in the groups, because youth often come up with better options than the leader herself or himself. Some members will enter a group more skilled than others in some areas, and those persons should be used to model and provide feedback to others. Group members are also often in the best possible position to evaluate the effectiveness of a coping strategy and should have an opportunity to do so. Hayes, Kohlenberg, and Melancon (1989) discovered that "global feedback" by group members ("on a scale of 1 to 10, how effective was that performance?") is among the most useful techniques, producing better performances than trying to determine in detail whether a role play met some preexisting set of rules. Such feedback must, of course, be delivered in respectful ways.
- *Focus and overlearning.* Learning complex skills requires considerable exposure and practice. One mistake often made in skills training is to try to cover everything in too short a period; for example, recognizing that many skills might be useful, some program planners try to cover two or more major skills in a single session. Unfortunately, this strategy generally leads to limited learning of anything, and little or no transfer to participants' everyday lives. Using several strategies to teach a single skill and *overlearning* to the point at which skills become pretty much automatic is a much better approach, even though it may permit a focus on a more narrow range of skills. For example, the Duluth Model for work with batterers (Pence & Paymar, 1993), a group program that typically lasts for 24 sessions, emphasizes giving up problem behaviors and learning new alternatives in only eight specific areas. Two to three sessions per skill area is probably a useful guideline. If a program is to have eight sessions, then doing an adequate job in three or four skill areas is preferable to trying to cover more skills than can possibly be done well. Most *PEACE POWER* groups begin with work to deepen participants' experience with the four core practices; the leaders then select, sometimes with the group members,

171

from the additional skills included in the life and leadership skills package as time permits.

- *Planned generalization to natural settings.* Group members should not be pressured to use new skills practiced in group in their everyday lives. They should be encouraged to experiment with the new skills as they feel ready, however, because the real payoff for skills training occurs outside the group. Group discussion should include what kinds of situations new skills might be helpful in, when they may not be, and how group members should begin trying skills out in ways likely to be successful. Later group sessions should provide opportunities for participants to report back on their successes, as well as about problems that they have experienced. The group may then be able to help solve problems and identify better alternatives. Such reporting back can be structured as oral or written homework as well.

The entire program should be viewed as a process of *planned successive approximations.* Usually, participants will not immediately achieve mastery of every skill or use skills learned in the most effective and consistent ways. Learning is developmental and progressive, so progress along the way should be richly recognized. As always, recognition should be genuine and offered for real progress rather than an artificial, mechanical exercise.

The Skills Education Sequence

Although, as always, programming needs to be adapted to the local situation and the individuals participating, the following (adapted from Rose, 1998) is the general sequence used in skills education:

1. Orientation to the process to be used in the skills education group (including reminders at each session of group purpose, rules, and process).
2. Identification of the particular skill to be rehearsed, with discussion of how and when it may be useful to those present.
3. Modeling (demonstration) of the skill to be learned or refined.
4. Rehearsal (practice) of the skill by participants.
5. Coaching during the rehearsal and feedback from leader and other members after it is complete. Both coaching and feedback should

include recognition for positive actions. In addition, those observing should identify refinements that the person might try. Suggesting (and in some cases modeling) refinements is not the same thing as criticizing "errors"; suggestions move the participant toward improvement, whereas criticism does not provide guidance about what to do, only about what not to do.

6. Another round of rehearsal to experiment with suggested changes, followed by additional cycles of feedback and practice as needed and time allows.

7. Discussion of plans to experiment with the skill outside the group.

Observing others go through this sequence is a major source of learning, complementing learning by rehearsing oneself. All members, however, should have opportunities to rehearse. In a few cases, a young person may strongly prefer to watch for a while before becoming involved in a role play; this preference should be honored, but the person should be given an opportunity to participate later. In addition, participation can be shaped gradually during the feedback process. The following is an example:

> Sarah, a member of the group, has been observing another (Joyce) being pressured to drink in a role play. Sarah might suggest, "You could say that you really don't want to do that right now." The group leader can then say something like, "Good! So if Jamie were to say to Joyce, 'Here, take a drink,' Joyce could say, 'I really . . .'" (turning and pointing to Sarah). Usually, Sarah will at that point repeat, "I really don't want that right now."

As Rose (1998) points out, not all modeling needs to involve role-playing, although this is a primary technique. Discussions of how to handle situations effectively can bring up additional ideas, and as their assignments, group members can watch how other people handle tough situations and report on both useful tactics and those that do not work well. These steps can expand the universe of possible skills.

Although modeling/rehearsal/role-playing is a central technique, it should not be viewed as the only avenue for skills training. Some life skills are best learned through other processes than modeling and rehearsal, often through experimentation in the young person's world. Some skills, for example, "finding a passion" or "honoring diversity," are likely to require other procedures, such as reinforcer sampling (i.e., trying new possibilities to see if they are rewarding) or critiquing of videotaped events. "Skills," in other words, often go beyond simply learning what to say under particular circumstances and involve broader repertoires.

Moving toward Leadership

Once young people have at least made a beginning in learning a particular skill, they can often help others use that skill, thus moving toward leadership. Young people can relatively easily identify actions that they could take to encourage others to act more respectfully, for example, or to act more assertively. Friends can frequently find ways to help others say "no" to inappropriate demands or pressures, and they can model moral decision making as well. The moral development literature suggests that doing so may help those observing achieve new developmental cusps (Goldstein et al., 1998). Planned role plays can include situations in which the person is asked to help others act in positive ways, or at least to move them away from destructive actions. (Suggestions for possible ways to include leadership behaviors are included in the discussions of each skill area in the following.)

Demonstrating Enthusiasm and Commitment

Twenty-five years ago, the author had contact with an outstanding substance abuse and violence prevention program organized and led by a young, dynamic social worker who emphasized skills education, values clarification, and service. The leader very clearly loved and was loved by the youth she was working with; the level of authentic affection, humor, and energy present was palpable. The written manual for the program was well done, but relatively standard. What was different was the tremendous enthusiasm generated, the result of extremely high levels of personal respect, recognition, and, yes, shared power. The young social worker who led the group gave so much emotionally that participating youth were inspired to do so as well. There is simply no substitute for this level of leadership, which guided the group to exceptional levels of exchange and communication. Without such energy and authenticity in the leader, no amount of brilliant programming will change behavior.

174

Basic Life and Leadership Skills

There are many, many valuable life skills that could be included in a life and leadership skills education program. Given the importance of focus and overlearning, however, the *PEACE POWER* strategy emphasizes eight skill areas, eight critical repertoires, that can be valuable in supporting a culture of nonviolent empowerment (Figure 18).

This wheel roughly maps onto the *PEACE POWER* wheel. Skills in the upper quadrant of Figure 18 can contribute to increasingly high levels of recognition, for example, while those in the right quadrant can

Figure 18

Life and leadership skills.

contribute to high levels of respectful action. (The correspondence is not perfect; skills shown in many cases can contribute to a *PEACE POWER* culture in many ways.)

Finding a Passion

Both theory and empirical data indicate that youth who are deeply immersed in positive activities are at reduced risk for many problems, including violence, substance abuse, and mental health issues. Behavioral science has discovered a mathematical law that is nearly as precise, and perhaps even more useful, than Einstein's "$E=mc^2$." This is called the "matching law" (McDowell, 1988). Although there are slightly more precise ways to state this law using complex mathematics, the basic equation for the matching law is $B = kr/(r+r_e)$. This formula may look complicated at first glance, but it really is not; further, it is worth the limited effort required to understand it. B here is the rate of behavior. The equation states that the rate of behavior can be predicted if the level of reward for that behavior (r) and the total amount of other rewards available for other behavior at this particular time and place (r_e) are known. (k is a constant and is not a matter of concern here.) The results of this formula are shown on the graph in Figure 19.

As seen on the graph, if few rewards are available for prosocial behavior, the level of problem behavior is high; if a medium level of rewards is available, the rate of problem behavior drops significantly; and in cases where very rich alternatives exist, the rate of problem behavior is very low. (Of course, only if the person has the skills to access the reward is it "available.") This equation accounts for over 90% of the variation in even complex social behavior like conversation—people spend proportionally more time with those whose company is very enjoyable, for example (McDowell, 1988). The equation also applies to academic behavior and to problem behaviors like aggression. (Aggression is rewarding for many people, especially those for whom it has "worked" socially.)

Therefore, a primary way to reduce problem behavior (B) is to increase other available rewards.

Perhaps the most important and practical application of the matching law is that someone who "finds a passion" in life often devotes much less energy to problem behavior. Youth who discover something else very rewarding are less likely to spend much time engaged in antisocial behavior. This "something else" may be a job, a sport, music, a deep relationship, or any of an unlimited range of other behaviors. It is es-

Figure 19

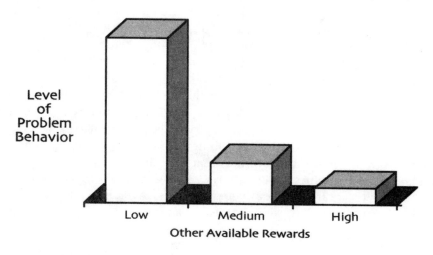

Higher rates of reward for prosocial behavior produce lower rates of problem behavior.

sential, though, that the activity be *genuinely* rewarding for the individual; often, the only way to find the appropriate activity is to experiment. Youth often can, with some help, come up with a rich range of ideas for themselves and for each other. They may need considerable encouragement, models of people who love what they are doing, and opportunities to try new activities until something "clicks." This can be done through individual consultation or in small groups—quite small groups may be the most useful here.

Many activities can be helpful. Trips, tours, visits by persons deeply involved in almost any activity—all of these can expose youth to possibilities that they may never have thought about, seen, or even known about before. (Career exploration groups and service opportunity groups are examples.) Group discussions in which youth have an opportunity to share what they love doing or think they might enjoy doing, to dream, and to explore new possibilities can be an important core of a leadership skills training program. Brainstorming that does not rule out consideration of even "crazy" notions (so long as they are prosocial!) can be really helpful; many individuals respond to activities that, to others, may appear to be peculiar. Ultimately, the goal is to help all young people identify one or preferably a number of positive and rewarding activities toward which they can direct their energy and for which they can receive recognition—from themselves as well as from others.

As do all of the skills addressed here, activities that support the effort to find a passion also offer youth opportunities for leadership; in this case, for example, they can help each other choose a rewarding activity. Youth who have a good sense of each other and a creative bent can work with peers struggling to find anything that they might really enjoy. Youth who are hesitant to try something new may benefit from having others accompany them. In the group, structuring role plays related to responding when a peer says, "there's nothing to do" can give young people opportunities to suggest to others that they dive into life and experiment. These activities should always be viewed as experimental; some things will capture and hold young people's attention, and some will not. This is to be expected. Constructing an enriched and enriching life is a lifelong experiment.

Envisioning a Path

One of the most crucial of life and leadership skills for youth involves the ability to identify goals toward which they want to work and then to envision the steps needed to get them from where they are to where they want to go. Goals may include interpersonal goals (e.g., making a friend or resolving a conflict), vocational goals, or the achievement of a "passion," as described in the previous section. According to research conducted by Shure (1999), the author of a well-validated curriculum for reducing antisocial behavior (*I Can Problem Solve*; Shure, 1992), one crucial aspect of problem solving is learning "means-end" thinking, being able to realistically describe how to reach a goal in a step-by-step manner. Shure indicates also that it is useful to be able to identify possible obstacles to reaching a goal and to learn the patience needed to accept a gradual process.

The notion of "envisioning" can be used literally in work with small groups of young people or with individuals. The general process includes the following steps:

- Clarifying a goal, putting it into words
- Identifying differences between the current situation and the goal situation

- Drawing a "time line" or, perhaps better, a curving path on a large sheet of paper, blackboard, etc., with the current situation on one end and the goal on the other
- Identifying steps along the way and noting those steps on the time line
- Noting on the time line points where obstacles might come up
- Making brief notes about how to address those obstacles, if necessary
- Discussing how long each step might take
- Identifying supporters for taking those steps, as it is initially difficult for many youth to sustain long processes without social support
- Making a plan to physically trace progress along the path—a form of self-monitoring.

Actually drawing the process of reaching a goal is likely to make it clearer for youth than talking about it in abstract terms. Discussion should keep returning to "why" this process is being followed, with reminders to those involved of the goal, the end to be achieved. This process can be used as a progressive learning experience, following these steps:

- A leader or teacher can lead a small-group exercise, first identifying a hypothetical goal (e.g., someone wanting to become a professional basketball player), and taking the group through the process, actually drawing out the path with markers or chalk.
- Actual goals of some of the youth participating can be identified, and the same process used to trace out a path, beginning with simple goals that can be achieved in a few days or a few weeks.
- One of the youth can then take over as leader and trace out one or more possible paths for a new goal of one or more members. (There is a movement here from life skills for oneself toward leadership skills.)

The same process and the same language (e.g., What path could you take to get there?) can be used in advising individuals. Discussing and rehearsing how the process might be used in informal conversations with friends can increase generalization to young people's day-to-day lives. In addition, occasional formal booster sessions may be helpful, in which the process is practiced again with new or more challenging situations (e.g., becoming a teacher).

Asserting Oneself

Assertiveness involves learning to speak with power in a way that maintains respect for everyone, rather than passively giving up power or aggressively demanding one's own way (Alberti, 1977; Rakos, 1991). Learning to act assertively means learning to speak and act in ways that are most likely to influence others positively, in ways that are honest and authentic. Assertive skills are best learned through modeling and practice, using role plays that are realistic reflections of young people's life situations. Some youth are already skillful at handling certain situations, and others can then learn from them. It is not enough to just discuss or give examples of these skills; the research indicates people actually need to practice the skills to be prepared to use them when necessary (Rakos, 1991).

Assertiveness training can teach youth new skills that they can use when a potential conflict situation arises. The goal is to learn to become assertive (powerful) rather than aggressive (demanding). The general procedures for this kind of assertiveness training are the same as those for other skills education:

1. Working with a small group (or occasionally an individual), label and describe the skill to be practiced (one at a time).
2. Discuss situations where and when the skill might be useful.
3. Demonstrate (model) the use of the skill.
4. Have young people role-play common situations from their lives in which the skills may be useful, and work together in the group to develop better and better responses to high-risk or provocative situations, as well as a peer culture supporting this approach.
5. Discuss in detail how these skills may be applied in participants' daily lives.

It is always best if participants develop many of the scenarios, so they seem as realistic as possible. Not only the words used but also tone of voice and nonverbal performance are important. The following are among the assertive skills that can be learned and strengthened by means of these procedures:

- Using "I" statements (e.g., I want . . ., I would like . . ., I feel . . .), which are assertive, rather than "you" statements, which are often experienced as blaming

- Making requests rather than demands
- Listening to what the other person says and repeating it to show real attention
- Admitting mistakes when one is wrong or has hurt someone—this takes real courage
- Refusing unreasonable requests, offers (e.g., to use drugs), and demands (to become involved in gang activities) in ways that are not likely to provoke the other party
- Letting other people save face
- Making honest, positive statements to others (recognizing their contributions and successes).

Although acting in all of these ways can provide useful modeling for other youth (an important dimension of leadership), an additional set of assertive skills involves redirecting peer groups, for example, when some youth are behaving in a bullying or threatening manner. Common approaches in this case are redirecting the group toward different activities in ways that allow youth to save face ("Aw, it's not worth it. Come on, let's go to the mall . . ."), distracting the attention of the group, and introducing humor to lighten the mood at critical moments. There are no standard approaches that always work under such circumstances, which is why progressive refinement using role play can be so powerful. One other important related skill is meeting privately with someone involved in problem behavior (e.g., drinking or hazing), and sincerely asking that person to stop. This is an advanced, but very critical, assertive behavior.

Honoring Diversity

One of the areas that causes particular difficulty among both young people and adults and that contributes to significant amounts of violence is bias—racism, sexism, homophobia, and other prejudices. Contemporary youth need to learn how to deal respectfully with people who are different from themselves, how to appreciate and celebrate diversity, how to recognize and refuse to participate in hate and oppression, and how to redirect others away from such participation. Many schools and organizations already have significant multicultural curricular materials and may also provide intercultural activities. All such activities are consistent with the *PEACE POWER* strategy. The ideas suggested for *PEACE POWER* programs are simply a beginning; there are many creative approaches that a community, organization, or school can initiate to increase the extent to which youth talk about and honor diversity. This is a prime area for shared power, in which members of different communities and cultures can contribute to planning.

Group or class activities related to diversity are a useful start. Members of a youth group can design a project in which they explore their own and each other's cultural heritage. One way to do this is to give an assignment to dyads, who study the similarities and differences in their two cultures together as part of regular assignments or group activities and then report back to the group. Assignments to interview family members, neighbors, persons at community centers, and so forth, can also be valuable.

In addition, the larger community can offer many resources that expand attention to cultural and other forms of diversity. The following are just a few examples:

- Schools and organizations can invite persons who are members of and knowledgeable about different cultures to visit and share their lives and experiences.
- Trips to ethnic events and communities to broaden exposure and curiosity can often be included in regular programming.
- An organization can plan and conduct a community holiday celebration, in which youth, families, and other community members share holiday traditions (e.g., Christmas, Kwanzaa, Hanukah), including food, music, celebrations, and deeper meanings. Even a simple multicultural potluck dinner can be a starting point.

Many of these activities are simply starting points, because a culture is not primarily food and entertainment. Subsequent activities should explore values and experiences among groups, with clear-eyed recognition of historical and current oppression and its wide-ranging effects on all. Although appreciating and honoring differences in cultures, religions, and lifestyles are extremely valuable, it is also important that youth learn about hate and oppression and make personal decisions about refusing to tolerate or participate in them. This can be a difficult area to open up, so it is useful to have some well-prepared materials available.

One excellent source for such materials is the Southern Poverty Law Center (see note 8). They offer a free subscription to the magazine *Teaching Tolerance* to educators and also can provide a free video-and-book kit (*The Shadow of Hate*) and other related curriculum materials. The Center also offers small grants to educators with new and creative ideas in this area. Beginning with such materials, youth can develop and expand their own projects to call attention to and combat hate and oppression.

Knowing One's Power

The *PEACE POWER* strategy begins with the premise that every young person has gifts, strengths, and talents on which he or she can construct a fulfilling life and has something truly valuable to contribute to the collective. As noted earlier, power is potentially unlimited; shared power is not a win–lose proposition. Many young people, however, have not yet "found" or "created" their power—they do not know what they have to contribute or how to make a contribution. Developmentally, one task for adolescents is to find, refine, and create their own power in this sense. Life and leadership skills groups offer a context for this work.

The goal in a *PEACE POWER* culture is that every young person can answer the question, What am I contributing to the community?, and every teacher, parent, or professional can answer the question, What does (young person's name) contribute? Reaching this point requires multiple iterations of (1) honest dialogue directed at identifying young people's gifts and potential contributions, as well as ways to learn additional skills that will increase their power; (2) opportunities for youth to test their power in collective activities; and (3) reflections on the experience. This is, perhaps, the most challenging group work of any—requiring real honesty, respect, and recognition. Helping youth find and create their power is also one of the most important contributions that adults can make, because it provides young people with meaning and recognition that go beyond egotism.

Choices and Consequences

Another critical developmental task for young people is learning to make decisions, to make choices, based on the short-term and long-term consequences of the alternative choices available. Many aggressive youth, in particular, tend to respond impulsively to immediate conditions, without consideration of longer term consequences. Choices and Consequences is an approach for helping students learn more effective problem-solving repertoires. The key steps in Choices and Consequences are the following (the words in all caps may be posted as reminders of the steps during skills training):

1. In a challenging situation, stop and realize that there are choices (multiple options). This is often a new way of thinking for youth (STOP).
2. Identify all possible choices (CHOICES).
3. Examine the *short-term* and *long-term*, *positive* and *negative* consequences of each choice (CONSEQUENCES).
4. Act based on the consequences (ACT). (It may not be realistic to ask youth to make a final decision immediately in many cases; they may need time to weigh the consequences for themselves.)

These are not easy repertoires for young people (and many adults) to learn, and they require extensive practice. In particular, recognizing consequences is not by itself enough; acting based on those consequences (Step 4) is a surprisingly advanced developmental cusp with which many youth struggle.

One useful tool is the choices and consequences matrix drawn on large sheets of newsprint or a chalkboard (Figure 20). In a small group, youth can be asked to complete a matrix for several typical problems. The idea is first to identify at least several options and then to complete the other cells in the chart as well as possible. Brainstorming in which no choices are immediately ruled out (e.g., "well, I could just quit school") and including some humorous choices may be useful to loosen up thinking. It should be clear, however, that this is an important exercise. In using this matrix, the leader should begin by offering one or two examples, like the following, then ask youth in the group to develop their own:

- Your boyfriend (girlfriend) says that he (she) wants to break up with you, but you don't want to do this. What are your choices, and what might the consequences of each be?
- You are visiting a friend's house, and his father is very drunk. The father threatens you. What are your choices, and what might the consequences of each be?
- You are at a store with a friend. She asks you to stand guard for her while she shoplifts a piece of clothing. What are your choices, and what might the consequences of each be?

184

Figure 20

Choice	Positive Short-term Consequences	Negative Short-term Consequences	Positive Long-term Consequences	Negative Long-term Consequences
1.				
2.				
3.				
4.				
5.				
6.				
7.				
8.				

Choices and consequences matrix.

This matrix can be useful whenever a young person has a decision to make; counselors and teachers may find it helpful to keep some blank forms available for use at such times.

After using the matrix a few times, students are ready to move to the next, more challenging step, which is to role-play simulated situations like those listed and then real situations. The leader can model real decisions that he or she has made or is making (being careful not to do this in a self-absorbed manner—"it's not about me"). In discussion, it may be useful to ask students about people that they themselves know who have made poor choices—what other choices there might have been and how the consequences may have been different.

In helping others to elaborate choices and consequences matrices, young people are learning a valuable leadership skill—which they may generalize into their everyday life. This is even more likely if youth are asked to experiment with these new skills and report about times that they have used them. In a follow-up session, young people can be asked individually to complete a matrix for a decision that they have made in the last few days (whether or not they made a good choice and acted on it); this may encourage generalization.

Defusing Anger

Skills for defusing anger, in combination with the learning of prosocial skills, have in a number of studies substantially reduced the rate of aggressive incidents and recidivism among the most difficult populations (see Nugent et al., 1998, for a brief review). Programs for defusing anger emphasize learning and extensive practice of a few simple skills, along with the provision of social and other rewards for using them. Although there are a number of somewhat different anger management programs available, the core repertoires are essentially similar. One crucial factor common to all of these programs is extensive practice under realistic conditions. On the other hand, the available data suggest that without the larger structure of rewards and recognition provided by the *PEACE POWER* strategy, teaching anger management skills is a relatively weak intervention (DeJong, Spiro, Wilson-Brewer, Vince-Whitman, & Prothrow-Stith, n.d.; Reiss & Roth, 1993).

There are four key sets of skills required to cope with potentially anger-producing situations: (1) avoidance skills, (2) physical defusing, (3) self-talk, and (4) defusing of others.

Avoidance Skills. The first skill is primarily preventive: avoiding high-risk situations to the extent possible. Training of these skills begins with the identification, with the youth involved, of the kinds of situations in which they may encounter potential provocations. Next, the group discuss and practice avoiding high-risk locations, ignoring provocations that can reasonably be ignored, and using distraction and attention refocusing in potentially provocative situations.

Physical Defusing. The second set of skills critical to defusing anger are those of recognizing and reducing the physiological arousal characteristic of anger. Youth first learn to identify the physiological signs of anger, from sweating and shaking to muscle tightness. This is important, because these experiences will then become cues for the new physical defusing skills.

One useful physical defusing skill is deep muscle relaxation that once learned can be cued with a simple self-instruction like "relax." Learning deep muscle relaxation requires several practice sessions in which youth close their eyes while the leader gradually directs them to move through the major muscle groups of the body, in each case first tensing the muscles about halfway, then letting go of the tension (any medical problems should be taken into account before using this procedure). Instructions begin with the leader saying in a slow and calming voice, using long pauses, something like the following:

> Now just settle back, close your eyes and relax . . . breathe slowly and evenly . . . even a bit slower . . . good . . . Now turn your attention to your right hand . . . make a fist, tensing your hand about halfway, and hold the tension . . . just notice the tension in your hand . . . hold it . . . and now slowly relax your hand . . . just let go . . . further . . . further . . . until your hand feels very, very relaxed . . . . Now turn your attention to your left hand . . . .

Similar instructions are given as the youth tenses and relaxes one set of major muscles after another. One useful sequence is as follows:

- Right hand (clench, hold, and release)
- Left hand (clench, hold, and release)
- Lower arms (push on chairs, hold, and release)
- Upper arms (tense arms bringing fists near shoulders, hold, and release)
- Feet (push toes into floor, hold, and release)
- Calves (lift toes, hold, and release)
- Upper legs (tense, hold, and release)
- Stomach (suck in, hold, and release)
- Chest (stick out, hold, and release)
- Back (arch, hold, and release)
- Shoulders (lift toward ears, hold, and release)
- Neck (push chin into chest, hold, and release)
- Face (tense by grimacing, hold, and release).

An alternative, more rapid approach to learning relaxation is the "relaxation response" (Benson, 1975). This procedure again requires several practice sessions, after which again a simple self-instruction like "relax" or "defuse" can bring on the relaxed state. The leader explains the procedure as follows:

- Sit in a quiet, comfortable position, and close your eyes.
- Slow your breathing.
- Each time you breathe out, repeat the word "relax," "defuse," or "peace" (or something else that works for the individual) silently.
- Continue the procedure for 10 to 20 minutes.

Once the young people have reached a very relaxed state using either of these procedures, they should repeat the key word they are using (i.e., "defuse," "relax") to themselves in a slow, relaxed way, while really paying attention to what being relaxed feels like. As a next step, they can then practice getting back into that relaxed state quickly while simply saying the word "defuse" to themselves. Then they can use this procedure when needed.

A final alternative is to select and practice one of several simple emergency relaxation exercises, like taking three very slow, very deep breaths, or noticing the tension in one's shoulders and focusing attention on letting it melt away. Some youth will be quite creative about identifying approaches that will work for them, once they begin to notice the differences between the physical experiences involved in anger and arousal, and those associated with calm control.

Self-Talk. When faced with a provocation, many people respond cognitively or verbally with self-talk (often covert). They say things like, "I can't let him get away with that!" or "She is disrespecting me—she can't do that!" Alternative kinds of self-talk are one step toward the goal of "nonprovocability," because it is not what someone else does that makes a person angry. Rather, our own reactions to someone else's actions are the root of our anger. No one else can "make" a person angry—we make ourselves angry by what we tell ourselves (Ellis & Dryden, 1997).

Each youth needs to identify several messages that he or she can say in self-talk when faced with a provocation, for example:

- "Defuse . . . "
- "Just stay cool . . . "
- "I can deal with this . . . "
- "I won't let him get to me . . . "
- "I'm doing fine, just stay with it . . . " (self-reinforcement)

- "This will be over soon . . . "
- "Let it go—this is not my problem"
- "I'm in control if I stay cool."

Once each youth has identified messages likely to be useful for himself or herself, the next step is to role-play using new self-talk out loud, followed by subvocal practice.

Defusing Others. Best learned *after* the self-management repertoires are the defusing skills involved in calming others, especially peers. The core skills include the following, all of which are best learned by discussion, modeling, and role-playing:

- Modeling calmness
- Encouraging talking (as an alternative to physical expression of frustration and anger)
- Listening calmly and nondefensively
- Expressing hope for resolution
- Helping save face (e.g., by acknowledging that the other is partly right)
- Assisting in the identification of options and choices (likely to be effective only *after* the other steps—modeling calmness, encouraging talking, etc.)

As usual in a *PEACE POWER* environment, everyone involved should use common language (e.g., "defuse anger"), so this becomes a natural part of the social environment within which youth live. Other environmental prompts—posters, contests, pencils, and t-shirts, for example—can repeat and reinforce this language. Drawn from marketing research, these strategies can be used to encourage defusing and other positive coping behaviors.

Recruiting Mentors

Among the better established approaches for helping youth through the challenges of childhood and adolescence is the use of mentors (Grossman & Garry, 1997). Big Brothers/Big Sisters, for example, is a longstanding program that has been identified as a Blueprint Program nationally. Adequate numbers of formal mentors are often difficult to recruit, however. Therefore, it can be valuable to help youth learn the skills necessary to recruit their own mentors, who may sometimes function in informal and limited, but still very beneficial ways. Adults and older youth can often function as "wise advisors" if given the opportunity (Embry, Flannery, Vazsonyi, Powell, & Atha, 1996), and there appear to be many cases in which young people have sought out adults or older youth from whom they can learn and who can concurrently function as role models for youth.

Many violence prevention programs may wish to establish and support formal, structured mentoring programs. Even if they do not, there are at least three advantages to teaching youth in life and leadership skills groups how to recruit mentors. First, young people need to be able to identify mentors who can be helpful in particular areas. For example, peers may be very helpful in dealing with problems in relating to other young people, but adult advisors are usually required to sort out issues like an unplanned pregnancy. Second, youth often say it is difficult to ask for help. They may require practice to reduce their anxiety about turning to someone else for help. Third, adults in the environment can benefit from opportunities to reflect on what they can do to help as mentors and advisors.

Although determining whether to seek a mentor may not seem to be a very difficult question, actually talking about it can be critical. This initial conversation begins to normalize the idea of turning to a teacher, or a relative, or someone associated with a church. Even apparently very "forward" youth may be surprisingly shy about turning to an adult for help, so it is useful for them to think about and discuss this beforehand. In addition, youth can discuss specifically who they may approach for particular kinds of challenging situations in life skills groups. Such discussion functions as "practice" for times of need. Discussions may also be helpful in identifying strategies for locating mentors in areas of career or recreational interest. Direct requests and polite persistence are often important components of establishing such connections.

Many youth find it very difficult actually to approach an adult and ask for help. This skill is best learned through role plays, beginning with relatively easy situations and moving to more challenging ones. For example, youth in a small life and leadership skills group may begin practice by asking a teacher for help with difficult schoolwork, then move to selecting someone to talk to about problems balancing school and work, or about dropping out of school. For the more difficult issues, the group may first role-play asking a friend who to talk to, then suggesting to a friend that he or she talk to an adult or other mentor, and finally actually approaching the adult, including practice in "what to say first"—for example, "Excuse me, Ms. ___, could I talk to you about something serious?" Similarly, role-playing may be helpful in preparing youth for approaching, say, a teacher who is known to be an expert in woodworking or backpacking, if these are areas that the young person is interested in learning. Exercising patience may be another skill that must be shaped and encouraged in such situations, because the adult may first simply suggest reading or other activities related to the area, but may be willing to become more actively involved with sustained interest. Youth also, in the course of these role plays, practice encouraging each other to identify and recruit mentors, yet another valuable leadership skill.

It can be helpful to organize discussions among the adults that youth come into contact with about the satisfactions and responsibilities of acting as mentors and wise advisors. Adults do not always stop to think about how important what they say may be to young people or about how hard they may be to approach. It does not hurt to think through together some of the advice that adults sometimes give. Discussion about the importance of helping young people examine choices and consequences, as well as about making it easy for them to approach adults, may be particularly useful.

Conclusion

Group work has long been recognized as a powerful modality for work with youth, and there is considerable research and experiential support for the utility of such groups for learning and practicing life skills. Although such groups may be particularly important to youth who have very few life and leadership skills, youth who do have those skills already may also benefit from the opportunities to discuss and practice ways that they can lead others to more effective action. In most systems, there are also a handful of young people who are quite involved in antisocial activities and only very slightly involved in prosocial behavior. These individuals are likely to be less affected by organizational or community *PEACE POWER* efforts unless they receive more intensive attention. The material in the next chapter provides guidance for such attention.

9

Intensive *PEACE POWER* Work with High-Risk Youth

Embry and Flannery (1999) argue persuasively that the distinction often drawn between violence prevention and intervention is nonproductive and problematic. The same basic strategies (e.g., increasing rates of recognition and respect) apply to achieving both goals—the difference is really only one of dose level. In addition, an integrated program is more powerful and can avoid the damage associated with labeling some youth as "problems" who require repair ("therapy"), while others need only something considered enhancement. Reframing "treatment" or "intervention" as simply more intensive *PEACE POWER* involvement, a normalization strategy, helps avoid these issues. All efforts continue to be directed toward constructing a single culture of nonviolent empowerment in which everyone participates. Generalization to the natural environment outside of the counseling situation is also more likely if the same language and prompts are used in both. Intensive *PEACE POWER* support, therefore, is grounded in the same four core practices as the rest of the strategy.

This chapter outlines a number of data-based procedures for such intensive services for the small number of youth who may require such intensity. The material that follows sketches possible approaches for providing more intensive support for high-risk youth, organized according to each of the core *PEACE POWER* practices; some, of course, can contribute to more than one practice concurrently. Intensive services require the ongoing involvement of skilled professionals (e.g., social workers, counselors, child care workers) for program design, as well as implementation of those plans with the necessary integrity. Frequent, even daily or hourly, contact may be required initially; intensity of involvement can be faded over time.

The core *PEACE POWER* practices can serve as the organizing principle for this intensive work. In this work, however, the emphasis is on variations not with whole cultures but with individuals who are often quite isolated from those cultures. The goal of intensive *PEACE POWER* work is to engage those isolated young people as active, productive members of peer, school, and other community cultures. Even for gang-involved youth, there is evidence that constructing positive community connections and using shared power may be effective in helping them to successfully move out of the deviant peer group. Research cited by Henggeler and colleagues indicates, for example, that most gang-involved youth remain in the gang culture only for limited periods and can form positive peer associations after leaving (Henggeler, Schoenwald, Borduin, Rowland, & Cunningham, 1998).

Increasing Experiences of Recognition and Reward

The most crucial component in intensive *PEACE POWER*, consistent with the rest of the strategy, is ensuring that young people who are at high risk for violence and coercion ultimately receive high levels of recognition and reward for prosocial behavior. This is, for most such youth, very uncommon. They may associate even the apparent praise that they have received with manipulation and predatory intentions (Embry & Flannery, 1999), so learning to recognize and accept recognition may be an important objective. (Written recognition, being less familiar, can be useful here.) Many of these young people also have come to associate personnel of youth-serving organizations and schools with punishment, threats, and reprimands. Overcoming such history will require very powerful and consistent experiences of reward and recognition.

Much more than with other youth, it may be necessary to offer additional and tangible rewards to high-risk youth and to associate those rewards with praise and natural reinforcers so that over time the latter are potentiated. Many high-risk youth have experienced a very narrow range of reinforcers and have limited behaviors for producing them. Reinforcer sampling and personal coaching to encourage exposure to new possibilities, as well as the kinds of activities discussed in chapter 8 (see above under "Finding a Passion"), can be critical here. Someone must work with the young person to identify possible prosocial ways to access experiences and items that the youth really values. Without appropriate reinforcers, behavior change will inevitably be minimal and short-lived.

Self-management, contracting, and point systems may all be useful tools for increasing access to recognition and reward. The goals of *self-management*, which are discussed in the following section, include increasing respectful behavior, accessing recognition and reward, and acting with respect; these goals are tightly intertwined in intensive *PEACE POWER* work. *Contracting* is a very useful tool with preadolescents and adolescents, so long as it is based on "clean contracts" to which the young person freely assents (Mattaini, 1999). Many so-called contracts are actually statements of the punishments that will be used if a young person violates a rule established by someone else; not surprisingly, such contracts typically produce only weak effects. By contrast, if a young person has a real voice in determining what behaviors are desirable; what positive, desirable consequences will follow positive behaviors; and what negative consequences will occur if positive behavior does not happen, contracts can be very powerful. Clearly spelled out contracts can reduce conflicts about what was agreed, and enforcement can usually be consistent with only minimal emotional side effects. The elements of effective contracting are well-established (Kazdin, 1994):

- Clear statements of what each party expects to gain;
- Specific description of the behaviors to be performed;
- Descriptions of the rewards (desired by the young person) to be earned and how they will be earned;
- Descriptions of sanctions for failing to honor the contract;
- A "bonus clause" for consistent compliance over a period of time;
- A plan for monitoring the behaviors involved and the consequences received; and
- Frequent and accessible opportunities for success and reward.

DeRisi and Butz (1975) offer excellent examples of clear and workable contracting.

Point systems can provide an extensive, precise, and flexible form of contracting. One advantage of point systems is that a young person can receive points for many behaviors, providing options and choices. Sanctions can involve small point fines, some of which the young person can earn back by practicing more positive behavior. Point systems can also be modified over time by adding new goals, removing those no longer needed, stretching out intervals between rewards as youth learn self-control over longer periods, and otherwise being shaped to fit the realities of changing situations.

In contracts and point systems, bonus clauses of one kind or another can often increase power. The arrangement used may be similar to a lottery. In addition to small regular rewards, larger rewards can be offered on an intermittent basis. Every 100 points earned, for example, might result in one ticket for a regular drawing for a new CD player, a dinner out with staff, or something else particularly valuable that cannot be offered every day, but can be every so often.

Increasing Respectful Action

To others in the youth's social environment, increasing respectful behavior is often regarded as a primary objective of intensive services. This is natural and reasonable. At the same time, it is important to remember that punishment or threat cannot effectively shape respectful action. Many adults pay little attention to their own behavior toward youth. For example, the author observed a male teacher in an alternative school "affectionately" punch a young man about 12 years old in the center of the chest with enough force for the sound to resonate down the hall and perhaps to leave a mark. The teacher, who did this in front of several witnesses, would have described his behavior as entirely innocent, but the message—establishing physical dominance—was clear.

Many young people have seldom observed respectful behavior. None of the procedures discussed in this section will be very effective in an atmosphere of disrespect and coercion, however; all will work far better in the context of relationships in which positive exchanges continually occur. Whatever procedures are used, the young person involved must be treated with respect, because disrespect will almost certainly be reciprocated—a counterproductive outcome. Of course, respectful action does not mean quiet compliance regardless of circumstances; appropriate assertion is one facet of acting with respect.

Contracting, Group Rewards, and Guided Self-Correction

Within a matrix of respect, a number of procedures can be useful for increasing respectful action. In addition to *proactive teaching* and *self-management*, which are described in detail later in this section, valuable tools include contracting, group rewards, and guided self-correction.

(Guided self-correction is discussed in chapter 10.) Adults can contract with young people for increasing periods of respectful action, with clear definitions of respectful and disrespectful behavior in the contract. Eventually, youth (and adults) can learn that respectful action produces the best outcomes for everyone. Immediate rewards may be required to increase a young person's experience with respectful behavior and its natural consequences, but discussion that helps to elaborate the connections should accompany the rewards.

Group rewards can also encourage respectful behavior. There are several possible variations. A leader of a small group of youth who are all receiving intensive services may offer a common reward if all group members are able to maintain positive behavior for a specified interval (e.g., an hour, a day, a week); intervals established should begin with a length of time that will be relatively easy and gradually be extended. Team-based rewards, in which two or more small teams "compete" to see which can go the longest with only positive behavior ratings, may be beneficial (Kazdin, 1994), but every team should be able to win if a certain level is achieved. In *consequence sharing* (Kazdin, 1994), all group members receive a payoff if the behavior of an individual reaches the established standard—the role of the others in such a case is to "help" in any way they can. Group rewards can be collaboratively designed with youth, and in some cases peer-administered rewards can also be useful. Discussion should accompany any of these options to ensure that they are implemented in respectful ways.

Proactive Teaching

Developed by Boys Town researchers and staff, proactive teaching is a simple, logical approach that may already be in use without being labeled as such, perhaps in partial and unstructured ways. Proactive teaching "is a way to prevent problems by telling students what to do and having them practice before they encounter a specific situation" (Davis, Nelson, & Gauger, 2000, p. 90). There are many variations of proactive teaching. For example, many high-risk youth experience problems at home or elsewhere that they bring with them to the program. A status check first thing in the morning demonstrates caring and offers opportunities to talk out issues before they bleed into the program day—often a valuable preventive. When specific types of behavior would help the young person manage his or her situation better, a structured proactive teaching process can be very effective. In this procedure, expectations are clarified and skills that may be required are learned. The five basic steps in proactive teaching are as follows:

1. Introducing the expected behavior (e.g., respectful assertion) and discussing what it involves and when it might be useful;
2. Discussing the reasons that using this skill can be useful, with emphasis on relatively immediate positive consequences;
3. Requesting acknowledgment (e.g., "Does that make sense to you?") and making sure the rationale is clear and appears reasonable to the young person;
4. Providing an opportunity to practice, either in a role play (e.g., "Let's try it—if I'm a friend of yours, and say, 'Hey, man, let's skip class,' and you don't want to do that, what could you say?"), or *in vivo* as the young person goes about his or her daily life (e.g., when the adult meets the student in the hallway, "Here we are by the stairs you guys often take outside when you skip class—what might you do instead when you're here and you're tempted to split?");
5. Providing recognition (and other rewards, if needed) for positive participation.

Proactive teaching of this kind is a preventive form of skills training, and the general training sequence is similar to that of other forms of such training. For example, if a young person receiving intensive *PEACE POWER* support has a history of struggling to control her anger, and if a particular time is likely to be stressful (say, a field trip or holiday period), some preparation and practice for the possible high-risk times may be very useful. Proactive teaching may also be useful for groups of students, for example, if a class is expecting a substitute ("guest") teacher or if problems often occur during a specific time of day.

Proactive teaching is a flexible strategy that requires little preparation. In cases where there are serious and longstanding problems, for example, if a young person is on-task very little of the time in class or often experiences problems in managing and defusing anger during recreational activities, a more structured and extremely powerful set of procedures known as self-management training may be indicated.

Self-Management Training

Self-management procedures have proved to be very powerful and consistently robust when used with youth to encourage prosocial behavior and decrease problem behavior (e.g., Ninness, Ellis, Miller, Baker, & Rutherford, 1995; Ninness, Fuerst, Rutherford, & Glenn, 1991). Even with quite disruptive youth, these procedures can rapidly and dramatically change behavior. Self-management training, therefore, should be regarded as among the best practices for providing intensive intervention with youth at high risk. Self-management procedures are, in fact, very useful for adults and other youth as well, because they help to structure and support actions that the person wants to take but finds difficult to pursue consistently. Exercise and nutrition programs, long-term projects, and other goals that require constant effort without much immediate payoff are prime targets for self-management.

The basic steps in self-management, whether for youth or adults, are as follows:

1. Establish the *goal* (e.g., being healthier).
2. *Pinpoint* actions that will contribute to reaching the goal (e.g., walk five miles at least four times a week).
3. *Track* the performance (in writing or on a graph). In some cases, these steps are all that is required, but this plan is quite similar to the infamous New Year's Resolution. As a result, for more difficult goals, a fourth step is usually needed.
4. Arrange *consequences* for taking or not taking the pinpointed actions—this is an active feedback mechanism. In many cases of self-management, regularly sharing data from Step 3 with someone else is an adequate consequence, but other procedures involving small rewards, small costs, or both are often needed to maintain consistency (Malott, 2000).

The *goal, pinpoint, track*, and *consequences* model is a generally useful paradigm for all forms of self-management.

Extensive work in self-management by youth has consistently demonstrated that teaching adolescents how to monitor their own behavior and rewarding them *both for accurate monitoring and for appropriate behavior* can produce dramatic changes (Young, West, Smith, & Morgan, 1991). For example, the graphs shown in Figure 21 from one of a series of similar single-case studies conducted with severely behaviorally disordered youth demonstrates typical results (Ninness et al., 1991): student behavior changed rapidly and relatively consistently when the program was initiated in the classroom (upper panel). When the program was extended to transitions between classes (lower panel), similar results appeared.

Figure 21

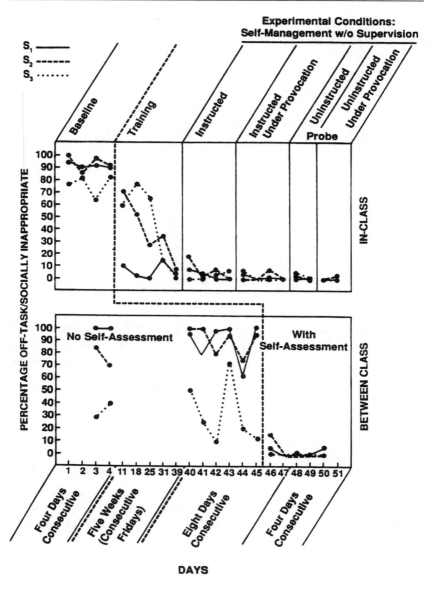

Percentage of off-task and socially inappropriate behavior across conditions of a study in which high-risk youth were trained in self-management skills, first in class, then for transitions between classes. Source: Reprinted with permission from Ninness, Fuerst, Rutherford, & Glenn, 1991.

The behaviors to be constructed involved both social skills like avoiding distractions from other students (e.g., waving them away without engaging) and respectfully accepting corrections from the teacher, as well as self-management skills like self-instruction and self-rating (e.g., on a scale of 1 to 4 for socially appropriate behavior). In the study conducted by Ninness and colleagues (1991), youth earned points based on teacher ratings of behavior and on their accuracy in ratings of their own behavior (i.e., within one point of teacher rating for the same period at initial levels, exact match for more advanced). Points were exchangeable for rewards and activities.

Students in this program progressed through four levels, beginning with assessments by student and teacher every 20 minutes and then moving gradually to assessments at lengthening intervals. Maintaining high point totals for a period of four weeks led to graduation to the next higher levels of privileges. Rewards and privileges (which should be designed in collaboration with the youth involved) in this study ranged from a choice of seats at lunch and an unaccompanied walk to the restroom, to extra computer use and placement in desired classrooms.

There are many ways to design a self-management program, so long as it meets certain basic requirements. First, the young person involved should be willing to try the program at least as an experiment to see if it may be helpful for him or her. Second, the rewards and privileges must not be too difficult to earn in the beginning, and the youth must value them. Third, the young person should receive points *both* for positive behavior and for accurately rating his or her own behavior, because self-assessment is a key skill for self-management. Fourth, the system should allow youth, as they learn to manage their own behavior under some circumstances, to earn even more valued rewards by progressing to a more challenging level (e.g., maintaining positive behavior for longer periods or in more difficult circumstances like during unstructured time). Fifth, very careful and consistent records are essential, and the young person involved should be able to see his or her progress on those records at any time. Finally, although more tangible rewards may be necessary for a period of time to help the student structure and manage his or her behavior, the program should provide high levels of authentic social recognition as well. At the highest level, the program can be faded so that the young person has continued access to positive privileges and experiences without tracking points, so long as satisfactory overall performance is maintained.

Procedures designed to provide intensive support should be creatively individualized to fit both the setting and the person involved. One creative variation is to videotape segments of classroom or other activities, then to sit down individually with the youth involved and review brief (e.g., 30-second) segments one at a time, and together to identify occurrences of appropriate behaviors and occurrences of inappropriate behavior (for which better alternatives can then be identified).

The core components of a student self-management program, then, are as follows:

- Teach and rehearse appropriate behavior.
- Teach self-monitoring and provide simple behavior rating forms.
- Graph the results.
- Reward both accurate self-monitoring and acceptable behavior as part of an ongoing system of positive structure, moving gradually from immediate, often somewhat artificial, rewards toward more delayed and natural reinforcers.

Self-management systems range from the simple to the complex. Self-management programs can be implemented at the level of a single student and can also be extended to groups of young people. For those who are implementing these procedures, exploration of more detailed literature and examples may be very helpful (see, e.g., Malott, 2000; Ninness et al., 1995; Ninness et al., 1991; Young et al., 1991).

Finding and Using One's Power to Contribute

Many youth who are involved with or at high risk for antisocial behavior, including coercion and violence, have very little awareness of any way to influence their worlds except through coercive power. Assisting them to find and create alternative forms of power is, therefore, crucial (see "Knowing One's Power," in chapter 8). Many of the activities discussed in chapter 5 can be used as part of an intensive plan; in particular, helping high-risk youth to take on leadership roles will dramatically shift their experiences and, ultimately, their actions. There are also several other procedures that may be especially valuable for this group of youth, including service learning, involvement in mentoring, and shadowing (all of which provide substantial opportunities for modeling and social learning processes).

The term *service learning* actually covers a range of activities, including those that students undertake as core parts of school curricula, those that are options within formal curricula, and those that are based in institutions and communities separate from formal education (Waterman, 1997). Learning to recognize and value one's talents and gifts through such processes fits very naturally into service activities. Particularly interesting are preliminary data suggesting that service learning activities can be differentially effective with high-risk youth. Blyth, Saito, and Berkas (1987) report that, in their pre-post study looking at youth involved in 10 service learning projects,

> [Y]outh who were most engaged in risk-taking behavior at Time 1 were more likely at Time 2 to see service class as less boring than regular classes and to believe that what they did contributed to the community. . . . Furthermore, youth at risk initially also showed differential changes over time in that they became more accepting of diversity and more engaged in academic tasks. . . . With respect to those youth who at Time 1 had higher levels of disengagement from school (e.g., skipping class, suspended) . . . the youth who were most disengaged became significantly more engaged than they were in both academic tasks and general learning. (p. 53)

These findings are encouraging. Some forms of service are probably more likely to produce positive outcomes than others. The literature suggests that such activities as tutoring younger children; working to improve housing for poor or older people; or helping with community improvement projects that produce visible, obvious change are often very motivating, while projects seen as busy work or janitorial may be less so (Waterman, 1997). Service learning certainly can also be viewed as overlapping with prevocational training, so long as the emphasis on contributing for the sake of the community as well as oneself remains.

Mentors who can expand the exposure of young people to adult roles and activities can be particularly useful for high-risk youth. Not surprisingly, individual youth who are moved into an adult environment often act very differently than they do when surrounded by peers who may encourage antisocial or immature behavior. High-risk youth may require more than the usual assistance and support for making such connections when they recruit their mentors (see chapter 8). The ideal situation is one in which an adult and a young person who share a common interest are paired, but this is not always (at least immediately) possible. Unlike younger children, adolescents are likely to engage over the long term only with an adult whose company they find rewarding. Adults and youth may, therefore, need to begin by sharing recreational experiences that both enjoy, while being encouraged to get to know each other.

A related option is shadowing. Young people can be sequentially linked for brief periods to adults involved in a range of activities, just to open their eyes to new possibilities. For example, youth can spend an afternoon with the mayor or other political figure, or with a business leader, or with a nurse, or with a telephone technician, or, in fact, with anyone who is making a productive contribution to the community. Those involved in community service are particularly good choices, because the purpose of these activities is to encourage youth to use their gifts to strengthen community. A long-term commitment may not be required here; rather, the procedure can be viewed as a form of reinforcer sampling.

Ideally, those serving as mentors or being shadowed should have something in common with the youth—for example, similarities in early life experience, race and ethnicity, and gender may be helpful in opening dialogue. Such similarities have been shown to increase the power of modeling (Bandura, 1986). Mentors and models linked with high-risk youth should receive specific training in the core PEACE POWER practices and language, including the importance of recognition and its use; honest, respectful communication; peacemaking; and, particularly important here, identification and discussion of the talents and gifts that they observe in the youth. The reason for this kind of program, after all, is to encourage youth to learn about and use their power.

In many communities, mentoring programs of some kind are already available. In those cases, it may make the most sense for people wishing to establish a PEACE POWER program to connect with the existing programs, rather than trying to invent new ones. In providing intensive PEACE POWER support, however, it is sometimes necessary to make very individualized arrangements. Consistent with shared power, individual youth can and should participate in planning and implementing mentoring activities, since they are likely to have the best sense of what may work for them. At the same time, because these experiences are likely to be very new for them, youth may need considerable encouragement and, in some cases, additional incentives to begin the process.

For example, some *PEACE POWER* projects offer modest stipends for cooperative involvement in these activities for a certain number of hours. All such activities should be presented and discussed as experiments, as it may take several tries to find connections that will be a good fit.

Making Peace

There are several ways to provide intensive support around making peace. One is through proactive teaching; another is through the standard five-step peacemaking tool and process, which can be extremely useful for work with high-risk youth (see chapter 6). Many high-risk youth particularly lack peacemaking repertoires, while other youth (and adults) have skills in this area, but simply need a structure (the five-step model) for using them. By contrast, high-risk youth may need considerable skills training to prepare them. Knowing this, proactive teaching is an obvious choice. The basic process, consistent with the proactive teaching process described earlier in this chapter, is as follows:

1. Introduce the skills involved in the five-step making peace model, and discuss when using them can be helpful.
2. Discuss the advantages of using this process, particularly how it can reduce negative consequences and produce immediate positive results.
3. Request acknowledgment (e.g., "Does that make sense to you?"), making sure that the rationale is clear and that the young person agrees at least to try it.
4. Provide opportunities to practice, by role-playing first each of the five steps individually then, as those are learned, the entire sequence.
5. Provide recognition and other rewards if needed for positive participation in the proactive teaching, as well as for using the process in real-world interactions.

Once this teaching has occurred, regular practice as issues arise in the setting and in "booster" role-playing sessions, if this appears necessary, can gradually refine the skills learned. Initially, first approximations (e.g., a willingness to listen or to respectfully state one's own thoughts) warrant recognition, because becoming very skilled in all five steps is a complex process that will take time. Strong recognition and extra rewards, if necessary, are appropriate for the first positive steps, because youth will not continue to use these behaviors unless they experience them as producing positive consequences.

Although many coercive and violent incidents do not begin with (and sometimes do not involve) out-of-control anger, many do, and high-risk youth often have particular trouble in defusing anger. The basic anger-defusing skills described in chapter 8 are very valuable for these young people, but they may also require more intensive training. For example, they may need 8 to 12 individual or group sessions focused on defusing skills, in contrast to the one or two sessions that a general program of life and leadership skills often includes. Overlearning, in which the new skills are learned to automaticity, is the best approach here. Because working to that level is demanding, extra rewards are likely to be required for active participation. Intensive programs may involve daily contact over a school semester, for example, and practice in defusing may be included once a week.

An even more intensive program that has strong empirical support for work with aggressive and violent youth is aggression replacement training (ART) as developed over several decades by Goldstein and colleagues (Goldstein, Glick, & Gibbs, 1998). Conducted in groups (one of the few situations in which it may be valuable to group youth involved in coercive behaviors together), ART is a multichannel strategy carried out over a period of weeks or months. Implementing ART is a professional function, requiring a trained social worker, counselor, or other professional not only with general expertise in group work, but also with specific expertise (through training or intensive study) in conducting an ART program. Finally, conferencing, discussed in detail in chapter 6, is a powerful intervention that should be regarded as a tool of choice in work with high-risk youth. Traditional disciplinary procedures usually are of only limited value for youth who, having experienced them over and over again for many years, have often become inured to their effects. In fact, many such youth find demonstrating their immunity to standard threats and punishments rewarding. Although the making peace tool can be very useful for minor conflicts, more powerful intervention is often necessary for major problems. The full conferencing model, definitely including parental figures and other supporters of each of those involved, should be regarded as best practice when repeated, serious incidents occur. The impact of experiencing the effects of one's behavior on parent, grandparent, sibling, close friends, and others important to the perpetrator is far more powerful than the disapproval of youth workers or school staff, and more likely to produce change. Similarly, the support of the networks of the youth involved is often required to ensure that agreements are kept and that steps toward reconciliation are taken and maintained.

Variations of the conferencing model may sometimes be needed. The standard model assumes one or more victims and one or more perpetrators, for example. In some cases, it may be inaccurate or impossible to determine whether each of multiple youth involved in an incident is a victim or a perpetrator. Determining the effects of the incident on each youth and their supporters and developing a plan for healing remain completely relevant under such circumstances, however. In other cases, the "victim" may be the school community, and representatives of that community should be included. In general, then, approaches for helping high-risk youth learn the skills for making peace are not qualitatively different than for anyone else, just, once again, more intensive.

Conclusion: Constructing an Individualized Plan

Planning intensive *PEACE POWER* support with an individual young person should ordinarily involve attention to all four of the core *PEACE POWER* practices. An adequate plan should include specific answers to all of these questions:

1. Recognition
   - What steps will be taken to identify really rewarding activities in which this person can participate?
   - What procedures will be used to ensure that positive actions are recognized?
2. Respect
   - What procedures will be used to proactively teach respectful and effective behavior repertoires?
   - What motivating procedures (e.g., recognition, incentives, self-management) will be used to encourage experimenting with those behavior repertoires?
3. Sharing power
   - What procedures will be used to help the young person identify current talents and gifts, and learn new ones?
   - What opportunities will be available to the young person to contribute, and what encouragement and incentives will be provided?

4. Making peace
- What procedures will be used to ensure that the young person knows and can use the steps involved in making peace?
- What motivating procedures will be used to encourage the young person to actually use the making peace procedures?

If all of these questions can be answered, the outlines of a reasonable plan will be clear; ongoing monitoring and evaluation will be essential, however, because most such plans require refinement and modification. Intensive *PEACE POWER* support, therefore, cannot be standardized. At least one skilled staff person will need to be continuously involved to implement the intensive support process with each young person in the context of a caring, respectful relationship.

Many high-risk youth experience challenges and stresses in many areas of life, and some may require help to increase their exposure to positive experiences and reduce their exposure to aversives across multiple domains, including in the family, in school, and in the community. The best researched approach for work with youth involved in serious antisocial behavior who require such support is *multisystemic treatment*, developed by Henggeler and colleagues (Henggeler et al., 1998; Mattaini, 1999). The approach has demonstrated substantial power for reducing delinquency, out-of-home placement, and recidivism, as well as for reintegrating youth into positive community systems. Multisystemic treatment is based on nine principles, reproduced in Table 8.

The focus in multisystemic treatment is constructional, emphasizing, as does the *PEACE POWER* strategy, the construction of networks that support positive behavior.

Brief strategic family therapy (BSFT; Robbins & Szapocznik, 2000) is an approach that has demonstrated effectiveness for work with Latino families and is among the best practices for work with that population. "The goal of BSFT is to improve youth behavior by:

- Improving family relationships that are presumed to be directly related to youth behavior problems.
- Improving relationships between the family and other important systems that influence the youth (e.g., schools, peers). (Robbins & Szapocznik, 2000, p. 3)

This approach combines elements of several existing family intervention models with multicultural effectiveness training, producing a cul-

Table 8. Multisystemic Treatment Principles

Principle 1: The primary purpose of assessment is to understand the fit between the identified problems and their broader systemic context.

Principle 2: Therapeutic contacts emphasize the positive and use systemic strengths as levers for change.

Principle 3: Interventions are designed to promote responsible behavior and decrease irresponsible behavior among family members.

Principle 4: Interventions are present-focused and action-oriented, targeting specific and well-defined problems.

Principle 5: Interventions target sequences of behavior within and between multiple systems that maintain the identified problems.

Principle 6: Interventions are developmentally appropriate and fit the developmental needs of the youth.

Principle 7: Interventions are designed to require daily or weekly effort by family members.

Principle 8: Intervention effectiveness is evaluated continuously from multiple perspectives with providers assuming accountability for overcoming barriers to successful outcomes.

Principle 9: Interventions are designed to promote treatment generalization and long-term maintenance of therapeutic change by empowering caregivers to address family members' needs across multiple systemic contexts.

Reprinted from Henggeler et al., 1998, used with permission.

turally specific approach for working with families that include youth involved in delinquent or antisocial behavior. Given its emphasis on constructing improved relationships, BSFT, like multisystemic treatment, can be highly congruent with *PEACE POWER*, and incorporated as part of intensive *PEACE POWER* services.

Intensive, constructive *PEACE POWER* support, or something very much like it, has the potential to bring youth who may be at high risk for perpetrating (and being victimized by) violence and coercion back into the larger community. It is dangerous for everyone to exclude and isolate very aggressive and threatening youth, since this may lead to escalating antisocial behavior. In addition, however, society ultimately cannot afford to lose the contributions of so many young people. Witness, for example, the enormous costs (financial and social) of incarcerating growing numbers. We don't know enough yet to effectively integrate everyone into society, but we can help many more than we currently do. The procedures discussed in this chapter can be a powerful beginning.

10

Environmental and Behavioral Supports for *PEACE POWER*

Beyond the basic *PEACE POWER* strategy, there are a number of other procedures that can support a culture of nonviolent empowerment within organizations and communities. Such supports can be very important in establishing an environment of safety and justice. Among these are the establishment and maintenance of positive, consistent structure; changes in the physical environment; analytic mapping of violent or abusive incidents; and well-learned, standard procedures for dealing with residual behavior problems when they arise. Probably the most important is positive structure, which actually is one way to institutionalize recognition and respect within an organization.

Establishing and Maintaining Positive Structure

Schools and youth-serving organizations obtain the best results from their violence prevention programs if they embed their activities in consistent systems of disciplinary practices (Walker, Colvin, & Ramsey, 1995). Positive structure involves ensuring that the results of behavior (both positive and negative) are predictable. Such predictability is developmentally essential at a time when youth are experimenting with new repertoires and dealing with many changes internally and socially.

Lack of positive structure can be severely problematic in a number of ways. For example, if distributed in ways that youth see as unfair, rewards may produce effects contrary to those intended. Organizations also need to have clear, definite procedures in place for dealing with undesirable behaviors when they do occur; these procedures should be part of an overall discipline plan that youth perceive as both fair and protective of their safety. Many of the youth who bring weapons to school, for example, report that they do so for protection; if young people feel safe, they are less likely to take that risky action. Youth need to know that when they act in prosocial ways, their behavior will be regularly recognized, and when they do not, the consequences are predictable. In the context of a generally positive system, inescapable penalties should be clear, and in such a system, paradoxically, quite small penalties usually are more effective than more severe punishments that may produce emotional side effects.

An Environment of Recognition

Surprisingly to many, structure is useful only in an environment that is primarily positive and has a high level of recognition. If a recognition plan is not currently in place, that lack must be addressed first and should be the first aspect of structure implemented. Definite rules with clear penalties will be useful in this context, but the research is clear: No amount of limit setting and rules will work in the long run in a recognition-poor environment. And no amount of political rhetoric can overcome this reality (Sidman, 2001).

Positive structure is another way of predictably increasing the level of reward in a setting like a school. Everyone involved can contribute to the design of a system of positive structure, establishment of rules, and identification of rewards. Those with the best sense of what will work are usually staff who work directly with youth and the youth themselves. Participating in planning positive structure can be a valuable activity for student councils, for example. Parents, administrators, security staff, and other staff also may have creative, useful ideas. Participation in designing positive structure is a significant opportunity for shared power.

Rules

Assuming a positive environment, rules are always necessary. There should be as few as possible, however, and a good reason for each one that does exist. Rules that function only to assert authority are likely to backfire. Rules should be very clear, with the penalties explicitly stated so that a young person who violates a rule makes that choice with knowledge of the consequences. Relatively modest sanctions, so long as consistently applied, typically produce better results than more severe penalties; further, the more modest sanctions are less likely to elicit undesirable side effects while still producing behavior change. In most settings, at least in many areas, young people can be realistic and effective partners in rule development, and they are more likely to view as reasonable and to respect rules that they helped to establish than rules that adults imposed on them. Once rules have been developed, they should be enforced every time; rules that are only sometimes enforced will be constantly tested. By the same token, it is necessary to deal with apparently "minor" infractions immediately; otherwise, problem behaviors are likely to escalate, and respect for the entire system of positive structure may decrease.

Monitoring

Problem behavior is more likely when situations are unstructured than when structured positive activities and supervision are taking place. Among children and preteens, for example, aggressive behavior is particularly likely during unsupervised activities on playgrounds, and the most common responses (reprimands by adult monitors and, perhaps, peer mediation) may focus attention on those undesirable behaviors (Embry & Flannery, 1999). Such attention may, paradoxically, *increase* the incidence of those behaviors. Structured activities and monitoring for *positive* behavior (Dougherty, Fowler, & Paine, 1985; Embry, Flannery, Vazsonyi, Powell, & Atha, 1996) can dramatically reduce such problems. For older youth, such unstructured times and unsupervised places as class transitions, stairwells and restrooms, and waits for cafeterias to open (e.g., Ninness, Ellis, Miller, Baker, & Rutherford, 1995) increase risk, and structure and monitoring (especially monitoring for positive behavior) of those times and places are often important.

Point Systems

Many youth programs, particularly those for youth who have learned only limited personal and social behavior repertoires (e.g., those in many juvenile justice and residential treatment settings) incorporate the use of point (or token) systems. These arrangements take positive structure to a more specific level. If well-designed, they can be very powerful tools; the Achievement Place Teaching Family Model developed at the University of Kansas, for example, which has been widely disseminated by Boys Town, has extensively documented the value of such arrangements (Wolf, Braukmann, & Ramp, 1987). The limitations and requirements of such arrangements have also been carefully elaborated. A number of principles are useful for developing these systems:

- The primary emphasis of point systems should be on earning points for positive behavior, rather than on losing points for negative behavior. This principle cannot be overemphasized; most point systems fall short in this area.
- Point systems should allow youth to earn incentives and rewards that they value. Youth must receive those incentives and rewards quickly enough to be meaningful, as many youth find it difficult to defer gratification. If a point system is not working well, the first place to look is at the quality and scheduling of incentives.
- It is critical to involve youth in planning point systems in a shared power framework. Youth are generally good at helping to resolve problems that come up in the design of point systems and in determining appropriate and meaningful consequences.
- Negative consequences should be modest, as small point fines may actually work better than large ones. They should be inevitable and nonnegotiable, however. Boys Town (Davis, Nelson, & Gauger, 2000) and the teaching family model from which many of the Boys Town procedures have emerged have demonstrated that "positive correction" can take much of the sting out of negative consequences. The basic notion is that the young person receives an opportunity to practice a better way to handle the situation and, thus, to earn back some of what he or she has lost. This procedure shifts attention quickly back toward positive behavior.
- Point systems can be fine grained; they need not, for example, use only small numbers like 3 points or 10 points. In the same way that youth can understand the difference between $1 and $10,000, even youth with very limited academic skills can quickly adapt to systems using hundreds or thousands of points. This may permit the fine-tuning of a system.
- Point systems should gradually move young people toward deferring gratification. Some youth have learned to defer gratification, but many have not. If a weekly system does not work for some

youth, it may be necessary to go to a daily system; for some, an hourly or even shorter system may be necessary for a time. Then, as youth come under the control of relatively immediate consequences, these reward schedules can be stretched over time. In addition, most such systems culminate in an "honor system" level, in which most rewards are freely available so long as behavior does not deteriorate. When youth reach this level, they are typically operating under "natural consequences"—the more deferred consequences that are typical in mainstream settings. It would be counterproductive in most cases to teach youth to function only under the tight structure of point systems.

- Regular review of the system is necessary to ensure both that the rewards used are still effective and that the correct behaviors are targeted. For example, some youth generally work once they are present in the classroom, but others may need to be rewarded for actually working, not just being present or quiet.

Those who plan to develop point systems and token economies should carefully mine the behavioral literature for principles and options (e.g., Kazdin, 1994; Sulzer-Azaroff & Mayer, 1991). Data should be carefully and regularly reviewed to ensure that a system as designed is actually shaping improved behavior reliably; if it is not, outside consultation may be needed.

Modifying the Physical Environment

People are dramatically affected by their physical environment. Youth act differently in a setting that feels comfortable to them than in one that feels cold or institutional. Some schools, for example, have the feel and sound of prisons—noisy, threatening, in poor repair. One of the important things that outstanding residential treatment programs have discovered is that an environment that communicates respect evokes respect (Bettelheim, 1974). Youth treat attractive surroundings, furniture, dishes, and so forth better than those that are less attractive, for example. In some cases, uniforms or dress codes can be helpful; if their clothing is somewhat more formal than other clothing that young people wear, youth may then act more formally. (Another advantage of uniforms is that they can shift attention from competition over clothes and accessories to more important areas. On the other hand, among youth in the United States, clothing often functions as a way of individualizing one's identity. Uniforms may therefore be counterproductive with older youth or in particular situations.)

Many youth are afraid in school. In surveys, youth often report that they perceive classrooms, hallways, restrooms, recreation areas outside, and the neighborhood and streets around the school as dangerous. Ensuring adequate monitoring and building a community of respect are important to prevent this problem. In addition, poor facilities communicate very clearly to young people that they are not valued. As noted by a 14-year-old African American girl quoted by Kozol (1991):

> Every year in February we are told to read the same old speech of Martin Luther King . . . "I have a dream." . . . We have a school in East St. Louis named for Dr. King. . . . The school is full of sewer water and the doors are locked with chains. Every student in that school is black. It's like a terrible joke on history. (p. 35)

The quality of the environment, physical and social, is not just cosmetic; it is in many cases a matter of social justice and human rights.

Conducting an Environmental Audit

There is an entire subfield of psychology that examines the effects of the physical environment, and there is much to learn from the extensive research conducted in environmental psychology. Those at any school or youth-serving organization can conduct an environmental audit of building(s) and surrounding areas. Such an audit is possible in a single classroom, certainly, but ideally is a community project, in which young people, staff, and perhaps parents and community members can be active planners and participants. Teams can develop special forms, to be completed on-site, for each area, and team members with clipboards or handheld computers can fill them out during the audit. Areas that the audit team can examine include the following:

1. Classrooms or program areas (to be examined for each room):
   - Is the room decorated in attractive ways? Are the furniture and other furnishings (e.g., carpets, floors, cabinets) in good repair? How could this room be improved?
   - Is there any apparent damage? Research indicates that damage, particularly vandalism, is likely to recur in areas previously dam-

aged, but not repaired quickly (see Goldstein, 1997, for a review of such environmental factors affecting vandalism). What could be done to improve this area?

- Is the room clean? Are the windows and floors clean? What could be done to improve this?
- Is the room decorated with attractive posters, artwork, learning materials, and particularly things prepared by the young people who use the space? Are these materials new, changed often, and in good condition? What could be done to improve this?
- Are areas for academic work simple, clean, and free of unnecessary distractions? This can be particularly important for students who experience learning challenges. What could be done to improve this?

2. Hallways, lunchrooms, and public spaces (to be examined separately for each area):

- Are these areas decorated in attractive ways? Are there new, fresh, meaningful decorations and artwork present, particularly those prepared by youth? How could this be improved?
- Is there any apparent damage or vandalism present? What could be done to improve this area?
- Is the area clean? Are the windows and floors clean? What could be done to improve this?
- Are high traffic areas free of distracting materials that people passing by may reach for or damage easily, resulting in a poor appearance?

3. Restrooms:

- Are restrooms clean, in good repair, and well lit? Adults sometimes think that youth do not care much about restroom cleanliness, but lack of clean restrooms is one of their most common complaints. How could these areas be improved?
- Is there sufficient monitoring so youth feel safe in the restrooms?

4. Noise:

- When walking down the hallway, or in a classroom, how much noise can be heard? Does that noise include loud voices, pounding, apparent arguments, or fighting? High levels of noise can make an environment overly physically stimulating, producing responses consistent with conditions of threat. What could be done to reduce noise levels if they seem high?

5. Outdoor spaces:
  - Is the building in good repair on the outside? What could be done to improve this?
  - Are the grounds well kept and attractive? What could be done to improve this?
  - Do outside areas feel safe? Are there accessible areas that are isolated and difficult to monitor? What could be done to improve this?
6. Neighborhood:
  - Does the neighborhood feel safe? Is there adequate monitoring (e.g., police, parents, community volunteers) to reassure students? Are there safe havens (e.g., stores, homes) where children or youth can go if they do not feel safe on the street? What could be done to improve this situation?
  - Is the neighborhood in good condition? Are there service projects in which youth from the school could become involved to improve the area around the school? Some schools have become involved in cleanup and beautification projects that can build commitment to the community and allow youth to demonstrate to themselves and others that they can make a difference.

Making a Plan

After an audit (of a single room or an entire program) is complete, it is necessary to develop a plan to address some of the areas for potential improvement. This is an ideal way to involve youth, staff, families, community members, businesses, and anyone else with a stake in the program. Participation in this activity builds a sense of community and commitment to that community, as well as improving the environment for learning and other programming. Those involved may need considerable creativity to obtain the resources required to make changes and may not be able to address everything at once; however, all of this is useful experience for young people. The plan should list clear priorities based on what is most important and most doable, with action steps developed for at least the highest priority items. The plan should also have a time line, with an established date to review and evaluate progress. Real communities do not rely only on maintenance departments or capital budgets to construct safe, attractive communities.

Mapping Violent and Threatening Incidents

Astor, Vargas, Pitner, and Meyer (1999) have developed a very creative approach for understanding and preventing violence in a particular location, such as a school. Their mapping approach is similar to crime mapping, which law enforcement officials often use to identify and plan for high-risk locations in urban settings. As applied in a school (variations for other settings are easy to imagine), the approach calls for focus groups of students, teachers, staff members, and administrators to work with maps of the school. Each participant marks the location of the three most violent events that occurred during a term (rated subjectively), along with data about time, gender and grade, and organizational response to each event. On separate maps, participants note the most "dangerous" (from their own perspective) areas in and around the school.

The completed maps are then used to structure discussion about where, when, and why violence occurs; this knowledge makes it possible to move toward understanding and eventually planning to prevent violent events. The developers of this approach then discuss how to aggregate the data to produce larger collective maps (Figure 22) and matrices that organize comments in ways useful for planning.

Consistent with many other approaches in this book, mapping can elicit and refine suggested preventive and interventive strategies that not only originate in the data, but also leave a great deal of room for creativity and experimentation. Such mapping is an inexpensive strategy that structures input from many voices and shares power to co-construct collective solutions, and the technique certainly deserves careful testing.

Handling Residual Behavior Problems

Although it is natural for those concerned with violence to think, "What do I do if a young person 'goes off' on me?", it is possible to prevent the vast majority of such incidents by firmly establishing a culture that incorporates the core *PEACE POWER* practices. Establishing such a culture, therefore, should be the priority, rather than immediate behavior management. Nevertheless, some incidents will certainly occur in all circumstances, and a good deal is known about ways to manage them

219

Figure 22

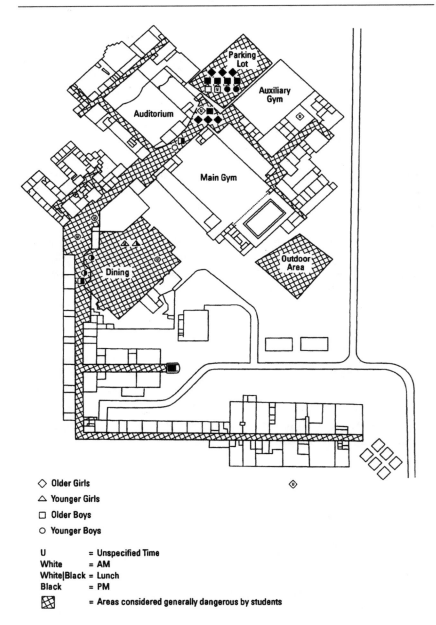

◇ Older Girls

△ Younger Girls

□ Older Boys

○ Younger Boys

U	= Unspecified Time
White	= AM
White|Black	= Lunch
Black	= PM
▨	= Areas considered generally dangerous by students

Violent events marked by location, time, gender, and age. Source: Reprinted from Astor, Vargas, Pitner, & Meyer, 1999.

effectively. There are entire volumes and programs directed to such management (e.g., Wood & Long, 1991), some of which also discuss physically managing violent behavior (e.g., Goldstein, Palumbo, Striepling, & Voutsinas, 1995). Organizations need to develop policies for physical intervention, with attention to legal and liability issues.

There are some skills that anyone can learn from dealing with such incidents; in very nearly every case, these skills will move those involved toward resolving the problem and preventing serious damage— either physical or social. Most such incidents can be defused without physical intervention. In a culture of shared power and shared responsibility, all participants, both youth and adults, are responsible for acting respectfully and for resolving issues that do arise. Adults, however, are expected to "act like adults" and to handle challenging behaviors in ways that lead to problem solving and collective well-being. Considerable research is available to guide such efforts.

Several years ago, Patterson and his group (e.g., Patterson, 1976; Patterson, Reid, & Dishion, 1992) identified a very important pattern in the coercive behavior of children. This pattern has since been observed among adolescents and adults as well (Mattaini, 1999). The basic pattern is as follows. Person #1 makes a demand that Person #2 act in some particular way. Person #2, not wanting to comply, becomes irate or threatening. Person #1 often backs down at that point (teaching Person #2 to become irate or threatening). Or, Person #1, instead of backing down, becomes irate and threatening. At that point, Person #2 either capitulates (teaching Person #1 to become irate or threatening) or escalates further. Eventually, someone will back down, teaching the other that escalating aversive or coercive behavior is a way to escape unwanted demands. There is no healthy way out of this pattern once it has begun to escalate, unless someone steps outside the spiral and does something different. Finding ways to avoid even the first steps down that path is very important. Many of the procedures recommended in sections that follow offer alternatives to this coercive spiral.

Wood and Long (1991), in their *life space intervention* model, explain the issue in a slightly different but also very helpful way. Like Patterson and associates, Wood and Long identify a pattern that can progressively spiral out of control, as well as procedures that an involved adult can take to prevent or de-escalate the potential crisis. In their words, "Stress arouses feelings. Feelings trigger behavior. Behavior incites others. Others increase stress. And around it goes!" (p. 32). This spiraling cycle is shown in Figure 23.

Figure 23

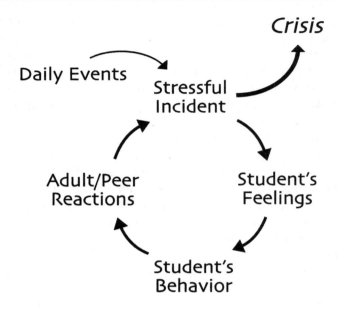

The conflict cycle. Source: Adapted with permission from Wood and Long, 1991.

As Wood and Long (1991) indicate, intervention at any of the four points in the cycle (reducing the stress, alleviating the young person's emotional responses, changing the young person's behavior, or modifying the reactions of others) may be possible. Procedures like separating the youth from observing peers (decreasing stress), empathic statements (moderating feelings), providing choices (opportunities to escape without losing face), and responding calmly (an unexpected adult reaction to challenge) are examples at each point on the circle.

Principles for Defusing Emotional Incidents

The following relatively simple principles, drawn from a variety of sources (e.g., Davis et al., 2000; Gordon, 1970) are useful for defusing volatile episodes:

- Remember that you are the adult. Project strength rather than emotional upset, and in particular, do not allow yourself to be pulled into acting like another adolescent.
- Having everyone involved in the conflict take a few minutes to cool off can be valuable for everyone, so long as further immediate intervention to protect someone is not required.
- Use a calming touch if a youth knows you well and is likely to be responsive to you. This and many of the other procedures and principles here rely on a strong relationship, based on a history of recognition and respect.
- If the young person is not responsive to you at the moment, "give him or her space," maintaining a reasonable distance and moving slowly. Although something like this may sound obvious, many people regularly violate this principle, instead "getting in the young person's face"—a setup for physical confrontation.
- Stay at or below the young person's eye level. Sitting down itself often defuses the situation significantly (unless your own safety requires you to be ready for immediate escape).
- "Turn down the volume." Speak respectfully, quietly, privately, firmly, and briefly, using the young person's name. Each of the five adverbs in the previous sentence is important, and each is commonly ignored. Role-playing may be necessary to prepare to respond in this way.
- Verbally recognize feelings early and express concern (e.g., "You look pretty hassled, can you make it through the period?"). This is, of course, "active listening" or empathic responding, among the most powerful of all possible tools for dealing with any strong emotion.
- Calmly repeat requests or options; do not engage in debate, or attempt to repeat what you said "longer, louder, and meaner" (Daniels, 2000), which is likely to lead to escalation.
- Isolate the problem by moving the young person away from peers, or peers away from the situation. There should be a strong focus on normal activity with other students.
- Use a prompt for physical relaxation (e.g., "Let's take three deep breaths . . ."), especially if the young people have previously practiced prompts in the setting, so the technique is well-learned and available. Well-learned responses can often interrupt an emerging and escalating situation: for example, siblings or other groups of

youth may stop many kinds of problem behavior simply because an adult they respect enters the room.

- Offer the young person a choice (e.g., "Would you rather go to time out to cool off, or should we go for a walk and talk about this?"). Choices are less coercive than "orders," because they leave the young person with latitude to exercise at least some control.
- Use the "when . . . then . . ." procedure (e.g., "When we talk about this, then you can go back to class or have some time by yourself to calm down"). This procedure moves toward an improved situation, promising immediate positive consequences for steps in the right direction.
- Acknowledge cooperation by recognizing the behavior (e.g., "Thank you for sitting down. Now maybe we can solve this thing.").
- Change environments. "Walking and talking" provides a change of stimuli and often attenuates feelings. The "talk" occurring should certainly address the young person's feelings; this is also an excellent opportunity to move toward guided self-correction.
- When the situation has become calmer, provide the expected or an appropriate negative consequence. Emotional outbursts should not be reinforced with positive attention and no negative consequence, but reasonable, relatively mild consequences produce better results under most circumstances than do very severe ones. Whenever possible, a young person should be allowed to "earn back" some of what he or she has lost by beginning to cooperate or by practicing a new way to handle the situation that got out of control.
- "Wipe the slate clean" (Davis et al., 2000, p. 67) after the crisis. Once consequences have been applied, let go of your own residual emotions and move quickly toward normalcy.

Behavior Strategies Developed at Boys Town

Father Flanagan's Boys Town, an organization with special expertise in managing difficult behavior, has developed and tested a range of strategies for dealing with incidents as "teaching moments." Rather than seeing problems as challenges to adult authority or their own ego, staff members view problem behaviors as evidence that the young person has not learned certain necessary life skills. Conflicts offer "teaching moments" in the ongoing flow of living. Boys Town has refined a number of strategies for this teaching, including the *teaching interaction, corrective teaching, preventive teaching, guided self-correction,* and *crisis teaching* (Connolly, Dowd, Criste, Nelson, & Tobias, 1995; Davis et al., 2000). Two of these approaches, guided self-correction and crisis teaching, are of general utility.

In guided self-correction (Davis et al., 2000), the adult uses a series of questions or requests for information to guide the young person through the process of learning from mistakes. The process needs to occur in an atmosphere of calm respect; it is likely to be effective only if grounded in an underlying positive relationship (built through a history of recognition). A major advantage of this procedure is that it clarifies the shared responsibility involved in behavior management: the adult and the young person together are responsible for the outcome. The adult's responsibilities include guiding the process, and the young person's responsibilities include working toward a solution; both are responsible for maintaining an atmosphere of respect.

The first request in guided self-correction is usually quite general, something like "Tell me what happened here." Subsequent questions address why the problem unfolded as it did (e.g., "Why do you think she reacted so strongly?"); what the likely consequences may be (e.g., "How do you think your parents will take this?"); and what options are available at this point (e.g., "What choices do you have now, as you see it?"). Davis and associates (2000) indicate that it is often necessary to help students answer these questions, especially before they have developed extensive problem-solving repertoires. Although variation to fit the situation is important, the basic questions to examine in guided self-correction are:

1. What happened here?
2. Why did people act as they did?
3. What were the consequences of what happened?
4. What can you do now?

Crisis teaching (Davis et al., 2000) is a simple, four-step process for defusing situations in which young people are losing emotional control:

1. Addressing the behavior. The adult interrupts the behavior and provides an instruction as to what to do instead (e.g., "Julie, I need

you to sit down now"). Although many negative behaviors are best ignored, out-of-control behavior cannot be ignored because it is likely to escalate if there is no response.

2. Monitoring one's own self-control. As noted in the discussion of life space intervention, an adult's reaction can go a long way toward either calming or escalating a potentially out-of-control situation. An adult who is not in control of herself or himself cannot help a young person regain control and almost surely will contribute to further confrontation. Anger-defusing skills, including viewing the situation as a teaching moment rather than as a challenge to one's own authority or ego, can be very helpful. If adults involved find they are losing control, they may need to take a few minutes to calm down or ask someone else to take over.

3. Ensuring youth self-control. The Boys Town staff suggest simply and calmly describing what the young person is doing and asking for a change (e.g., "Your voice is getting louder. Please sit down so we can talk this out"). Calming and empathic statements, recognition and praise for steps toward calmness, offering choices for immediate action, and reminders of the improved consequences of calmer behavior (e.g., "If you can calm down now, we can work this out without having to take it any further") may be part of this process. It is essential, of course, that any other young people present be safe, even if this requires turning to physical intervention or involving other staff, according to the policies of the organization.

4. Engaging the student in follow-up teaching once emotions have moderated. Follow-up teaching can involve direct instruction as to what the problem behavior is, why it is a problem, and what the consequences are, or it can be conducted through guided self-correction. A consequence (e.g., a small loss of privileges) is also established at this point.

Both guided self-correction and crisis teaching are relatively easy procedures to understand, but using them under pressure can be challenging. It is, therefore, very valuable to offer those who will be using these techniques various opportunities to practice them in role plays (as realistic as possible), with the steps outlined on wall charts, so that they become familiar parts of the adults' repertoire before they are needed.

Conclusion

The approaches and tools presented in this chapter, if used as components of and adjuncts to the core *PEACE POWER* strategy, hold considerable promise for further reducing coercive, threatening, and violent actions in organizational and community settings. Each, by itself, is probably of real value, but the real power lies in a comprehensive project that substantively changes the world in which young people live, shaping them and their futures. At the same time, larger cultural forces also have profound impacts.

Conclusion:
Toward Cultures of
Nonviolent Power

The *PEACE POWER* strategy and other similar programs, if collaboratively and creatively pursued, are likely to have a significant effect on the levels of violent, coercive, adversarial, and antisocial behavior in family, peer, organizational, and community cultures. At the same time, larger sociocultural forces that shape and structure violence, oppression, and social injustice are likely to set an outside limit on the effectiveness of local prevention and intervention programs. Youth who are constantly exposed to coercive and violent media, who are continuously oppressed because of the color of their skin or their sexual orientation, who are beaten in what are supposed to be loving relationships, or who are encouraged or required by their jobs and social networks to oppress others or to value only the interests of those in a position to oppress them will naturally continue to be at high risk for perpetrating violence and other forms of coercion toward themselves or others.

These larger sociocultural issues can be addressed only through advocacy and social action directed toward social and institutional policy. Researchers and policy advocates have identified a number of central recommendations for work at these levels. Flannery and Huff (1999), for example, suggest the following policy initiatives:

- Establishment of communitywide prevention councils (Hawkins & Catalano, 1992) as part of integrated projects aimed at strengthening currently struggling and disorganized communities.
- Development of integrated, holistic family support systems that are universally available and consistent with the state of the art

(Biglan, 1995). Biglan and Taylor (2000) review the extensive evidence supporting the utility of programs like these for producing reductions in violence in the long term.

- Tighter restrictions on the availability of firearms.
- Establishment of programs oriented toward discouraging gang involvement and providing support for those who are ready to leave gang life. As discovered by Henggeler and colleagues (Henggeler, Schoenwald, Borduin, Rowland, & Cunningham, 1998), involvement in gangs need not be, and often is not, a lifelong phenomenon.
- Increased emphasis on rigorous evaluation of policy and program initiatives.

Jenson and Howard (1999a) generally concur and offer additional recommendations, including the establishment of community continua of prevention, early intervention, and long-term treatment services to meet the needs of multiple groups of youth. In addition, they emphasize the need to dramatically reduce exposure to violence in the media—and in real life. Increased funding for school-based services is essential, because youth at risk may be most easily identified early in schools, but often are not so identified because of overworked pupil services personnel.

The National Research Council, in its extensive four-volume survey of the science of violence prevention (Reiss & Roth, 1993), suggested six major focuses for emphasis:

1. An extensive research initiative studying ways of intervening in biological and psychosocial processes that may be associated with potential for violence (e.g., reducing the rate of low birth weights, and certain cognitive behavioral educational procedures, including problem–solving [choices and consequences] and anger management);
2. Actions to modify places, activities, and situations that may promote violence (e.g., factors contributing to commercial robberies or high-risk locations in schools);
3. Action to disrupt illegal drug and weapons markets;
4. Shifts in firearms and substance laws to decrease the lethality of confrontations and to reduce intoxication and other substance-related contributors to violence;
5. Targeted initiatives related to bias crimes, gangs, and communities in transition; and
6. Comprehensive initiatives to reduce partner violence.

This is a very challenging policy agenda, and yet over time and with continued effort, it might dramatically shift the rate and intensity of violence in our society. The purpose of many of these components is to reduce reliance on coercive action by those at high risk for perpetrating violence, either by increasing the costs of such behavior or by increasing access to alternatives. The second approach is likely to have longer lasting effects, but there certainly is a place for both.

We as a society must, however, remember the larger issue—our heavy sociocultural reliance on coercion as a primary strategy for maintaining social institutions. For example, when violent crimes occur, the most common first reaction is to suggest more severe penalties. Similarly, when large media corporations are targeting (the word is used advisedly) young children in efforts to market violent films and music to maximize profits, the first response is to condemn corporate actors, threaten them to make them stop, and punish them if they do not. The same underlying process is operating in both cases, with the same results. Because the rewards of continuing the behavior remain, the perpetrators try to find ways to avoid observation; they deny their actions and continue to perform them when they believe that they can escape surveillance. So long as society teaches its members that personal and corporate self-interest is more important than collective welfare, and that coercion and threat are the best ways to protect their self-interest, violence will continue to be a serious issue. Efforts to reduce reliance on coercion throughout society (see Sidman, 2001, for a serious alternative) could complete the circle of prevention begun in local programs.

Science tells us that *PEACE POWER* is consistent with the way things are. Coercion is also a natural and powerful phenomenon, but scientific findings, the practical wisdom of non-European (particularly indigenous) peoples, and millennia of human sociocultural history all converge to teach us that in the long run, constructive peace-in-action that relies on shared power is even more potent. Our hope is that programs emerging from the *PEACE POWER* strategy will provide at least modest support for recognizing, revering, and preserving the one web of life.

He gave the original people peace and power.

Joanne Shenandoah, *Peacemaker's Journey* (2000)

Notes

1. The PeaceBuilders web site is located at http://www.peacebuilders.com.
2. Further information about all of the Blueprint Programs can be obtained at http://www.colorado.edu/cspv/blueprints/.
3. The Community Tool Box web site is located at http://ctb.lsi.ukans.edu.
4. Twenty-five sheet pads of preprinted, self-adhesive recognition notes are available at www.bfsr.org/PEACEPOWER.html.
5. Wallet-sized plastic cards with the *PEACE POWER* Pledge are available at www.bfsr.org/PEACEPOWER.html.
6. The erasable white-board planner (5.5" x 8.5") is available at www.bfsr.org/PEACEPOWER.html.
7. The erasable white-board home recognition record (5.5" x 8.5") is available at www.bfsr.org/PEACEPOWER.html.
8. The Southern Poverty Law Center web site is located at www.splcenter.org.
9. For links to environmental organizations, see the Behaviorists for Social Responsibility web site at www.bfsr.org.
10. The Student Pledge Against Gun Violence web site is located at http://www.pledge.org.
11. The Families and Schools Together (FAST) web site is located at www.wcer.wisc.edu/fast.
12. The Making Peace Tool is available in pads of 50 sheets at http://www.bfsr.org/PEACEPOWER.html.
13. The Real Justice web site is located at www.realjustice.org.
14. Information about Real Justice training sessions is available at www.realjustice.org.

References

Aber, J. L., Brown, J. L., Chaudry, N., Jones, S. M., & Samples, F. (1996). The evaluation of the Resolving Conflict Creatively program: An overview. *American Journal of Preventive Medicine, 12* (5, Suppl.), 82–90.

Akwesasne Notes. (1978). *Basic call to consciousness.* Summertown, TN: Book Publishing Company.

Alberti, R. E. (1977). *Assertiveness: Innovations, applications, issues.* San Luis Obispo, CA: Impact Publishers.

Alexander, J. F. (1973). Defensive and supportive communication in normal and deviant families. *Journal of Consulting and Clinical Psychology, 40,* 223–231.

Allen, K. D., & Warzak, W. J. (2000). The problem of parental nonadherence in clinical behavior analysis: Effective treatment is not enough. *Journal of Applied Behavior Analysis, 33,* 373–391.

Allen, L., Jones, S. M., Seidman, E., & Aber, J. L. (1999). Organization of exposure to violence among urban adolescents: Clinical, prevention, and research implications. In D. J. Flannery & C. R. Huff (Eds.), *Youth violence: Prevention, intervention, and social policy* (pp. 119–141). Washington, DC: American Psychiatric Press.

American Psychological Association. (1993). *Violence and youth: Psychology's response.* Washington, DC: Author.

Anderson, E. (1999). *Code of the street: Decency, violence, and the moral life of the inner city.* New York: W. W. Norton.

Aristide, J.-B. (2000). *Eyes of the heart.* Monroe, ME: Common Courage Press.

Armstrong, B. (1997). The young men's clinic. In M. Hanson (Ed.), *Maternal and child health program design and development—From the ground up: Collaboration and partnership* (pp. 23–32). New York: Columbia University School of Social Work.

References

Astor, R. A., Vargas, L. A., Pitner, R. O., & Meyer, H. A. (1999). School violence: Research, theory, and practice. In J. M. Jenson & M. O. Howard (Eds.), *Youth violence: Current research and recent practice innovations* (pp. 139–171). Washington, DC: NASW Press.

Balsam, P. D., & Bondy, A. S. (1983). The negative side effects of reward. *Journal of Applied Behavior Analysis, 16,* 283–296.

Bandura, A. (1986). *Social foundations of thought and action.* Englewood Cliffs, NJ: Prentice-Hall.

Barton, C., & Alexander, J. F. (1991). Functional family therapy. In A. S. Gurman & D. P. Kniskern (Eds.), *Handbook of family therapy* (Vol. 1, pp. 403–443). New York: Brunner/Mazel.

Bay-Hinitz, A. K., Peterson, R. F., & Quilitch, H. R. (1994). Cooperative games: A way to modify aggressive and cooperative behaviors in young children. *Journal of Applied Behavior Analysis, 27,* 435–446.

Bell, C., & Jenkins, E. (1993). Community violence and children on Chicago's southside. *Psychiatry, 56,* 46–54.

Benson, H. (1975). *The relaxation response.* New York: Avon Books.

Bernardi, P. (1992). *Improvisation starters: A collection of 900 improvisation situations for the theater.* Cincinnati, OH: Betterway Publications.

Bettelheim. B. (1974). *A home for the heart.* New York: Knopf.

Biegon, A. (1990). Effects of steroid hormones on serotonergic systems? *Annals of the New York Academy of Sciences, 600,* 427–434.

Biglan, A. (1995). *Changing cultural practices.* Reno, NV: Context Press.

Biglan, A. (1996). Sexual coercion. In M. A. Mattaini & B. A. Thyer (Eds.), *Finding solutions to social problems: Behavioral strategies for change* (pp. 289–316). Washington, DC: American Psychological Association.

Biglan, A., Metzler, C. W., & Ary, D. V. (1994). Increasing the prevalence of successful children: The case for community intervention research. *The Behavior Analyst, 17,* 335–351.

Biglan, A., & Taylor, T. K. (2000). Why have we been more successful in reducing tobacco use than violent crime? *American Journal of Community Psychology, 28,* 269-302.

Bloom, M., Fischer, J., & Orme, J. G. (1999). *Evaluating practice: Guidelines for the accountable professional* (3rd ed.). Boston: Allyn & Bacon.

Blyth, D. A., Saito, R., & Berkas, T. (1997). A quantitative study of the impact of service-learning programs. In A. S. Waterman (Ed.), *Service-learning: Applications from the research* (pp. 39–56). Hillsdale, NJ: Lawrence Erlbaum Associates.

Bosworth, K., Espelage, D., DuBay, T., Dahlberg, L. L., & Daytner, G. (1996). Using multimedia to teach conflict-resolution skills to young adolescents. *American Journal of Preventive Medicine, 12* (5, Suppl.), 65–74.

References

Briggs, H. E., & Paulson, R. I. (1996). Racism. In M. A. Mattaini & B. A. Thyer (Eds.), *Finding solutions to social problems: Behavioral strategies for change* (pp. 147–177). Washington, DC: American Psychological Association.

Briscoe, R. V., Hoffman, D. B., & Bailey, J. S. (1975). Behavioral community psychology: Training a community board to problem solve. *Journal of Applied Behavior Analysis, 8,* 157–168.

Bureau of Justice Statistics (2000). Teens experience the highest rates of violent crime. Available at: *http://www.ojp.usdoj.gov/bjs/glance/vage.htm.*

Canada, G. (1995). *Fist stick knife gun.* Boston: Beacon Press.

Capra, F. (1996). *The web of life.* New York: Anchor.

Carlson, N. R. (1998). *The physiology of behavior* (6th ed.). Boston: Allyn & Bacon.

Carnegie, D. (1936). *How to win friends and influence people.* New York: Pocket Books.

Carton, J. S. (1996). The differential effects of tangible rewards and praise on intrinsic motivation: A comparison of cognitive evaluation theory and operant theory. *The Behavior Analyst, 19,* 237–255.

Carton, J. S., & Nowicki, S., Jr. (1998). Should behavior therapists stop using reinforcement? A reexamination of the undermining effect of reinforcement on intrinsic motivation. *Behavior Therapy, 29,* 65–86.

Catalano, R. F., & Hawkins, J. D. (1996). The social development model: A theory of antisocial behavior. In J. D. Hawkins (Ed.), *Delinquency and crime: Current theories* (pp. 149–197). New York: Cambridge University Press.

Cavanaugh, M. (2000). What is religious naturalism? A preliminary report of an ongoing conversation. *Zygon, 35,* 241–252.

Chapin, M., & Singer, M. I. (1999). Principles of military combat stress treatment related to children in high-risk environments. In D. J. Flannery & C. R. Huff (Eds.), *Youth violence: Prevention, intervention, and social policy* (pp. 99–118). Washington, DC: American Psychiatric Press.

Chesney-Lind, M., & Brown, M. (1999). Girls and violence: An overview. In D. J. Flannery & C. R. Huff (Eds.), *Youth violence: Prevention, intervention, and social policy* (pp. 171–199). Washington, DC: American Psychiatric Press.

Cohen, H. L., & Filipczak, J. (1971). *A new learning environment.* Boston: Authors Cooperative.

Colby, I. C. (1997). Transforming human services organizations through empowerment of neighbors. *Journal of Community Practice, 4*(2), 1–12.

Comer, E. W., & Fraser, M. W. (1998). Evaluation of six family-support programs: Are they effective? *Families in Society, 79,* 134–148.

Connolly, T., Dowd, T., Criste, A., Nelson, C., & Tobias, L. (1995). *The well-managed classroom.* Boys Town, NE: Boys Town Press.

References

Dahlberg, L. L., Toal, S. B., & Behrens, C. B. (Eds.). (1998). *Measuring violence-related attitudes, beliefs, and behaviors among youths: A compendium of assessment tools.* Atlanta, GA: Centers for Disease Control and Prevention.

Daniels, A. (2000). *Bringing out the best in people* (2nd ed.). New York: McGraw-Hill.

Davis, J. L., Nelson, C. S., & Gauger, E. S. (2000). *Safe and effective secondary schools: The Boys Town model.* Boys Town, NE: Boys Town Press.

DeJong, W., Spiro, A., III, Wilson-Brewer, R., Vince-Whitman, C., & Prothrow-Stith, D. (n.d.). *Evaluation summary: Violence prevention curriculum for adolescents.* Newton, MA: Educational Development Center.

Delgado, M., & Barton, K. (1998). Murals in Latino communities: Social indicators of community strengths. *Social Work, 37,* 346–356.

DeRisi, W. J., & Butz, G. (1975). *Writing behavioral contracts.* Champaign, IL: Research Press.

Dickinson, A. M. (1989). The detrimental effects of extrinsic reinforcement on "intrinsic motivation." *The Behavior Analyst, 12,* 1–15.

Dougherty, B. S., Fowler, S. A., & Paine, S. C. (1985). The use of peer monitors to reduce negative interactions during recess. *Journal of Applied Behavior Analysis, 18,* 141–153.

Earls, F. (1994). Violence and today's youth. *Critical Health Issues for Children and Youth, 4,* 4–23.

Einstein, A. (n.d.). *The world as I see it.* New York: Wisdom Library.

Elliott, D. S., & Tolan, P. H. (1999). Youth violence prevention, intervention, and social policy: An overview. In D. J. Flannery & C. R. Huff (Eds.), *Youth violence: Prevention, intervention, and social policy* (pp. 3–46). Washington, DC: American Psychiatric Press.

Ellis, A., & Dryden, W. (1997). *The practice of rational emotive behavior therapy* (2nd ed.). New York: Springer.

Embry, D. D., & Flannery, D. J. (1999). Two sides of the coin: Multilevel prevention and intervention to reduce youth violent behavior. In D. J. Flannery & C. R. Huff (Eds.), *Youth violence: Prevention, intervention, and social policy* (pp. 47–72). Washington, DC: American Psychiatric Press.

Embry, D. D., Flannery, D. J., Vazsonyi, A. T., Powell, K. E., & Atha, H. (1996). PeaceBuilders: A theoretically driven, school-based model for early violence prevention. *American Journal of Preventive Medicine, 12* (5, Suppl.), 91–100.

Fawcett, S. B. (1991). Some values guiding community research and action. *Journal of Applied Behavior Analysis, 24,* 621–636.

Fawcett, S. B., Francisco, V. T., Paine-Andrews, A., Fisher, J. L., Lewis, R. K., Williams, E. L., Richter, K. P., Harris, K. J., & Berkley, J. Y. (1994). *Preventing youth violence: An action planning guide for community-based initiatives.* Lawrence, KS: Work Group on Health Promotion & Community Development, Department of Human Development, University of Kansas.

Fawcett, S. B., Mathews, R. M., & Fletcher, R. K. (1980). Some promising dimensions for behavioral community technology. *Journal of Applied Behavior Analysis, 13,* 505–518.

Federal Trade Commission (2000, September). *Marketing violent entertainment to children: A review of self-regulation and industry practices in the motion picture, music recording & electronic game industries: A report of the Federal Trade Commission.* Available at: *http://www.ftc.gov/reports/violence/vioreport.pdf.*

Finn, J. L., & Checkoway, B. (1998). Young people as competent community builders: A challenge to social work. *Social Work, 43,* 335–345.

Flannery, D. J., & Huff, C. R. (1999). Implications for prevention, intervention, and social policy with violent youth. In D. J. Flannery & C. R. Huff (Eds.), *Youth violence: Prevention, intervention, and social policy* (pp. 293–306). Washington, DC: American Psychiatric Press.

Forman, S. G. (1993). *Coping skills interventions for children and adolescents.* San Francisco: Jossey-Bass.

Franke, T. M. (2000). Adolescent violent behavior: An analysis across and within racial/ethnic groups. *Journal of Multicultural Social Work, 8,* 47–70.

Freire, P. (1994). *Pedagogy of the oppressed* (rev. ed.). New York: Continuum.

Garbarino, J. (1995). *Raising children in a socially toxic environment.* San Francisco: Jossey-Bass.

Garbarino, J. (1999). *Lost boys: Why our sons turn violent and how we can save them.* New York: Free Press.

Ginsburg, E. H. (1990). *Effective interventions: Applying learning theory to school social work.* New York: Greenwood.

Glenn, S. S. (1991). Contingencies and metacontingencies: Relations among behavioral, cultural, and biological evolution. In P. A. Lamal (Ed.), *Behavioral analysis of societies and cultural practices* (pp. 39–73). New York: Hemisphere Publishing.

Goldfried, M. R., & Davison, G. C. (1994). *Clinical behavior therapy* (expanded ed.). New York: John Wiley & Sons.

Goldiamond, I. (1974). Toward a constructional approach to social problems. *Behaviorism, 2,* 1–84.

Goldstein, A. P. (1997). Controlling vandalism: The person-environment duet. In A. P. Goldstein & J. C. Conoley (Eds.), *School violence intervention: A practical handbook* (pp. 290-321). New York: Guilford Press.

Goldstein, A. (1999). Teaching prosocial behavior to antisocial youth. In D. J. Flannery & C. R. Huff (Eds.), *Youth violence: Prevention, intervention, and social policy* (pp. 253–273). Washington, DC: American Psychiatric Press.

Goldstein, A., & Glick, B. (1994a). Aggression replacement training: Curriculum and evaluation. *Simulation and Gaming, 25,* 9–26.

Goldstein, A. P., & Glick, B. (1994b). *The prosocial gang: Implementing aggression replacement training.* Thousand Oaks, CA: Sage.

Goldstein, A., P., Glick, B., & Gibbs, J. C. (1998). *Aggression replacement training: A comprehensive intervention for aggressive youth* (rev. ed.). Champaign, IL: Research Press.

Goldstein, A. P., Palumbo, J., Striepling, S., & Voutsinas, A. M. (1995). *Break it up: A teacher's guide to managing student aggression.* Champaign, IL: Research Press.

Goodenough, U. (1998). *The sacred depths of nature.* New York: Oxford University Press.

Gordon, T. (1970). *Parent effectiveness training.* New York: Wyden Press.

Grossman, J. B., & Garry, E. M. (1997). *Mentoring—A proven delinquency prevention strategy* (Report No. NCJ 164834). Washington, DC: U.S. Department of Justice, Office of Justice Programs.

Gunnoe, M. L., & Mariner, C. L. (1997). Toward a developmental-contextual model of the effects of parental spanking on children's aggression. *Archives of Pediatrics and Adolescent Medicine, 151,* 768–775.

Gutierrez, L. (1997). Multicultural community organizing. In M. Reisch & E. Gambrill (Eds.), *Social work in the 21st century* (pp. 249–259). Thousand Oaks, CA: Pine Forge.

Hagedorn, J. (1998). Gang violence in the postindustrial era. *Crime and Justice: A Review of Research, 24,* 365–419.

Hawkins, J. D., & Catalano, R. F. (1992). *Communities that care.* San Francisco: Jossey-Bass.

Hayes, S. C., Kohlenberg, B. S., & Melancon, S. M. (1989). Avoiding and altering rule-control as a strategy of clinical intervention. In S. C. Hayes (Ed.), *Rule-governed behavior: Cognition, contingencies, and instructional control* (pp. 359–385). New York: Plenum.

Hazel, J. S., Schumaker, J. B., Sherman, J. A., & Sheldon-Wildgen, J. (1981). *ASSET: A social skills program for adolescents* (leader's guide). Champaign, IL: Research Press.

Henggeler, S. W., Schoenwald, S. K., Borduin, C. M., Rowland, M. D., & Cunningham, P. B. (1998). *Multisystemic treatment of antisocial behavior in children and adolescents.* New York: Guilford Press.

Howard, M. O., & Jenson, J. M. (1999). Causes of youth violence. In J. M. Jenson & M. O. Howard (Eds.), *Youth violence: Current research and recent practice innovations* (pp. 19–42). Washington, DC: NASW Press.

Jenson, J. M., & Howard, M. O. (1999a). Advancing knowledge for practice with aggressive and violent youths. In J. M. Jenson & M. O. Howard (Eds.), *Youth violence: Current research and recent practice innovations* (pp. 229–240). Washington, DC: NASW Press.

Jenson, J. M., & Howard, M. O. (1999b). Prevalence and patterns of youth violence. In J. M. Jenson & M. O. Howard (Eds.), *Youth violence: Current research and recent practice innovations* (pp. 3–18). Washington, DC: NASW Press.

Jenson, J. M., & Howard, M. O. (Eds.). (1999c). *Youth violence: Current research and recent practice innovations.* Washington, DC: NASW Press.

Jonson-Reid, M. (1999). Child abuse and youth violence. In J. M. Jenson & M. O. Howard (Eds.), *Youth violence: Current research and recent practice innovations* (pp. 87–112). Washington, DC: NASW Press.

Josephson Institute of Ethics. (2001). *2000 report card: Violence and substance abuse. http://www.josephsoninstitute.org/Survey2000/violence2000-commentary.htm.*

Kaplan, N. M. (1997). Mediation in the school system: Facilitating the development of peer mediation programs. In E. Kruk (Ed.), *Mediation and conflict resolution in social work and the human services* (pp. 247–262). Chicago: Nelson-Hall.

Kaufman, P., Chen, X., Choy, S. P., Chandler, K. A., Chapman, C. D., Rand, M. R., & Ringel, C. (1998). *Indicators of school crime and safety, 1998* (Report No. NCES 98-251/NCJ 172215). Washington, DC: U.S. Departments of Education and Justice.

Kazdin, A. E. (1984). Statistical analyses for single-case experimental designs. In D. H. Barlow & M. Hersen (Eds.), *Single case experimental designs: Strategies for studying behavior change* (pp. 285–324). New York: Pergamon.

Kazdin, A. E. (1994). *Behavior modification in applied settings* (5th ed.). Pacific Grove, CA: Brooks/Cole.

Kazi, M. A. F. (1998). *Single-case evaluation by social workers.* Burlington, VT: Ashgate.

Kohn, A. (1993). *Punished by rewards: The trouble with gold stars, incentive plans, A's, praise, and other bribes.* Boston: Houghton Mifflin.

Kozol, J. (1991). *Savage inequalities: Children in America's schools.* New York: HarperPerennial.

Kruk, E. (Ed.). (1997). *Mediation and conflict resolution in social work and the human services.* Chicago: Nelson-Hall.

Lane, R. (1997). *Murder in America.* Columbus, OH: Ohio State University Press.

Lawler, M. K. (2000). School-based violence prevention programs: What works. In D. S. Sandhu & C. B. Aspy (Eds.), *Violence in American schools: A practical guide for counselors* (pp. 247–266). Alexandria, VA: American Counseling Association.

LeBaron, M. (1997). Intercultural disputes. In E. Kruk (Ed.), *Mediation and conflict resolution in social work and the human services* (pp. 315–335). Chicago: Nelson-Hall.

LeCroy, C. W. (1994). *Handbook of child and adolescent treatment manuals.* New York: Lexington Books.

Lee, J. (1993). *Facing the fire: Experiencing and expressing anger appropriately.* New York: Bantam Books.

Lloyd, J. W., Eberhardt, M. J., & Drake, G. P., Jr. (1996). Group versus individual reinforcement contingencies within the context of group study conditions. *Journal of Applied Behavior Analysis, 29,* 189–200.

Louis Harris and Associates, Inc. (1993). *The Metropolitan Life survey of the American teacher 1993.* New York: Author.

Lowery, C. T. (1998). American Indian perspectives on addiction and recovery. *Health and Social Work, 23,* 127–198.

Lowery, C. T., & Mattaini, M. A. (1999). The science of sharing power: Native American thought and behavior analysis. *Behavior and Social Issues, 9,* 3–23.

Lowery, C. T., & Mattaini, M. A. (2001). Shared power in social work: A Native American perspective. In H. Briggs & K. Corcoran (Eds.), *Foundations of change: Effective social work practice* (pp. 109–124) Chicago, IL: Lyceum.

Luvmour, S., & Luvmour, J. (n.d.). *Everyone wins!: Cooperative games and activities.* Gabriola Island, British Columbia: New Society Publishers.

Malott, R. W. (2000). *I'll stop procrastinating when I get around to it* (version 3.2). Unpublished manuscript available from Department of Psychology, Western Michigan University, Kalamazoo, MI.

Malott, R. W., Whaley, D. L., & Malott, M. E. (1997). *Elementary principles of behavior* (3rd ed.). Englewood Cliffs, NJ: Prentice-Hall.

Martin, C. L. (1999). *The way of the human being.* New Haven, CT: Yale University Press.

Mattaini, M. A. (1996). Envisioning cultural practices. *The Behavior Analyst, 19,* 257–272.

Mattaini, M. A. (1999). *Clinical intervention with families.* Washington, DC: NASW Press.

Mattaini, M. A., & Lowery, C. T., with the *PEACE POWER* Working Group (1999). *Youth violence prevention: The state of the science.* Behaviorists for Social Responsibility. World wide web document: *http://www.bfsr.org/violence.html.*

Mattaini, M. A., & Thyer, B. A. (Eds.). (1996). *Finding solutions to social problems: Behavioral strategies for change.* Washington, DC: American Psychological Association.

Mattaini, M. A., Twyman, J. S., Chin, W., & Lee, K. N. (1996). Youth violence. In M. A. Mattaini & B. A. Thyer (Eds.), *Finding solutions to social problems: Behavioral strategies for change* (pp. 75–111). Washington, DC: American Psychological Association.

Mayer, G. R., Butterworth, T., Nafpaktitis, M., & Sulzer-Azaroff, B. (1983). Preventing school vandalism and improving discipline: A three-year study. *Journal of Applied Behavior Analysis, 16,* 355–369.

Mayer, G. R., Mitchell, L. K., Clementi, T., Clement-Robertson, E., Myatt, R., & Bullara, D. T. (1993). A dropout prevention program for at-risk high school students: Emphasizing consulting to promote positive classroom climates. *Education & Treatment of Children, 16,* 135–146.

McCold, P. (1997). *Restorative justice: An annotated bibliography*. Monsey, NJ: Criminal Justice Press.

McDonald, L., & Frey, H. E. (1999). *Families and schools together: Building relationships* (Report No. NCJ 173423). Washington, DC: U.S. Department of Justice, Office of Justice Programs.

McDowell, J. J. (1988). Matching theory in natural human environments. *The Behavior Analyst, 11,* 95–109.

Miczek, K. A., Mirsky, A. F., Carey, R., DeBold, J., & Raine, A. (1994). An overview of biological influences on violent behavior. In A. J. Reiss, Jr., K. A. Miczek, & J. A. Roth (Eds.), *Understanding and preventing violence: Vol. 2. Biobehavioral influences* (pp. 1–20). Washington, DC: National Academy Press.

Mirsky, A. F., & Siegel, A. (1994). The neurobiology of violence and aggression. In A. J. Reiss, Jr., K. A. Miczek, & J. A. Roth (Eds.), *Understanding and preventing violence: Vol. 2. Biobehavioral influences* (pp. 59–172). Washington, DC: National Academy Press.

Moore, M. (1994). *Violence in America: Mobilizing a response*. Washington, DC: National Academy Press.

Moore, M. H., Prothrow-Stith, D., Guyer, B., & Spivak, H. (1994). Violence and intentional injuries: Criminal justice and public health perspectives on an urgent national problem. In A. J. Reiss, Jr., & J. A. Roth (Eds.), *Understanding and preventing violence: Vol. 4. Consequences and control* (pp. 167–216). Washington, DC: National Academy Press.

Muller, J., & Mihalic, S. (1999). *Blueprints: A violence prevention initiative* (Report No. FS-99110). Washington, DC: U.S. Department of Justice, Office of Justice Programs.

Murphy, H. A., Hutchison, J. M., & Bailey, J. S. (1983). Behavioral school psychology goes outdoors: The effect of organized games on playground aggression. *Journal of Applied Behavior Analysis, 16,* 29–35.

Napoleon, H. (1991). *Yuuyaraq: The way of the human being* (edited by E. Madsen). Fairbanks, AK: Center for Cross-Cultural Studies, University of Alaska, Fairbanks.

Ninness, H. A. C., Ellis, J., Miller, W. B., Baker, D., & Rutherford, R. (1995). The effect of a self management training package on the transfer of aggression control procedures in the absence of supervision. *Behavior Modification, 19,* 464–490.

Ninness, H. A. C., Fuerst, J., Rutherford, R. D., & Glenn, S. S. (1991). Effects of self management training and reinforcement on the transfer of improved conduct in the absence of supervision. *Journal of Applied Behavior Analysis, 24,* 499–508.

Nugent, W. R., Bruley, C., & Allen, P. (1998). The effects of aggression replacement training on antisocial behavior in a runaway shelter. *Research on Social Work Practice, 8,* 637–656.

O'Connell, T., Wachtel, B., & Wachtel, T. (1999). *Conferencing handbook.* Pipersville, PA: The Piper's Press.

O'Donnell, S. M., & Karanja, S. T. (2000). Transformative community practice: Building a model for developing extremely low income African-American communities. *Journal of Community Practice, 7*(3), 67–84.

Olweus, D. (1993). *Bullying at school.* Cambridge, MA: Blackwell.

Orlick, T. (1978). *The cooperative sports and games book.* New York: Pantheon.

Orlick, T. (1982). *The second cooperative sports and games book.* New York: Pantheon.

Patterson, G. R. (1976). The aggressive child: Victim and architect of a coercive system. In E. J. Mash, L. A. Hamerlynck, & L. C. Handy (Eds.), *Behavior modification and families* (pp. 267–316). New York: Brunner/Mazel.

Patterson, G. R., DeBaryshe, B. D., & Ramsey, E. (1989). A developmental perspective on antisocial behavior. *American Psychologist, 44,* 329–335.

Patterson, G. R., Reid, J. B., & Dishion, T. J. (1992). *Antisocial boys: Vol. 4. A social interactional approach.* Eugene, OR: Castalia.

PEACE POWER Working Group (1999). *PEACE POWER manual.* New York: Walden Fellowship, Inc.

Pence, E., & Paymar, M. (1993). *Education groups for men who batter: The Duluth model.* New York: Springer.

Perkins, C. A. (1997). *Age patterns of victims of serious violent crime* (Report No. NCJ-162031). Washington, DC: U.S. Department of Justice.

Potter, C. C. (1999). Violence and aggression in girls. In J. M. Jenson & M. O. Howard (Eds.), *Youth violence: Current research and recent practice innovations* (pp. 113–138). Washington, DC: NASW Press.

Rakos, R. F. (1991). *Assertive behavior: Theory, research, and training.* London: Routledge.

Reid, W. J. (1985). *Family problem solving.* New York: Columbia University Press.

Reiss, A. J., Jr., & Roth, J. A. (1993). *Understanding and preventing violence.* Washington, DC: National Academy Press.

Richters, J., & Martinez, P. (1993). The NIMH community violence project: Children as victims and witnesses to violence. *Psychiatry, 56,* 7–21.

Robbins, M. S., & Szapocznik, J. (2000). *Brief strategic family therapy* (Juvenile Justice Bulletin, NCJ 179285). Washington, DC: U.S. Department of Justice, Office of Justice Programs.

Rose, S. D. (1978). *Group therapy: A behavioral approach.* Englewood Cliffs, NJ: Prentice-Hall.

Rose, S. D. (1998). *Group therapy with troubled youth: A cognitive-behavioral interactive approach.* Thousand Oaks, CA: Sage.

Ross, L., & Coleman, M. (2000). Urban community action planning inspires teenagers to transform their community and their identity. *Journal of Community Practice, 7*(2), 29–45.

References

Ross, R. (1992). *Dancing with a ghost: Exploring Indian reality.* Toronto: Reed Books Canada.

Ross, R. (1996). *Returning to the teachings: Exploring aboriginal justice.* Toronto: Penguin Books Canada.

Rossi, P. H., Freeman, H. E., & Lipsey, M. W. (1999). *Evaluation: A systematic approach* (6th ed.). Thousand Oaks, CA: Sage.

Rottschaefer, W. A. (2000). Naturalizing ethics: The biology and psychology of moral agency. *Zygon, 35,* 253–286.

Rushforth, N. B., & Flannery, D. J. (1999). Role of firearms in youth violence. In D. J. Flannery & C. R. Huff (Eds.), *Youth violence: Prevention, intervention, and social policy* (pp. 201–228). Washington, DC: American Psychiatric Press.

Samples, F., & Aber, L. (1998). Evaluations of school-based violence prevention programs. In D. S. Elliott, B. Hamburg, & K. Williams (Eds.), *Violence in American schools: A new perspective* (pp. 217–252). New York: Cambridge University Press.

Sandhu, D. S., & Aspy, C. B. (Eds.). (2000). *Violence in American schools: A practical guide for counselors.* Alexandria, VA: American Counseling Association.

Schuster, M. A., Franke, T. M., Bastian, A. M., Sor, S., & Halfon, N. (2000). Firearm storage patterns in US homes with children. *American Journal of Public Health, 90,* 588–594.

Serna, L. A., Schumaker, J. B., Sherman, J. A., & Sheldon, J. B. (1991). In-home generalization of social interactions in families of adolescents with behavior problems. *Journal of Applied Behavior Analysis, 24,* 733–746.

Sharpe, T., Brown, M., & Crider, K. (1995). The effects of a sportsmanship curriculum intervention on generalized positive social behavior of urban elementary school students. *Journal of Applied Behavior Analysis, 28,* 401–416.

Shenandoah, J. (2000). *Peacemaker's journey* (sound recording). Boulder, CO: Silver Wave Records.

Shonkoff, J. P., & Phillips, D. A. (Eds.). (2000). *From neurons to neighborhoods: The science of early child development.* Washington, DC: National Academy Press.

Shure, M. B. (1992). *I can problem solve.* Champaign, IL: Research Press.

Shure, M. B. (1999). *Preventing violence the problem-solving way* (Report No. NCJ 172847). Washington, DC: U.S. Department of Justice, Office of Justice Program.

Sidman, M. (2001). *Coercion and its fallout.* Boston: Authors Cooperative.

Silko, L. M. (1977). *Ceremony.* New York: Viking Penguin Books.

Singer, M., Miller, D., & Slovak, K. (1997). *The mental health consequences of children's exposure to violence.* Cleveland, OH: Cuyahoga County Mental Health Research Institute, Mandel School of Applied Social Sciences, Case Western Reserve University.

References

Skinner, B. F. (1981). Selection by consequences. *Science, 213,* 501–504.

Smokowski, P. R., Rose, S., Todar, K., & Reardon, K. (1999). Postgroup-casualty status, group events, and leader behavior. *Research on Social Work Practice, 9,* 555–574.

Snyder, H. N. (2000, December). Juvenile arrests, 1999. *Juvenile Justice Bulletin* (Report No. NCJ 185236). Washington, DC: U.S. Department of Justice, Office of Juvenile Justice and Delinquency Prevention.

Southern Poverty Law Center. (2000). Hate goes to school. WWW document, accessed 4/29/2001 at *http://www.splcenter.org/cgibin/goframe.pl?refname=/ intelligenceproject/ip-4n1.html.*

Stokes, T. F., & Baer, D. M. (1977). An implicit technology of generalization. *Journal of Applied Behavior Analysis, 10,* 349–367.

Straus, M. A., Sugarman, D. B., & Giles-Sims, J. (1997). Spanking by parents and subsequent antisocial behavior of children. *Archives of Pediatrics and Adolescent Medicine, 151,* 761–767.

Stuart, R. B., & Lott, L. A. (1972). Behavioral contracting with delinquents: A cautionary note. *Journal of Behavior Therapy and Experimental Psychiatry, 3,* 161–169.

Sulzer-Azaroff, B., & Mayer, G. R. (1991). *Behavior analysis for lasting change.* Fort Worth, TX: Holt, Rinehart and Winston.

The way of the spirit. (1997). Chicago: Time-Life Books.

Thompson, J. (1999). *Drama workshops for anger management and offending behaviour.* Philadelphia: Jessica Kingsley Publishers.

Tropman, J. E. (1996). *Effective meetings: Improving group decision making* (2nd ed.). Thousand Oaks, CA: Sage.

Tryon, W. W. (1982). A simplified time-series analysis for evaluating treatment interventions. *Journal of Applied Behavior Analysis, 15,* 423–429.

Umbreit, M. S., & Kruk, E. (1997). Parents and children. In E. Kruk (Ed.), *Mediation and conflict resolution in social work and the human services* (pp. 97–115). Chicago: Nelson-Hall.

United Nations. (1948). *Universal declaration of human rights.* New York: Author.

Vizenor, G. (1991). *The heirs of Columbus.* New York: Quality Paperback Book Club, originally published by Wesleyan Press.

Walker, H. M., Colvin, G., & Ramsey, E. (1995). *Antisocial behavior in school: Strategies and best practices.* Pacific Grove, CA: Brooks/Cole.

Waterman, A. S. (Ed.). (1997). *Service-learning: Applications from the research.* Hillsdale, NJ: Lawrence Erlbaum Associates.

Webster-Stratton, C. (1997). From parent training to community building. *Families in Society, 78,* 156–171.

Williams, J. H., & Van Dorn, R. A. (1999). Delinquency, gangs, and youth violence. In J. M. Jenson & M. O. Howard (Eds.), *Youth violence: Current research and recent practice innovations* (pp. 199–225). Washington, DC: NASW Press.

References

Wilson, J. Q., & Herrnstein, R. J. (1985). *Crime and human nature.* New York: Simon & Schuster.

Wilson, W. J. (1999). *The bridge over the racial divide: Rising inequality and coalition politics.* Los Angeles: University of California Press.

Wolf, M. M. (1978). Social validity: The case for subjective measurement or how applied behavior analysis is finding its heart. *Journal of Applied Behavior Analysis, 11,* 203–214.

Wolf, M. M., Braukmann, C. J., & Ramp, K. A. (1987). Serious delinquent behavior as part of a significantly handicapping condition: Cures and supportive environments. *Journal of Applied Behavior Analysis, 20,* 347–359.

Wood, M. M., & Long, N. J. (1991). *Life space intervention: Talking with children in crisis.* Austin, TX: Pro-Ed.

Young, K. R., West, R. P., Smith, D. J., & Morgan, D. P. (1991). *Teaching self-management strategies to adolescents.* Longmont, CO: Sopris West.

Peace Power for Adolescents
Strategies for a Culture of Nonviolence

Cover design by Metadog Design Group

Interior Design and Composition by
Cynthia Stock, Electronic Quill

Typeset in Berkeley

Printed by Victor Graphics
on 60# Victor offset

Index

ORDER FORM

Qty.	Title	Item #	Price	Total
___	Peace Power for Adolescents	3290	$39.99	_____
___	Making Choices	3231	$33.99	_____
___	Youth Violence	3118	$39.99	_____
___	Risk and Resilience in Childhood	274X	$44.99	_____
___	Clinical Intervention with Families	3088	$39.99	_____
___	Multicultural Issues in Social Work	2669	$39.99	_____
___	Multisystem Skills and Interventions in School Social Work Practice	2952	$39.99	_____

POSTAGE AND HANDLING
Minimum postage and handling fee is $4.95. Orders that do not include appropriate postage and handling will be returned.

DOMESTIC: Please add 12% to orders under $100 for postage and handling. For orders over $100 add 7% of order.

CANADA: Please add 17% postage and handling.

OTHER INTERNATIONAL: Please add 22% postage and handling.

Subtotal	_____
Postage and Handling	_____
DC residents add 6% sales tax	_____
MD residents add 5% sales tax	_____
Total	_____

❒ **Check** or **money order** (payable to NASW Press) for $ _____.

❒ **Credit card**
  ❒ NASW Visa* I ❒ Visa I ❒ NASW MasterCard* I ❒ MasterCard I ❒ Amex

Credit Card Number _____   Expiration Date _____

Signature _____

Use of these cards generates funds in support of the social work profession.

Name _____

Address _____

City _____ State/Province _____

Country _____ Zip _____

Phone _____ E-mail _____

NASW Member # (if applicable) _____

(Please make checks payable to NASW Press. Prices are subject to change.)

NASW PRESS
P. O. Box 431
Annapolis JCT, MD 20701
USA

Credit card orders call
1-800-227-3590
(In the Metro Wash., DC, area, call 301-317-8688)
Or fax your order to 301-206-7989
Or order online at http://www.naswpress.org

Visit our Web site at http://www.naswpress.org.

3290BC

IMPORTANT BOOKS ON CHILDREN, YOUTH, & FAMILIES FROM NASW PRESS

Peace Power for Adolescents: *Strategies for a Culture of Nonviolence,* Mark A Mattaini, DSW, ACSW, *and the PEACE POWER Working Group.* Recent school shootings have forced youth violence to the top of our national agenda. But these events are only one symptom of a greater problem—a toxic social environment that breeds isolation and rage among our children. This groundbreaking book looks at the wide range of risk factors and indicators for violence and translates the findings into an effective prevention and intervention system—**PEACE POWER!**

ISBN: 0-87101-329-0. July 2001. Item #3290. 272 pages. $39.99.

Making Choices: *Social Problem-Solving Skills for Children,* Mark W. Fraser, James K. Nash, Maeda J. *Galinsky, and Kathleen M. Darwin.* (The first volume in the NASW Practice Resource Series.) Based on a cognitive problem-solving approach, *Making Choices* addresses the urgent need for children to acquire competence in meeting the demands of childhood within social, school, and family parameters. The book is designed for children from kindergarten through middle school whose behavior is impulsive, oppositional, or aggressive. Recognizing that a great deal of children's behavior is tied to problem-solving, the volume focuses on how children solve instrumental and relational issues in differing social settings.

ISBN: 0-87101-323-1. 2000. Item #3231. 196 pages. $33.99.

Youth Violence: *Current Research and Recent Practice Innovations,* Jeffrey M. Jenson and Matthew O. *Howard, Editors.* A timely, eye-opening book from Colorado social workers on the youth violence that has galvanized the nation. This critical volume pinpoints and probes the etiology of this escalating trend, which is found in urban, suburban, and rural contexts. *Youth Violence* assesses the current situation and examines recent prevention and treatment innovations for violent youths.

ISBN: 0-87101-311-8. 1999. Item #3118. 280 pages. $39.99.

Risk and Resilience in Childhood: *An Ecological Perspective,* Mark W. Fraser, Editor. How is it that some children face enormous odds but prevail over adversity to become successful? How can you develop practice models that foster resilience and build exciting new knowledge about risk and protection in childhood? You'll find answers to these questions and more in *Risk and Resilience in Childhood,* a unique text that introduces and explores the concepts of protection and resilience in the face of adversity.

ISBN: 0-87101-274-X. 1997. Item #274X. 296 pages. $44.99.

Clinical Intervention with Families, *by Mark A. Mattaini* (Companion volume to *Clinical Practice with Individuals*). Written for social workers in family practice as well as for instructors and advanced-level students, this book is a state-of-the-art and state-of-the-science treatment guide of family practice. An essential volume for those seeking to understand the extrinsic family factors affecting the theory and practice of family social work!

ISBN: 0-87101-308-8. 1999. Item #3088. 312 pages. $39.99.

Multicultural Issues in Social Work, *Patricia L. Ewalt, Edith M. Freeman, Stuart A. Kirk, and Dennis L. Poole, Editors.* A collection of 38 articles from 1994 and 1995 issues of the four NASW Press journals. This resource examines the differences and similarities in the experiences, needs, and beliefs of people in different population groups.

ISBN: 0-87101-266-9. 1996. Item #2669. 578 pages. $39.99.

Multisystem Skills and Interventions in School Social Work Practice, *Edith M. Freeman, Cynthia G. Franklin, Rowena Fong, Gary L. Shaffer, and Elizabeth M. Timberlake, Editors.* This practical guide will help you meet the emerging needs of students, families, schools, and communities today. You'll learn about the skills and competencies you need to work effectively with new social work consumers. And you'll find out how you can change policies, gain funding, and otherwise influence large systems in the changing sociopolitical climate.

ISBN: 0-87101-295-2. 1998. Item #2952. 492 pages. $39.99.

(Order form and information on reverse side)